CHOOSING MY TOMORROW

SURVIVING MURDER, NAVIGATING MENTAL HEALTH, AND HARNESSING THE POWER OF CHOICE

JODIE BAULKHAM

Choosing My Tomorrow: Surviving Murder, Navigating Mental Health, and Harnessing the Power of Choice

First edition

Although the author and publisher have made every effort to ensure that the information in this book was correct at press time, the author and publisher do not assume and hereby disclaim any liability to any party for any loss, damage, or disruption caused by errors or omissions, whether such errors or omissions result from negligence, accident, or any other cause.

Adherence to all applicable laws and regulations, including international, federal, state and local governing professional licensing, business practices, advertising, and all other aspects of doing business in the US, Canada or any other jurisdiction is the sole responsibility of the reader and consumer.

Neither the author nor the publisher assumes any responsibility or liability whatsoever on behalf of the consumer or reader of this material. Any perceived slight of any individual or organization is purely unintentional.

The resources in this book are provided for informational purposes only and should not be used to replace the specialized training and professional judgment of a health care or mental health care professional.

Neither the author nor the publisher can be held responsible for the use of the information provided within this book. Please always consult a trained professional before making any decision regarding treatment of yourself or others.

For more information, email info@jodiebaulkham.com.

Library and Archives Canada Cataloguing in Publication

Title: Choosing My Tomorrow: Surviving Murder, Navigating Mental Health, and Harnessing the Power of Choice / Jodie Baulkham

Names: Baulkham, Jodie, author.

ISBN: 978-1-7380912-0-1 (paperback)| ISBN: 978-1-7380912-1-8 (hardcover)|

ISBN: 978-7380912-2-5 (ebook) | ISBN: 978-7380912-3-2 (audio book)

Dedication

This book is dedicated to those who have sacrificed themselves in the fulfilment of their duty to serve others, their communities, and their country.

I choose to remember them as I move forward with each of my tomorrows.

Get Your Free Gifts!

In the third section of this book, you'll find valuable insights and thought-provoking questions. These resources are conveniently packaged in a downloadable workbook, allowing you to capture your own reflections.

Using my skills as an experienced course designer, I've also created a mini course that I think you'll find incredibly beneficial.

Check them out today!

To obtain your free copies, simply visit:

www.jodiebaulkham.com

Table of Contents

Part 1: The Widow vii

Part 2: The Wife 197

Part 3: The Lessons Learned 307

33: The Importance of Self-Discovery and Strength of Character 312

34: Stop Taking Things Personally 317

35: Ask Questions That Support Communication 320

36: Use Helpful Language 324

37: Speak Authentically 329

38: Confide in Someone You Trust 332

39: Appreciate All Your Days 335

40: Talk Regularly about Mental Health 338

41: Hope Can Save A Life 341

42: Grief Is Complex 345

43: The Value of Seeking Professional Help 351

Conclusion 356

Epilogue 360

Appendix A 369

Mental Health Continuum 369

Acknowledgments 371

Your Next Best Steps 377

Foreword

•••••

Dr. Jody Carrington is a Clinical Psychologist, best selling author of "Feeling Seen," "Kids These Days", and "Teachers These Days," captivating speaker, and former Civilian Member of the Royal Canadian Mounted Police (RCMP).

You're only as okay as the people who hold you. I don't know if there's ever been a sentiment truer in the policing world. Particularly in rural or small-town posts, the community knows who you are the second you take up shop. The "cop's kid" is often as noticeable as the uniform and the spouse is held to the same expectations of conduct. The families who love the police officer are often exposed vicariously and sometimes can be the first alerted to the traumas that are an inevitability to those who do this holy work. What is never, ever talked about enough is the fact that in North America, there is very little (read none) training or preparation for the families of police officers.

You see, the job of a police officer has always been to rush to people who are at their worst. Rarely is a police officer called when things are going well. In their most difficult, scariest, or darkest moments, humans will always need another person to walk them through it. One of the most profound philosophers,

Ram Dass perhaps said it best, *"we are all here, walking each other home"*. Police officers are often the most prolific "walkers" in our lifetimes. In other words, from a neurophysiological perspective, when any of us gets upset, scared, or overwhelmed, we will become emotionally dysregulated (i.e., flip our lids). We will lose access to most parts of our memories, our kindness, sometimes even our words. It's biologically necessary, particularly during traumatic experiences (e.g., when you get in a car accident, during an abusive situation, or anything that induces terror) to flip all the extraneous stuff that's not necessary in that moment out of the way. Often, another human (who is regulated) is required to take charge and walk another through that experience; sometimes with force when necessary and with kindness and compassion if ever possible. The truth is, having emotional regulation skills is a privilege. You can't give away something you've never received. This means, often, police officers are doing the walking for marginalized people or those who have experienced abuse, neglect, or other trauma. They tend to, by virtue of their profession, see the worst parts of humanity. Every day.

By extension then, there will be a significant sequela of their work that will be experienced by those who hold them closest or see them the most. There is ample evidence to support this truth. And perhaps most critical in successfully coping with or healing from this often-traumatic exposure is how it is responded to immediately or in the days following some of the worst experiences. Who is present after the hardest calls will always be consistent: the families.

When a human being is asked, without question, to serve other humans who will be emotionally dysregulated, even when the risk might be their own life, is something that we as humans are wired for. In fact, humans with the most remarkable legacies have been the ones who walked others through horrific things. The most critical question is: what do we do with the emotion after we've done the walking? Because seeing emotions that result from trauma cannot kill you, but not talking about them or having a safe place to put them, just might.

There has been a push, particularly in the past decade, for a long-overdue "increased awareness and support" for the mental health of police officers. Lagging behind these initiatives is an understanding and support for the role of families and children. And I'll say it again: you're only as okay as the people who hold you.

In Jodie Baulkham's words that follow on these pages, you will experience what it's like to love and be loved in the midst of trauma and unimaginable grief. She eloquently outlines that there is life that happens in and around the confines of our jobs and that it will be impossible at times to separate the two. The esteemed and necessary job of a police officer, particularly in the unique world of Canada's national police force, is steeped in beautiful tradition. It is full of honour, identity, and nobility like no other on this planet. The job of a police officer, in some form, will always be necessary because humans will always need the walkers. In this book, you will find the beginnings of the resources to support family systems who serve our communities. The vulnerable, beautiful stories of Chris, Brent, and Alexis, as told through Jodie's incredible experience of breaking and healing a million times over, offers a raw insight into just what humans can endure.

To all of you reading these words who have done this work: thank you. I am in awe of your strength, I am so aware of your sacrifice, and like Jodie, I vow to continue to work towards honouring and building resources to support those of you who do this holy work of walking us all home.

Part 1: The Widow

1

•••••

THE KNOCK AT the door came shortly after 5:30 a.m.

I was up changing our eight month old daughter Alexis. Knowing that a houseguest at that hour of the morning was not usual, I placed Alexis back in her crib and answered the door. A colleague of Chris' and friend of ours, Constable Karla George, was on the other side. I could tell she had not been awake long as she still had a sleep line on her right cheek. In a rushed tone she asked:

"Is Chris home?"

"No, he was called out a few hours ago."

"We can't seem to reach him."

I walked up the four steps from our foyer and across the hall into the office. I could hear Alexis becoming restless. Chris had taken over the closet in that room to store his kit and uniform. He also used it as his private dressing room. It appeared as usual. A wooden desk and chair were on the wall adjacent to the door, with a dresser and bookshelf opposite. On the dresser I noticed Chris' portable radio. I yelled from the office, "Oh, I know why you can't reach him!" I picked up the radio and quickly carried it with me back to where Karla was waiting. I handed it to her. "He left his portable on the dresser." She received the radio from me and before promptly leaving the house she said, "We'll be in touch."

I closed the door behind her, feeling a strange sense of isolation wash over me. The sound of the latch clicking shut echoed in my ears as I made my way back to Alexis.

As I was bouncing our baby girl on my hip, my mind was racing. I called my friend Cindy, who lived just down the street. I knew that I would be waking her up. It was Saturday morning on Thanksgiving weekend, of course people without children would still be sleeping. Taking a deep breath, I dialled her number, my hands shaking as I held the phone to my ear.

As it rang, my heart pounded in my chest, the sound reverberating through every fibre of my being. Cindy finally answered, her voice groggy with sleep. I struggled to find the right words, my voice breaking as I tried to convey the news.

"Chris is missing. Karla just came by the house. They don't know where he is. Can you come over?" The weight of those words seemed to hang in the air, heavy and unyielding.

"I'm on my way."

As I anxiously waited for her, my gaze absentmindedly fixed on the sheer curtains hanging in the front bay window of our living room. Through the delicate fabric, I caught sight of someone walking up my driveway, carrying two cups of coffee. But before she could reach my door, a police car pulled in. Out jumped Corporal Mike Carter, and I realized that the person with the coffee was his wife, Carla. I guessed he was arriving with an update.

He met me at the door and told me they had found Chris.

He had been rushed to the hospital.

The gravity of the situation hit me like a tidal wave, and in my state of shock, I realized that I was still wearing my maternity pyjamas.

I murmured, "I need to change my pants."

Mike simply said, "Hurry."

I rushed to change my clothes as quickly as possible, my hands trembling as I struggled to compose myself. Cindy arrived just as I finished dressing. With Alexis under the care of Mike's wife, in a blur of emotions, Cindy, Mike and I all piled into the police cruiser and headed towards the hospital.

Hay River had a population of just 3,500, so the hospital was small and limited in its resources, providing only essential care and services. During emergencies, the staff worked to stabilize patients, preparing them for a medivac by air ambulance to larger centres like Yellowknife or Edmonton. Medivac transports were a regular part of life in the Northwest Territories, bridging the gap between remote communities and advanced medical facilities.

As we made our way to the hospital, my mind was overwhelmed with worry and fear. The hospital, once a place of joyful anticipation during my pregnancy ultrasound, was now a reminder of the fragility of life. The uncertainty of the situation weighed heavily on us as we awaited news of Chris' condition.

Together, we pushed through the heavy hospital doors, the cold air of anxiety embracing us as we entered. With each step, my heart pounded in sync with the urgency of the moment. With a mix of apprehension and anticipation, we approached the nurse's station. There, a compassionate nurse met us with concern etched across her face.

"Chris and the doctor are in the ER," she confirmed, her voice gentle yet laden with worry. My mind swirled with questions and fears.

Suddenly, my attention was diverted to the left by the sound of quick, heavy footsteps. My head snapped in that direction, and I saw a nurse sprinting towards us with a determination that mirrored my racing mind. Without hesitation, she veered sharply around a corner and disappeared into the depths of the ER's back room, undoubtedly attending to a pressing emergency. My heart pounded, and a knot formed in my stomach as I could sense the seriousness of the situation unfolding.

In that moment, the gravity of the situation became clearer. I braced myself for the possibility that Chris might need immediate medical transport, and my thoughts turned to our daughter. As the weight of responsibility settled upon me, I knew I had to plan to accompany him on a medivac.

It was my practice to puree Alexis' food and freeze it in ice cube trays. At eight months old she was eating a variety of food and I took pride in making most of it for her. I needed Cindy to know how to care for Alexis while I was away caring for Chris.

As we stood at the counter, my hands trembled uncontrollably as I put pen to paper. The gravity of the situation weighed heavily on me, and my emotions threatened to overwhelm my attempts at writing. Sensing my struggle, Cindy took the pen and asked me to dictate the details.

"Two cubes of banana for breakfast with barley cereal, two cubes of sweet potato, and one cube of chicken for lunch..."

I managed to say, my voice wavering as the words escaped my lips. Before I could continue with the dinner plans, Mike appeared and gently guided me away from the nursing station.

He led me down a small hallway, the same one where we had seen the nurse rushing earlier. The room he ushered me into was small, its cramped walls amplifying my sense of confinement and anxiety. It enclosed me in a space that mirrored the overwhelming weight of the news I was about to receive. With two chairs and a small table as the only furniture, Mike motioned for me to sit in the chair nearest to the door. As I lowered myself into the seat, the hard, cold plastic seemed to accentuate the harsh reality I was about to face. My body leaned forward in anticipation, as if seeking any clue or reassurance in the confines of the room. Mike closed the door behind him, creating a cocoon of privacy in which to deliver the news. He knelt down beside me, his hand gently resting on my right knee. I turned to look into his eyes, and in that moment, a wave of realization washed over me. I knew what he was about to say before the words ever left his lips.

"He's gone," Mike said softly.

My voice faltered, and I began to stammer, unable to form coherent sentences. Questions raced through my mind at lightning speed, each thought colliding with the next in a chaotic jumble.

As my body succumbed to the shock, I instinctively shook my head in disbelief, as if denying the truth could somehow make it less painful. My hands moved from my lap to my head, trying to soothe the storm of thoughts and emotions that threatened to overwhelm me. Seeking some semblance of stability, I leaned forward, resting my elbows on my knees, and cradled my head in my hands. Seconds felt like an eternity as the weight of reality bore down on me, leaving me raw and vulnerable.

In those brief moments, my world had been shattered, and the enormity of the loss was beyond comprehension. The room seemed to close in around me, echoing the confines of my heart as I grappled with the unfathomable truth that had forever altered the course of my life. Time seemed to stretch and compress, all happening in a breathless instant after Mike's revelation.

I sat back up, took a deep breathe, looked at Mike and formed a short, concise, coherent sentence:

"I want to see him."

"Jodie, I don't think that's a good idea."

"Tell the doctors to clean him up. I am going to see him."

The journey down the seemingly endless ER hallway felt like a slow, agonizing march towards an inevitable and devastating truth. With each step, the door ahead seemed to retreat further into the distance, as if trying to shield me from what lay beyond. Familiar faces dotted the scene, belonging to the tight-knit detachment and support staff, providing a sense of community in ordinary circumstances. But today was different.

Brad, one of the other constables, stood resolute in his uniform, guarding the ER door. His presence should have been a source of comfort, a reminder of camaraderie in times of crisis. But I knew that his duty was to preserve evidence, to ensure the continuity of the investigation, and this meant being there when I faced the unimaginable.

Crossing the threshold of the door, my heart weighed heavy with anticipation and dread. There, on a gurney, lay my beloved husband, Chris, covered by a stark white sheet. His sturdy black boots peeked out from underneath, a heartbreaking sight that emphasized the tragedy of the moment. An intubation tube protruded from his lifeless body, a cold reminder of the efforts made to save him.

Unable to take my eyes off Chris, I mustered the strength to make a simple request, my voice trembling with emotion.

"Can you take that tube out?" I sought a glimpse of his familiar face, hoping to find solace in the reassurance of his features.

The doctor, standing close to Chris' head, expressed his regrets. "No, I'm sorry. The tube has to stay." His voice was filled with compassion, but he was unable to grant my wish.

As the doctor began to reveal the extent of Chris' injuries, my heart clenched in anguish. Multiple gunshots had torn through his body, each wound a painful testament to the senseless act that had robbed him from us. I would come to learn from the autopsy report that Chris had been shot four times; in the upper left thigh, through the pelvic bone, through the left chest muscle, which also punctured his left arm, and the fatal blow was through his neck, nearly completely severing his jugular vein.

Despite the emotional turmoil surrounding me, I moved closer to Chris, my hands trembling as I reached for his. Holding his cold, lifeless hand in both of mine, I turned his wedding ring gently on his finger, cherishing the symbol of our love and commitment. A desperate longing to remove it from his finger filled my heart, but I didn't ask if I could take it off. I knew the answer would be no.

Whispering into his ear, I told him how much I loved him while my tears fell like gentle raindrops on his skin. With a tender touch, I stroked his smooth forehead, my thumb tracing the familiar contours. It felt as though he was just sleeping, his strong presence somehow still there.

In the background, Brad struggled to contain his emotions, a mirror to my own heartache. It was a surreal and devastating moment, one that would forever be etched in my memory.

Sitting beside Chris, holding his hand tightly, I could hear the rhythmic ticking of the clock in the background, a reminder of time slipping away. My eyes wandered to the wall opposite me, where containers and supplies adorned the space. The blue containers, each with crooked labels, seemed to draw my attention, and I couldn't help but imagine myself straightening them if I worked there. It was as if my mind was grasping for any semblance of normalcy among the chaos.

Amidst the heartache, a rational part of me questioned how long I should stay by his side. I knew that nothing I did could bring him back to life, and yet, leaving felt like an acknowledgment of the reality that awaited me—a future without him. The minutes passed like an eternity, and with each moment, the distance between the life I had known and the unknown future seemed to widen.

Summoning the courage to take a brief respite, I asked the nurse if I could use the washroom attached to the ER. Walking down the sterile hallway, I couldn't help but notice the crocs shoes I had hurriedly slipped on when I fled from the house, now tracking blood with each step. It was a reminder of the tragedy that had unfolded just a short time ago.

Glancing back at Chris one last time, I passed by Brad, his presence a silent testament to the reality of the situation. Returning to the small room where my life had been forever changed, I knew that this was just the beginning of a long and painful journey of grief and healing.

2

•••••

CHRIS AND I were introduced by a mutual friend in the late summer of 2000. We were headed into our last year of university, he at Wilfrid Laurier and I at the University of Waterloo. It was the beginning of football season. The Laurier Golden Hawks were in the middle of football tryouts and conditioning camp. My apartment was a short walk from the stadium, a convenient place to rest and eat during their two-a-day practice schedule. My first memory of Chris is of him entering my apartment wearing black dress pants with a silver buckled belt, a grey golf shirt and black dress shoes. His attire was in sharp contrast to what our friend was wearing, grey sweats with a purple and gold hawk emblem on the thigh. Chris was coming from an interview at the fast-food chain Wendy's.

His appearance was striking, especially for a twenty three year-old. He was 6'2" and bald. Granted, he shaved his head, but even if he chose to grow out his hair, he would have only been able to sport the Friar-Tuck look, where the hair grows around the lower ridge of the head. He had a huge, charming smile that highlighted his signature chicklets, his two front teeth. I learned in that initial conversation that he wanted to be a Mountie, and had begun the application process to join the Royal Canadian Mounted Police (RCMP). Chris' dream became a reality as he proudly tossed his cadet epaulettes into the air during his graduation. He finished his training at Depot in Regina in February 2002. That moment was filled with joy and pride, not only for Chris but for both of our families who gathered to witness this significant milestone in his life. For the first time since we began dating, our parents met each other, sharing in our happiness and excitement.

As the celebrations echoed around us, a bittersweet realization settled in our hearts. That night marked the beginning of a four-month separation. But we were no strangers to long-distance relationships, having faced such realities in the past.

In the spring of April 2001, Chris and I embarked on a romance that blossomed in the bustling nightclub where we both worked. He took on the role of a vigilant bouncer, while I served as a charismatic bartender, and amidst the vibrant energy of the club, our paths intertwined. It didn't take long for us to gravitate towards each other, and soon, we found ourselves spending more and more time together beyond the confines of work. My heart was captivated, and I was utterly smitten by this incredible man.

As we delved deeper into our relationship, the imminent possibility of being apart weighed on our hearts and minds, but we were ready to make this relationship work. I supported Chris as he embarked on the rigorous journey of becoming an RCMP officer. I stood by him through every step of the application process, from the stringent security screening to the demanding physical tests and the nerve-wracking interview. Each day was filled with a sense of anticipation, as we wondered if "today might be the day" when the long-awaited call would come, leading him closer to fulfilment of his dreams.

While the thought of him realizing his aspirations filled me with excitement, it also brought a tinge of fear and sadness for us to be separated. The training academy required all cadets to reside on the base, leaving little room for free time, and even when granted, it was a rare and treasured luxury. In mid-August, the pivotal call finally came, and with just two weeks to prepare, Chris readied himself for the momentous move from Ontario to Saskatchewan. He was now part of Troop Thirteen, a significant step on his life's path.

As the day of departure arrived, we stood at the airport, emotions swirling within us. Pride for Chris' accomplishment intertwined with the undeniable yearning to be together. We bid our farewells, knowing that this was a temporary parting. With a mix of admiration and longing, I watched him clear security, walking towards his dreams and a future that we knew we would face together, no matter the miles that separated us.

On Chris' second day of training, the world was forever changed by the tragic events of 9/11. As we watched in shock and disbelief, the horrifying attacks unfolded in New York, leaving a permanent mark on our hearts.

The events of that fateful morning served as a distressing reminder of the sacrifices made by first responders, and the profound impact their dedication has on the lives of their families as well. We knew from the beginning that Chris' path as an RCMP officer would come with inherent risks, but witnessing the bravery and selflessness displayed by those in the line of duty brought the weight of that reality crashing down upon us.

In our minds, we had always accepted the possibility that his chosen career might place him in harm's way, but like so many others, we never truly believed it would become our reality. We had forged our commitment to one another, knowing that love could conquer any challenges that lay ahead. However, the events of that day served as a reminder that life is unpredictable, and sometimes the path we choose can lead us into unexpected and difficult circumstances.

Our love continued to grow amidst the separation, as daily emails checked in a computer lab and frequent phone calls from the dorm payphone became our cherished routine. Despite the distance, we found comfort in our connection, sharing our hopes and dreams with each other, holding onto the promise of a future together.

In the beautiful autumn of October, I made a special trip from Toronto to Regina for a weekend visit, eager to be by Chris' side. The moment I arrived, the excitement was palpable—as I toured the base, met Chris' fellow troopmates and immersed myself in his world. To make the weekend even more special, we cheered on the Saskatchewan Rough Riders at a football game, creating beautiful memories as twenty-three and twenty-four-year-olds in love, relishing every moment together.

As December arrived, the holiday season brought Chris back to Ontario for a few precious days over the Christmas break, bringing us the joyous opportunity to be in each other's arms once again.

And then, in a magical moment beneath the mistletoe, everything changed. Dressed in his smart attire, donning dress pants, a collared shirt, and his RCMP-issued leather boots, Chris got down on one knee, his eyes sparkling with love and hope. With unwavering certainty, he asked the most important question of our lives.

"Will you marry me?"

Time seemed to stand still as my heart swelled with emotion. Overwhelmed by love and happiness, I said "yes!" without hesitation, embracing the journey that lay ahead as partners in life. With the joy of our engagement lighting up our souls, we spent the rest of the holiday season sharing our news with our delighted family and friends, their warm embrace and well-wishes surrounding us in love.

Our pattern of seeing each other every two months persisted, and I eagerly attended Chris' graduation in February. This visit felt distinct from the one I had made in October. With our engagement now official, new aspects were coming into play, and my health was being evaluated as they considered Chris' first posting. A psychological questionnaire and a joint meeting with a psychologist were required for us to navigate this stage. It was an unusual juxtaposition, discussing our future while the graduation weekend festivities buzzed in the background.

The psychologist began the session with an unexpected and somewhat disheartening statistic: "Police officers have a 54% divorce rate." As a newly engaged couple, it was not exactly the uplifting conversation we had anticipated. However, he went on to share invaluable advice about the importance of maintaining a life outside the all-consuming "blue-world" of policing. His words resonated deeply with us, as he emphasized the significance of finding hobbies, interests, and friendships that could offer an alternative perspective and healthy support.

At that moment, I didn't fully grasp the profound impact this piece of advice would have on my life moving forward. Little did I know that it would become an essential lifeline in my journey of survival. As we absorbed the psychologist's guidance, we realized that finding balance in our lives was crucial to nurturing our relationship and navigating the unique challenges that lay ahead.

After Chris' momentous graduation on a Monday, the following morning found us on a flight bound for Toronto. The day was bittersweet as we spent the afternoon at my sister Deb's apartment, knowing that it would be our last moments together for the next four months. That very night, I had a flight scheduled to Australia, where I had enrolled at the University of Western Sydney to pursue my desire of becoming an elementary school teacher. This had been my plan even before I met Chris—to travel the world and acquire the education needed to fulfill my passion for teaching.

The atmosphere in Deb's apartment was sombre, and my heart was heavy with sadness as I faced the prospect of leaving. I couldn't help but feel that I was missing out on the opportunity to lay down the foundation of a shared life and build a sense of community together in a new city. I longed to set down roots, but my journey to Sydney—literally on the other side of the world—seemed overwhelming and ill-timed.

For Chris, a different path awaited him as he was posted to Yellowknife, in Canada's far north. Unlike me, he exuded excitement and enthusiasm as he looked forward to stepping out into the world as Constable C.J. Worden, ready to utilize the skills he had honed during his training to help those in need. While I was struggling with leaving, he embraced this new adventure with fervour, eager to make a difference in his role as a law enforcement officer.

As the evening approached, the time came for us to part ways at the airport, our emotions mingling with hope and uncertainty. We knew we would see each other again in a few months, but the challenges of coordinating phone calls between his shift work and the different time zones lay ahead.

Each email and phone call we exchanged brought new layers of understanding and closeness to our relationship. While I was immersing myself in my studies and embracing my new surroundings in Sydney, Chris was doing the same in Yellowknife. We were both carving our paths in different corners of the world, yet our hearts remained intimately connected.

In June, during my school break, I had the opportunity to fly back to Canada for three weeks, and I eagerly embraced the chance to be with Chris again. He was living in Force housing, and as I stepped into the cozy abode, I couldn't help but be impressed by how far we had come. The accommodations were a far cry from our student days, and it filled my heart with pride to see how much we had grown as individuals and as a couple.

With excitement sparkling in his eyes, Chris showed me around Yellowknife, a city rich in cultural heritage and the traditional home of many of Canada's indigenous peoples. The capital and largest city in the Northwest Territories, it had a population of 18,500 at the time. It was a city built on rocks and surrounded by water. The landscape was beautiful and much enjoyed as we took full advantage of being in the land of the midnight sun. I marvelled at the detachment, the courthouse, and the places where Chris and his fellow officers would be called to assist, all of which I had heard about in our emails and phone conversations.

As I met his watch-mates and others working in the office, the world he had described to me through our digital exchanges came to life before my eyes. The future that I had eagerly anticipated was no longer a distant dream; it was here, taking shape in this vibrant community. Eager to fulfill my own aspirations of becoming an elementary school teacher, I introduced myself to school principals, making them aware of my impending certification and availability to teach in December 2002.

After that visit, I carried a profound sense of clarity in my heart. Our life together was on the right path, and the life we could lead as a united couple filled my soul with comfort and joy. Yellowknife embraced me with open arms, and I felt at ease in this community that Chris had come to love. With the future stretching out before us, we were ready to embrace it hand in hand.

In November 2002, I finally joined Chris permanently in Yellowknife. I had completed my degree, travelled the mesmerizing west coast of Australia, made cherished memories and formed bonds with amazing people along the way. As I embraced this chapter of my life, I knew I was ready to embark on the adventure of being the spouse of a first responder.

3

THE VISION WE had for our future was both inspiring and heartwarming. We saw ourselves as a dynamic power couple, each contributing in our own way to make the world a better place. Chris would be the protector, serving his community with unwavering dedication and courage. Meanwhile, I would be the nurturer, imparting knowledge and values to the young minds of tomorrow as an elementary school teacher. Together, we were poised to create a life that seemed like something out of storybooks, filled with love, purpose, and shared dreams.

Our hearts were filled with excitement and anticipation as we prepared to start this new chapter. As I settled into our life in Yellowknife, I marvelled at the beauty of the northern landscape and the warmth of the close-knit community. The support and camaraderie among the first responder families was uplifting, reminding me that we were not alone on this journey. We had found our place, and together, we were building a life that felt like a fairy tale come true.

On February 22, 2003, we exchanged vows in the heart of my hometown. It was a moment of immense pride and joy as

Chris stood tall in his ceremonial Red Serge uniform, and we walked out of the church under the dignified presence of the honour guard's flags, surrounded by a gentle mix of drizzle and snow creating a dreamlike atmosphere. The weather seemed like nature's way of showering us with blessings.

Finally, we had done it! Through all the challenges and months of being apart, we had persevered, and our love had brought us to this day. Over our twenty-two-month relationship, we had spent fifteen months apart, nearly sixty-eight percent of our time together separated by oceans and time zones.

As we returned to Yellowknife, we did so with a sense of pride, now united as Mr. and Mrs. Worden. The future we had dreamed of was now unfolding before our eyes, and we were eager to embrace the joys and challenges of life as a married couple.

With my teacher certification process underway, I had the opportunity to substitute teach while applying for permanent positions. It was an exciting time as I pursued my dream job as the physical education specialist at St. Joe's Elementary School. With my background in kinesiology, this role allowed me to do what I loved most: promote the importance of physical activity and bring joy and fun to each class for 40 minutes at a time throughout the day.

As I settled into my role at the school, I also began to build strong friendships with my co-workers, stepping outside the familiar boundaries of the "blue-world" and embracing a social life beyond the police community. Chris and I were finding a beautiful balance between our personal and professional lives, and the city of Yellowknife offered a unique backdrop for us to grow as a young couple.

We adapted to Chris' shift schedule, which comprised two days on duty, followed by two nights, and then four days off.

The predictability of this schedule allowed us to make the most of our time together, especially in the land of the midnight sun, where extended daylight hours seemed to make up for the time we had spent apart in the past. Our days were filled with love and laughter as we explored the wonders of Yellowknife and the surrounding landscapes. From adventurous hikes to quiet strolls, we made memories that would last a lifetime.

In the winter following our wedding, a unique opportunity presented itself for Chris to transfer to a fly-in settlement further north. Wha Ti, with a population of 652 people, was accessible by air all year round and by ice-road for two months during the winter. It was a place steeped in tradition, surrounded by the breathtaking beauty of a serene lake. The settlement housed a two-person policing detachment, a nursing station, a Co-op food store, and a school that served students from kindergarten to grade twelve, with an attached adult basic education wing for distance education courses run by Aurora College. Eager to embrace the experience of living on traditional lands, we wholeheartedly accepted this transfer.

Wha Ti was a breathtakingly beautiful place of raw, untouched wilderness and awe-inspiring landscapes. The settlement was perched on the shores of a pristine lake, its tranquil waters reflecting the vivid colours of the surrounding boreal forest. As the seasons shifted, the landscape transformed, offering a stunning display of nature's ever-changing canvas.

During the colder months, a thick blanket of snow covered the land, creating a winter wonderland that glistened under the shimmering northern lights. The icy lake became a frozen highway, facilitating access to the settlement via the ice-road during the coldest days. The winter months brought a sense of serenity, with the sound of crunching snow underfoot and the occasional soft rustle of wildlife navigating through the snow-covered trees.

As spring arrived, a sense of rejuvenation swept through the land. The temperatures rose, and the ice began to thaw, giving way to a new season of growth and renewal. The boreal forest came alive with an explosion of vibrant colours and the sweet scent of blossoms. Wildflowers dotted the landscape, and the once-frozen lake rippled with life as migratory birds returned to nest along its shores.

Throughout the summer, the sun remained a constant companion, never truly setting during the magical phenomenon known as the "midnight sun." The days stretched on endlessly, creating a surreal experience of eternal daylight. The community embraced the summer months with outdoor activities, from fishing and boating on the glistening lake to hiking through the dense forests, where the scent of pine and earth filled the air.

As autumn painted the landscape with warm hues of orange and gold, the settlement prepared for the arrival of winter once more. The fleeting beauty of the fall foliage served as a reminder of the cyclical nature of life in the North, where the changing seasons brought both challenges and marvels.

Living in Wha Ti allowed us to witness the incredible resilience of nature and the profound connection between the land and its people. The vastness of the wilderness provided a sense of freedom and an escape from the busyness of urban life, allowing us to truly appreciate the wonders of the natural world.

Over the course of our twenty-one months in Wha Ti, we had both sets of parents come to visit us at different times. Chris' parents arrived in early March 2005, during an unforgettable and upsetting moment in our lives. Their visit coincided with the tragic event that shook the entire country: the murder of four RCMP officers in the small Alberta town of Mayerthorpe. Constables Anthony Gordon, Leo Johnston, Brock Myrol, and Peter Schiemannn lost their lives in the line of duty, leaving behind grieving families and a nation in mourning.

I can still picture Chris' mom sitting on our couch, her face filled with empathy and sadness as we watched the news together.

"Oh, those poor families," she said.

Just that thought filled the room with heaviness. This tragedy hit close to home, reminding us of the sacrifices and risks that come with being a part of the law enforcement community. The loss of these brave officers underscored the importance of cherishing every moment we had with our loved ones and appreciating the time we spent together.

Isolated postings typically lasted for two years, and before long our time in Wha Ti had come to an end. In November 2005, we were moving to Chris' final posting in Hay River. Before settling into our new home, we decided to embark on a five-week adventure to South Africa, a journey that held special significance for Chris.

As a graduate of Wilfrid Laurier University with a major in political science, Chris had studied the history of South Africa extensively, particularly the era of Apartheid. He was eager to experience the country firsthand, to walk in the places he had learned about in textbooks, and to immerse himself in the culture and history of this remarkable nation. It was a deeply meaningful trip for him, connecting the academic knowledge he had acquired with the reality on the ground.

Beyond fulfilling Chris' educational aspirations, this trip also marked an important milestone in our journey as a couple.

We knew that we were ready to start a family, and the decision to explore South Africa was, in a way, a celebration of this new phase of our lives. We were aware that parenthood would bring new responsibilities and commitments, so we embraced this opportunity to venture into the world together for what we anticipated might be the last big adventure before our family expanded.

During those five weeks, we traversed the diverse landscapes of South Africa, from the bustling city streets of Cape Town to the vast savannahs of Kruger National Park. We marveled at the majestic wildlife, soaked in the breathtaking beauty of the Cape Winelands, and stood in awe before the powerful presence of Table Mountain. Beyond the tourist attractions, we took the time to engage with the locals, immersing ourselves in their traditions, cuisine, and stories. The trip was a profound experience that deepened our understanding of the country's history and its people whose resilience and spirit left a lasting impression on us.

Moving to Hay River, a town connected to the road system, was a game-changer for us. The accessibility of supplies and the ability to travel more easily brought a new level of excitement and convenience to our lives. We relished the fact that we could now stock up on essentials from Costco during our trips to visit my sister Sandy in Red Deer, just a twelve-hour drive away. Our truck would return loaded with all the necessities, making our daily lives in Hay River more comfortable and enjoyable.

The road system also made it possible for us to connect with friends in Yellowknife, just over a five-hour drive away. Reuniting with family and friends in person brought immeasurable joy, especially when living so far from our blood relatives. We quickly learned that our friends in the Territories became our chosen family. We became pillars of support for each other, forming strong bonds forged by shared experiences and the common challenges of life in the north. Many of our friends were imports from other provinces, working in the same unique environment. These connections became an essential part of our lives, offering us comfort and camaraderie in the face of the vast northern landscape.

I was fortunate to secure a part-time teaching position at Diamond Jenness Secondary School, which was affectionately known as the 'purple school.' This institution gained widespread recognition when Robert Munsch wrote the children's book 'Smelly Socks,' inspired by its purple-coloured exterior. I taught social studies in the mornings and also provided additional support to students who needed it. The flexible schedule was a blessing, especially when I became pregnant in May 2006. I could balance work and rest according to the needs of my changing body.

The news of my pregnancy filled us with immense joy and anticipation. We were thrilled to be embarking on the journey of parenthood. The support from our friends and the close-knit community made the experience even more special. As my belly grew, so did our excitement to welcome a new member into our family.

We were ecstatic to be starting our own family, and dreamed of becoming a family of six. Both of us grew up in families of that size, and the dynamics of a large family were something we cherished and wanted to recreate.

As my due date approached, we travelled to Yellowknife, eagerly awaiting the arrival of our newest family member. Fortunately, my pregnancy had been smooth and uncomplicated, and we were filled with anticipation as we prepared to welcome our baby into the world. On February 6, 2007, our lives changed forever when Alexis Marie was born. She was a beautiful and healthy baby, with a striking resemblance to her father. People couldn't help but notice the uncanny resemblance between them, often comparing them to the iconic duo of Austin Powers and Mini-Me. We even had a playful Halloween costume idea of Chris wearing a baby carrier with Alexis facing outward.

Life as a new family of three was pure bliss. Chris doted on Alexis with love and devotion, cherishing every moment spent together. It warmed my heart to see their undeniable connection. We were planning an epic road trip to Ontario in October to show the family how much Alexis had grown.

This trip was meant to be a joyous adventure, a chance for us to pick up the motorhome we had purchased and visit with our family. Our vision was to traverse the vast expanse of Canada, crossing provinces and territories in the RV, creating beautiful memories together along the way. We were excited to explore the breathtaking landscapes, connect with nature, and bask in the freedom of the open road during our time off.

However, the events of October 6, 2007, changed everything. The news of Chris' murder sent shockwaves through our world, shattering our dreams and plans. Our journey to Ontario would still take place, but for an entirely different reason.

4

COUNSELLOR AND PSYCHOTHERAPIST Belinda Sidhu's explanation of "survivor mode" resonates deeply with my experience after the tragic loss of Chris. She explains that "in simple terms, 'survivor mode' is our body's automatic response to danger….this can lead to that fight/flight/freeze response." It was as if my body and mind were on high alert, constantly scanning for danger and trying to cope with the overwhelming emotional turmoil. The fight, flight, or freeze response became a constant companion, and it took all my energy trying to navigate through each moment.

The passage of time during those first twenty-four hours after Chris' death was a surreal blur. Some moments felt like a whirlwind, where everything was moving at an alarming pace, while in other moments time seemed to drag on endlessly. My mind struggled to make sense of the immense grief, questions, and emotions that flooded it. I was stuck in a disorienting fog, unable to find a clear path forward.

Numbness and raw intensity coexisted within me. I could feel my emotions oscillating between feeling nothing at all and being overwhelmed by a tidal wave of pain and sorrow. It was an incredibly disorienting experience, as if my heart and mind were engaged in a constant battle.

Simple tasks that once seemed effortless now felt daunting and overwhelming. I knew there were things that needed to be taken care of, but I couldn't find the energy or focus to even start. The weight of grief and shock clouded my ability to make decisions or carry out basic actions. I needed help, and that's when my chosen family and the RCMP family came to my aid.

As my house filled up with friends and loved ones, the weight of their presence and the silence that hung in the air was heavy. Each person's sympathetic gaze spoke volumes, but there were no words that could bridge the chasm of grief that engulfed me. Amidst the sea of concerned faces, the silence felt deafening, leaving me grappling with the enormity of the tragedy that had befallen us.

I knew that I had to make phone calls, to reach out to those who cared for us and who would undoubtedly have the same burning questions that consumed my own thoughts. But the answers to their inquiries were as elusive to me as they were to them. *How did this happen? Where was the person responsible? What were the next steps?*

The lack of answers only added to the sense of helplessness and confusion that gripped my heart. It was as if I was standing at the edge of an abyss, searching for solid ground but finding none. I needed to have a plan, to know what to say, but the words escaped me. The reality was too painful, too raw, to be contained in a simple explanation.

I decided to make my first call to my friend Michèle. She and I had been friends since my first days substitute teaching in

Yellowknife. I took a deep breath and started to speak, asking her to listen without interrupting. My voice trembling, I told her the devastating news: "Chris was shot and killed last night. I don't know who did it, and they are looking for them. Can you get here?"

Michèle's immediate response was one of unwavering support. She understood the urgency and pain in my voice and didn't hesitate to be by my side during this unimaginable time. Without hesitation, she arranged a flight to Hay River, where she would stand by me through the dark days that followed.

The same rehearsed line was used when I called my parents back in Ontario. It was an indescribably difficult conversation to have, as I could feel their pain through the phone line. After delivering the devastating news, my father's emotions overwhelmed him, and the phone dropped from his hand. My mom picked up the call, and I found the strength to repeat the tragic truth, knowing that they too would drop everything to be by my side.

Two days later, my parents arrived in Hay River, standing strong with me as we faced the grief together. The support and love from both my chosen family and blood relatives helped me navigate through the darkest moments of my life. Their presence, without words, conveyed the unwavering commitment to walk beside me through the storm of sorrow.

The weight of the information I held, knowing that Chris' parents had not yet been informed of the tragedy, was excruciating. The RCMP had advised against me making that call as they were arranging for two police officers to deliver the devastating news in person. The three-hour wait felt like an eternity, each passing minute filled with heartache and the knowledge that they were blissfully unaware of the life-altering news that awaited them.

In Ottawa, Chris' parents John and Mary Ann, and two of their remaining children, Cathy and Michael, were enjoying a celebratory brunch for their thirty-fourth wedding anniversary, completely unaware of the impending visit from the officers that would shatter their world. Chris' youngest brother, Peter, was overseas in Europe, making it even more difficult to coordinate the flow of information.

The shooter remained at large, heightening the tension and fear in both communities we were a part of. As the investigation unfolded, the geographical search area for the shooter widened. In the Northwest Territories, where only a small number of police officers were stationed, the remoteness of the region presented challenges in managing the situation. Reinforcements from neighbouring provinces were brought in to support the investigation. I found some comfort in the knowledge that many of the lead investigators were people Chris had worked with in the past. Their presence provided a sense of familiarity and reassurance during this tumultuous time. Knowing that they were tirelessly working to find justice brought a glimmer of reassurance in the midst of the chaos. As the days passed, it was challenging to control the flow of information between the Northwest Territories and Alberta, where the investigation was taking place, and our family in Ontario.

The days following Chris' death were a whirlwind of activity and emotions. A command centre was established at the nearby hotel to coordinate efforts and support the investigation. For our safety, a police officer was stationed outside our house around the clock. The six-hour gap between Chris being called out and his body being found meant that the perpetrator had a significant head start in their escape. The news of the murder spread rapidly, leaving both the community and the media searching for information. However, little information was available, leaving everyone with more questions than answers.

In the community, there was an outpouring of support. Residents wrapped trees and light poles with blue ribbons as a symbol of solidarity and respect for Chris' service. People dropped off food and cards at our home, wanting to show their sympathy and care. However, the influx of visitors became overwhelming, and I asked Michèle to act as an intermediary, gently requesting people to give me space to process my grief in private.

Throughout this heartbreaking time, our baby daughter brought both comfort and challenge. She was too young to comprehend the magnitude of the loss, and her routine demanded my attention, forcing me to stay present and continue as her mother. Being there for her became my anchor, even as my world fell apart. Being her mom was the one thing I could control, and it provided a sense of stability during a time of chaos. Taking care of her, feeding her, giving her baths, and reading her stories became my sanctuary, even as tears streamed down my face.

The doctor at the hospital provided me with Ativan to help manage the overwhelming emotions and assist with sleep. Taking the pill made my body feel heavy and slow, but it did little to ease the overwhelming thoughts and emotions I was experiencing. The weight of being an only parent and losing my best friend and soulmate was crushing and there seemed to be no easy way to find relief from the pain.

5

THE SUPPORT FROM the RCMP during those first dark days was beyond anything I could have imagined. Not only were they tirelessly working on the operational side, handling the manhunt and investigation, but the administrative side also stepped up to offer incredible support to both me and the Worden family.

I was informed that someone from the Member/Employee Assistance Program (MEAP) would be arriving to provide guidance and support. When I saw a uniformed member at our doorstep, I assumed it was the MEAP, but to my surprise, it was the Commanding Officer of Chris' division. His presence brought a mix of emotions—gratitude for his condolences and support, but also a yearning for more information. Unfortunately, at that moment, he had very few details to share. I heard words like "everyone is working hard," "this case is their number one priority," and "Chris will always be remembered," but they seemed to fade into the background as I struggled to grasp the reality of the situation.

When people spoke about Chris in the past tense, I would further remove myself from reality. It was difficult to process their words, and I longed for concrete information and guidance on making funeral arrangements. I wanted to focus on facts, on what needed to be done, rather than dwelling on the overwhelming emotions that threatened to engulf me.

Thankfully, my MEAP did eventually arrive, accompanied by Sergeant Brent Baulkham, a member of the Staff Relations Representative (SRR) program. Brent had been involved in supporting families during the tragic funerals in Mayerthorpe and was experienced in dealing with the complexities of grieving families. He brought with him not only the expertise of a trained negotiator but also the compassionate ear of an excellent listener. These qualities proved invaluable as we navigated the regimental funeral process and the myriad of emotions that accompanied our grief.

In the aftermath of Chris' murder, I found myself grappling with an overwhelming flood of emotions and questions that seemed to have no easy answers. It felt as if I was observing everything from a distance, like I was floating above myself, disconnected from reality. The haze that surrounded me made it difficult to process the weight of the situation and the multitude of tasks that needed to be addressed.

I noticed that people began to speak to me in slow, simple language, as if I had regressed to a child-like state. Their eyes searched for any sign of acknowledgment or recognition from me, but I struggled to respond in the way that they expected. Some topics would immediately pull me into full alertness, like discussions about the ongoing investigation. In those moments, I was attentive and focused, trying to gain any understanding of what had happened.

However, when others approached me with words of sympathy and sorrow, I found myself tuning them out. I didn't want their pity or reassurance. My grief was too raw, and I felt a sense of resentment towards those seeking comfort from me when I needed it the most. In my fragile state, I couldn't fully comprehend their intentions.

Grief has a way of warping our sense of reality, making it difficult to navigate through everyday interactions. It felt as if I was wearing a thick emotional armour, shielding myself from anything that might exacerbate my pain. I was on auto-pilot, just trying to get through each day without completely unravelling.

The process of planning a regimental funeral from a distance was a daunting task. As the legal spouse, I was responsible for making decisions, but I made sure to include Chris' parents every step of the way. Regular communication between us was crucial as we navigated the logistics and other details of the funeral arrangements. Together, we decided that a regimental funeral in Ottawa, Chris' hometown and the nation's capital, would be the most fitting way to honour his memory and service.

Coordinating a large-scale formal service across provinces before the era of smartphones was no small feat. It required meticulous organization and collaboration between the RCMP members in both provinces to ensure everything went smoothly. While funerals for fallen officers were not common, they had become more frequent in recent years, leading to the establishment of procedures and policies to support the planning process.

The circumstances surrounding Chris' death added additional complexity to the planning. As an active murder investigation, Chris had to undergo an autopsy before he was transported across the country. Balancing the ceremonial considerations with the demands of an ongoing investigation required careful coordination and cooperation.

With all these factors in mind, we set the funeral date for October 15, 2007. It left me with just eight days to get everything in order, which felt like an impossibly short time frame for the magnitude of what needed to be done. Yet, I remained determined to give Chris the honourable farewell he deserved.

In the midst of the overwhelming grief and turmoil, the MEAP and SRR were there to guide me through the process of planning Chris' regimental funeral. They explained the rules of engagement, the aspects that could be adjusted, and those that were non-negotiable. In moments where I could find a sense of control, I seized the opportunity to make decisions and express my intentions clearly. It was a way for me to navigate the uncertainty and regain some semblance of power in an otherwise uncontrollable situation.

At times, when faced with choices where I felt no strong preference, I would involve Chris' parents and offer them the decision. For instance, whether to proceed with burial or cremation was a question that needed answering, as Chris and I had not discussed his preference. Both Chris and I were raised in practising Catholic families, where burial was the customary choice. When John and MaryAnn expressed their wish for Chris to be buried, I readily agreed. They researched options and chose Beechwood Cemetery in Ottawa, which is Canada's national cemetery, as Chris' final resting place. Again, I concurred with their decision, acknowledging that it would bring them comfort to be able to visit their son's grave close to where he grew up.

Throughout these difficult days, I was acutely aware of my youth, being only twenty-nine years old, and facing a life-altering tragedy. I knew my path had taken an unexpected and unexplained detour, and the future looked uncertain. But I remained hopeful that with time, I would find a new path that would eventually lead to happiness. While I couldn't predict where this new road would take me, knowing that Chris' parents found solace in the chosen resting place gave me reassurance that he would not be alone, even if I couldn't be there with him.

In the aftermath of Chris' death, I found myself grappling with the concept of the human experience after death. My belief in the existence of the soul led me to imagine that Chris' had been released and become part of a greater community of angels and spirits that guide and protect their loved ones. Despite this spiritual understanding, I couldn't help but project human emotions onto his deceased body. It was still too raw and new to accept that the vibrant man I had married and the father of our child was no longer experiencing the world as I knew it. In my heart, I wanted to believe that he was now in a better place, a place I called heaven, where he could continue to watch over Alexis and me from another plane of existence.

I grappled with my faith during those days. I struggled with the concept of God's plan. How could such a tragedy be part of any divine plan? I questioned why God would allow such evil and violence to occur in the world, why there was so much suffering and injustice. These questions had occurred to me for years, and now they intensified in the face of this tragedy. While organized religion had caused strife and conflict, I sought solace in spirituality, believing that Chris' essence and soul remained accessible to us. I clung to the idea that he would continue to guide me in parenting Alexis, even from beyond this earthly realm.

I wanted to feel his presence as I provided comfort to our daughter. In the nights that followed Chris' death, I would tell her,"Mommy and daddy love you and daddy is watching over you from heaven." This ritual continued for nearly a year, serving as a source of reassurance and hope for both of us in the midst of our grief.

My parents arrived Sunday afternoon. They'd flown overnight to be with me. While enroute they met reporters who were making their way to Hay River to report on the story of Chris' death and the circumstances around it. The shooter had still not been identified and their whereabouts was unknown. My parents spoke with a few members of the media and their quotes appeared in papers across the country the next day. My sister Deb had spoken to a reporter from her apartment in Toronto. Her words about Chris and my relationship were added to the story about the shooting, the ongoing investigation, and the man hunt. Facebook groups were created for people to share memories, stories, and condolences. I made a conscious decision not to engage in reading the posts. My capacity to absorb condolences was already reaching its limits as I focussed on the immediate decisions that needed to be made before I left Hay River for Chris' funeral in Ottawa. One of those immediate decisions was whether I was going to make a statement to the media.

The events surrounding Chris' murder brought a surge of curiosity and speculation about my life, leading to numerous requests from the media to speak with my family. Chris' parents responded with a simple "No comment" to protect their privacy. Meanwhile, RCMP news conferences offered limited new information, leaving gaps that were filled with assumptions and inaccuracies about our life. Feeling the need to set the record straight and express gratitude for the overwhelming support we'd received, I spent Sunday evening crafting a statement.

On a Monday afternoon, flanked by my parents, Michèle, and senior RCMP officers, I stood on our front lawn to address the public. With my mom holding Alexis in her arms, I spoke about Chris' love for family, life, and football. I expressed gratitude for the outpouring of support and outlined ways the public could honour Chris' memory through donations. I announced the creation of the Chris Worden Memorial Award, dedicated to supporting the football program and players at Laurier University. I worked with one of Chris' former football coaches to establish this award, which would honour athletes who exemplified the qualities that Chris cherished—accountability, teamwork, courage, compassion, justice, and a love of learning. It was my way of ensuring that Chris' values and legacy would continue to inspire others. As the press conference concluded, I held Alexis tightly in my arms, seeking comfort and strength from the presence of my daughter. At the end, I reiterated my plea for privacy as I retreated back into the house.

It seemed like every few hours, there was a new "person of importance" showing up at my door, believing that they should offer their condolences in person due to their position or experience. I put "person of importance" in quotes because that was how others perceived them, not necessarily how I saw them. These were individuals Chris and I had never met, and I struggled to understand why they felt entitled to be there during such a deeply personal and difficult time. My emotions were raw, and I had little desire or capacity to engage with even those I had known and loved for years.

The idea of expending my energy to sit with these strangers, just so their offices could report that they had "spoken with the widow," didn't sit well with me. I found it challenging to navigate these encounters, as my grief and devastation were so intense that I could barely maintain composure with my closest confidants. In the privacy of my circle of trust, the chosen few who sat with me in my living room, I expressed myself without filters. My emotions poured out as I tried to find some semblance of understanding and a path forward amidst the overwhelming pain.

In those moments, my thoughts were far from polished or professional. I was grappling with intense anger, grief, and the feeling of having my soul ripped open. Those who were there to support me listened to my raw and unfiltered dialogue, allowing me to vent and rage as I searched for some sense of resolution and clarity in the face of unimaginable loss.

Once these initial feelings were dispelled from my thoughts, I made a conscious effort to believe that the people arriving at our home to express condolences were sincere in their support and compassion. Despite my initial skepticism about their status, I chose to accept their offers of assistance and contact information, recognizing that I could reach out to them when needed. I understood that leveraging their positions could help amplify my voice and advocate for the causes that were important to me.

One of the first "persons of importance" to visit me was RCMP Commissioner William Elliot, who had recently been appointed as the first civilian in that post. His appointment had been a topic of discussion between Chris, myself, and the other detachment members. Chris had been supportive of having a sworn peace officer heading our national police force and had not agreed with the government's choice to place a civilian in the role. Chris' opinion was shared by many serving on the front lines. Because of that, I struggled with the decision of whether or not to meet with Commissioner Elliot.

Despite my mixed emotions, I chose to engage with him, hoping that this demonstration of dedication to the organization and compassion for our family's loss would have a positive impact on frontline members. I believed that he needed to show his commitment to protecting those in the force and their families. This reassurance was not only essential for the frontline's well-being, but also had another motive. I wanted the officers investigating Chris' murder to be reminded that their work family needed them at their very best so they could capture the shooter and restore a sense of safety in my life.

Hay River was crawling with RCMP police officers from neighbouring divisions. Specialized units had been brought in. Tactical, canine, forensics, and general duty members were working around the clock to process the scene, chase leads, interview townspeople and relieve the Hay River detachment members from duty. Among the specialists was RCMP psychologist, Barb Schmaltz.

I asked to see Barb. When we met, I sat across from her in her hotel room not knowing where to begin. My greatest concern at the time was whether Alexis would have any memories of Chris. She spoke calmly and quietly.

"No, she's too young."

I also asked about quelling my mind, to stop thinking about being alone. A week past my twenty ninth birthday, I was fearful of living a life alone. I didn't want to be preoccupied with the thought of finding another person to fill this void. It was too soon and too uncomfortable and I wanted it to stop. I wanted so many things to stop. Barb urged me to anchor myself in the present instant by directing my attention to my breath. She demonstrated a method called box breathing wherein you inhale for a span of four seconds, then hold for another four seconds, followed by a four-second exhale, and concluding with a four-second pause before commencing the cycle again. Additionally, she suggested that the repetition of a mantra might provide assistance. I chose "just breathe."

Chris' Sergeant, Ron Rose, and his wife Constable Karla George, hosted a gathering in their home the night before we left Hay River. It was a profoundly emotional event that brought together members of the RCMP detachment, their families, auxiliary constables, Commissioner Elliot, the divisional leadership team, and close friends of both the force and our family. It was an overwhelming mix of grief, love, and support that filled the room.

As I walked through the door, the weight of Chris' absence felt heavier than ever. But seeing the familiar faces and feeling the warmth of their embraces made me realize that I wasn't alone on this painful journey. As I stood in that gathering, surrounded by people who loved Chris and cared for our family, my heart was heavy with grief, but also filled with gratitude. Gratitude for the warmth and compassion that enveloped me, for the stories that brought back memories of the wonderful man I had lost, and for the understanding looks and embraces that conveyed more than words ever could.

As each person shared their cherished memories of Chris, I felt a mix of emotions swirling inside me. There were tears, yes, but also laughter through the funny anecdotes and quirks that made Chris the incredible person he was. In those moments, I saw a glimpse of the man I fell in love with, the man who could light up a room with his smile and make everyone feel at ease.

But amidst the laughter, there was still the pain of knowing that Chris was gone, and that we would never share another physical moment together. The ache in my chest was relentless, a constant reminder of the void that now existed in my life. I longed to have him back, to hear his voice, to feel his touch, and to watch him be the amazing father I knew he would have been to our daughter.

Throughout the gathering, there was a sense of raw vulnerability, and no one tried to hide their pain. It was a safe space to express our emotions, whether through tears or silence.

Despite the heaviness of my heart, being surrounded by this supportive community gave me a glimmer of hope. It made me realize that I was not alone in my grief, that others were mourning alongside me, sharing their own struggles, and finding strength in each other. In their presence, I felt a connection to Chris that transcended the physical realm, as if his spirit was there with us, embracing us all in its loving presence.

In those few hours, the weight of the world felt just a little lighter. The walls that grief had built around my heart seemed to soften just a little. It wasn't a magical cure for the pain, but it was a brief respite from the overwhelming weight of loss. I was reminded that life would go on, that somehow, I would find the strength to keep moving forward, even when the pain threatened to consume me. And as I looked around at the faces of those who cared, I knew that I could lean on them when the burden felt too heavy to bear alone.

This gathering became a beacon of hope in the midst of my darkest days. It showed me that healing was possible, that love and support could carry us through the most unbearable times. And as we shared stories, tears, and laughter, I felt a glimmer of peace, knowing that Chris would live on not just in my heart, but in the hearts of all those who loved him too.

The next morning I prepared to travel to Ottawa. Leaving my house felt like stepping into an unknown abyss of grief. As I boarded the RCMP plane, I couldn't help but feel a heavy ache in my chest, knowing that this departure marked the end of the life I once knew. It was a surreal feeling, almost as if I was leaving a part of myself behind in that house.

Amidst the busyness of packing and planning, I had managed to keep my emotions in check, but as the moment of departure approached, the floodgates of grief opened. I needed a few moments of solitude, away from the concerned looks and sympathetic glances of my loved ones.

"Everybody out, I just need a few minutes," I implored, needing the space to release the pent-up emotions that had been building inside me.

Alone in our bedroom, clutching Chris' white undershirt, I allowed myself to unleash the anguish I had been holding back. The sounds that escaped me were primal, raw, and gut-wrenching. The reality of his absence hit me like a tidal wave, and I realized that I had to face a future without him. In that moment, I made silent vows to him, promises that I would honour our plans, raise Alexis with love and share stories of our life together to keep his memory alive in our hearts.

I sought strength from him, desperately hoping that his spirit was watching over us, guiding us through the darkness. It was as if I was having a one-sided conversation with him, pouring out my heart, seeking his protection and support. In the midst of my tears and pleas, a newfound determination began to take root within me.

As I emerged from that private moment, my resolve had solidified. I knew that upon our return, the house would become our home, Alexis' and mine. I would find a way to move forward, to navigate this uncharted territory, and to honour the love we shared. While the pain of his absence would never truly fade, I knew I had to be strong for Alexis.

The flight felt like a step into a future that I had not asked for nor expected. I held Alexis close, and in her innocent eyes, I found a glimmer of hope and a reason to keep going. We were embarking on a path we had not chosen, but we would walk it together, hand in hand, as we faced whatever lay ahead.

The days that followed were a blur of funeral preparations, tributes, and mourning. Through it all, I clung to the strength I had found in that moment alone in our bedroom. As I stood before the world, sharing Chris' story and my pain, I knew that I had to be a beacon of resilience, not just for myself, but for all those who loved him.

In the midst of heartache, I discovered a newfound sense of purpose. I would carry Chris' memory in my heart and ensure that his legacy lived on through our daughter. And as I stepped back into that house, our house, after the funeral, I knew that I would find a way to turn the pain of loss into a guiding light that would lead us forward in the years to come.

6

•••••

AS WE CONTINUED our journey to Ottawa, the plane felt both spacious and confining at the same time. The hum of the engines provided a steady background noise, almost like a lullaby, and I found myself lost in my thoughts as I stared out the window. The passing clouds seemed to mirror the whirlwind of emotions swirling within me.

Alexis was blissfully unaware of the weight of our situation, content in her own little world with her stuffed giraffe and pacifier. Her innocence was like a soothing balm to my aching heart. As I watched her clutch her stuffed giraffe, I marvelled at how she seemed to embody the resilience that I so desperately sought. As her mother, it was my duty to protect her, but in this moment, it felt like I was falling short.

The brief stops for fuel in Winnipeg and London provided a much-needed break from the monotony of the flight, but they also brought a sense of anxiety as we drew closer to our destination. Dropping my parents off in London was both a relief and a burden. It meant we were getting closer to Chris' family and the funeral, but it also felt like I was leaving behind a safety net of support.

When we finally landed in Ottawa, the reality of the situation hit me like a tidal wave. This was the place Chris had called home, and yet, it now felt foreign and unfamiliar without him by my side. As we stepped off the plane, I held Alexis close, seeking comfort in her presence, while at the same time feeling a heavy weight on my shoulders.

With my heart pounding, Alexis and I began the drive to Chris' parent's house, the darkness and coolness of the evening adding an air of mystery and anticipation. My emotions were a mixture of excitement and trepidation as I wondered how the reunion with his family would unfold. Would I be able to compose myself, or would my feelings overwhelm me?

As we pulled up to Chris' childhood home, the warm glow of lights and drawn curtains welcomed us. Unstrapping Alexis from her car seat, I held her close, preparing to face his family. The door swung open before I even had a chance to knock, revealing a room filled with familiar faces. The sight of Alexis being lovingly embraced by them, her bright, curious eyes mirroring Chris', was both comforting and heart-wrenching. She embodied a living connection to him, a cherished reminder of the love we once shared.

Amidst the hugs and emotions, I fought back tears, determined to maintain some semblance of control. My hands found distraction in unpacking, a way to ground me. Alexis and I settled into an upstairs bedroom, the playpen beside the queen bed. I carefully hung our clothes in the closet. Her toys were brought down to the main living area, where she played and explored her surroundings with curiosity, as the unfamiliar faces around her showered her with love and attention.

The following morning, I woke up with a slight respite from the weight of decision-making. For the people coming from out of town, it was a travel day. Knowing that tomorrow was the day I'd have to face making the arrangements at the funeral home, cemetery, and church, I welcomed this temporary pause.

As I settled into the Ottawa environment, I found myself meeting new faces, members of the Worden family's support team. I had to remind myself of something crucial—I had to choose to believe that people are kind, genuine, and doing their best. Yet, I couldn't shake off the wave of frustration whenever I encountered the pitying glances from well-meaning individuals. Their words: "Everything happens for a reason," "Time heals," or "It's part of God's plan," brought me from sadness to anger in an instant. Those expressions felt like empty clichés that only added to my pain. Though I tried to be reasonable and respectful, hearing those phrases made my blood boil. I realized that these sayings were merely fillers, attempts to find something to say when the right words seemed elusive. Still, I vowed never to use those expressions myself in the future, knowing firsthand how painful they could be. In my grief, I longed for genuine connections, for people to simply be present without trying to make everything better with empty words.

As the days passed, I learned to navigate these interactions, to find a calming voice amid the turmoil, and to cling to the belief that genuine kindness could be found in unexpected places. While grief had altered my world, I was determined to face it with honesty and openness, courage and authenticity.

Delegating tasks became my lifeline during those overwhelming days. One of the responsibilities I entrusted to Michèle was finding appropriate readings for the mass.

Her experience as a teacher at a Catholic school made her the perfect candidate. I knew she and her friends would put together a thoughtful shortlist, sparing me from the burden of having to research options.

It was a delicate balance—making others feel useful while also lightening my own load. I recognized that leaning on the support of those around me was essential for both my well-being and the success of the funeral preparations.

Selecting the pallbearers, honorary pallbearers, and headdress pallbearers was an emotional journey. The pallbearers and headdress pallbearers were fellow RCMP officers, the honorary pallbearers included a mix of Chris' RCMP colleagues and childhood friends. Each of them held a special place in Chris' life, and I felt it was important to honour his connection with them. Each name on that list brought back memories of shared laughter, adventures, and bonds that could never be replaced. The sight of my husband's fellow officers practicing with such dedication to ensure a flawless tribute moved me to tears. They weren't just performing a duty; they were bearing the weight of loss and honouring a brother who would never return to their ranks.

As the early evening descended, a heavy veil of emotions surrounded me as we made our way to the RCMP hangar. Chris' body was arriving from Edmonton, the autopsy now complete. I carefully handpicked six fellow members who had worked alongside Chris to form a ceremonial troop, an honourable escort to receive him.

Dressed in their iconic Red Serge, they cradled the silver casket draped in the Canadian flag with profound reverence. In a solemn procession, they placed the casket on a wheeled frame, gently rolling it to the centre of the hangar. Our hearts weighed down with grief, each family member, including myself and Alexis, approached the casket to place a red rose near its head. As Alexis tenderly laid her pink rose, a unique touch of innocence and purity amid the sea of red, tears welled in my eyes.

In the sombreness of the moment, we were accompanied by a motorcade to the funeral home. Along the way, a memorable scene unfolded that etched itself deeply into my memory. A city bus halted to the side of the road, its driver standing outside, hand raised in a salute as we passed by. The sight of this unknown person honouring the sacrifice Chris had made was profoundly moving, a testament to the compassion and respect shown by strangers we might never have the opportunity to meet.

In that moment, I was overcome with a profound sense of gratitude and sorrow. The way people honoured Chris' memory, even those unknown to us, showed that his life had left an indelible mark on the world.

As we returned to the comforting embrace of the Worden family home, seeking solace in each other's presence, we turned on the National News. There, on the screen, stood Peter Mansbridge, the seasoned senior news anchor, his voice carrying the weight of the day's events. The preview of the top stories began, and there it was—the manhunt for Chris' shooter taking precedence as the number one story.

In the midst of grief and sorrow, an unexpected thought escaped my lips, a blend of dark humour and disbelief: "We beat the election!" On that very day, the nation had engaged in the critical process of selecting the next Prime Minister of Canada, yet the news of Chris' elusive assailant took centre stage, overshadowing even the gravity of the political decisions being made.

As I lay in bed that night, the urgency of the situation weighed heavily on my mind. The funeral was approaching, a day of remembrance and farewell to honour Chris' life and service, and all I could think was: *They need to find the shooter before the day of the funeral. They have to.* It felt like an imperative, a plea to the universe, knowing that closure and justice were crucial for Chris to rest in peace.

My sisters and their spouses arrived. Sandy had met an RCMP officer after the autopsy had concluded to receive Chris' wedding ring. She handed it to me that morning before I left for the funeral home. As I clutched the ring, I felt a mix of emotions overwhelming me. Sorrow for the future we had lost, gratitude for the love we had shared, and an ache for the life we would never get to live together. It was a bittersweet moment, knowing that this small ring held so much significance and carried the weight of a short lifetime of memories.

While I was away from the house that morning, a touching gesture unfolded as an RCMP tailor arrived to measure Alexis. The RCMP has arranged for her to have a custom Red Serge made, adorned with the same insignia as Chris'.. My parents, having arrived in their RV the day before, were there to provide support and care for Alexis during this time.

Looking back, the morning after Chris' body arrived stands out as one of the most arduous to endure, rivalling even the day of the funeral in its emotional intensity. As I was picked up from the Worden family house, my heart weighed heavily with the knowledge of what lay ahead.

As I stepped into the funeral home, the atmosphere enveloped me in an unusual sense of calm. The hushed tones and the faint scent of flowers mingling in the air created an eerie stillness that contrasted sharply with the emotions swirling inside me. The funeral home director approached with a gentle and understanding demeanour, ready to assist us in this sombre task.

Handing over Chris' wedding ring felt like surrendering a piece of my heart. The weight of its significance and the finality it represented was almost unbearable. The director carefully took the ring, recognizing the depth of its meaning, and assured me that everything would be done with utmost care and respect.

He gently guided me to a room displaying caskets, reminding me that I had to select one suitable for Chris' tall frame. As I looked at the two options before me, my heart sank. It was a decision I never thought I would have to make at this stage in my life. My mind raced, trying to imagine what Chris would have chosen. In the end, I settled on a dark cherry wood casket, hoping it reflected his taste and dignity.

Next came the task of designing the funeral card, a tribute to the man who meant the world to me. My emotions were raw as I flipped through verses and poems, searching for the words that could capture the essence of Chris' spirit. A poem pulled from Facebook caught my eye, and it resonated with my heart. I knew it was written just for him.

A Mountie's died, his family grieves
Amidst the autumn's falling leaves
Gentle smile, manner and wit
For you, for me, for all of us
Taken by a vicious crime
Taken long before his time
Sam Browne belt and Stetson hat

Scarlet tunic, ceased so flat
His horse stands by with empty saddle
Head hung low from the final battle
And now he lies with comrades near
Attention they stand, on their cheek a tear
As he starts his last parade
From our hearts he'll never fade
A Canadian son who gave his best
A Canadian hero now at rest

~Gareth Duguid, October 2007

In that quiet room, surrounded by caskets and funeral cards, I grappled with the reality of saying goodbye to the love of my life. Each decision felt like another step away from the life we had dreamed of together. But I knew that I had to be strong and make the choices that would honour Chris and his memory. I had three visitations to make it through; one on Saturday evening and two on Sunday.

Walking into the church, I couldn't shake the knot in my stomach as I met with the presiding priest. Michèle had prepared a list of readings, but the truth was that I didn't want to engage with any talk of God or religious reassurances. It felt like a painful reminder of the questions and anger that had been brewing inside me since Chris' death. I let others in the room handle the details, desperately trying to keep my composure.

One pressing issue dominated the discussion—the capacity of the church. We were expecting hundreds of police officers from different departments and countries to march in the parade from Parliament Hill to Notre-Dame Cathedral Basilica. The streets would be lined with even more people coming to pay their respects. To manage the crowd, we had to create a guest list. Only those with invitations would be allowed inside the church.

It was an daunting task, like debating with your parents about who gets invited to your wedding. I didn't want anyone to feel excluded, but the reality was that the space was limited. The logistics of delivering invitations to the selected guests added another layer of complexity. In a time before smart-phones were widely used, we couldn't simply send out a group text with a QR code. The RCMP stepped in to handle the practical arrangements, leaving us to wrestle with the emotional burden of deciding who would be there to honour Chris.

Two eulogies were planned for the service. Corporal Mike Carter would speak on behalf of the RCMP, representing the law enforcement family that Chris was part of. Cathy Worden, Chris' sister, would speak on behalf of the family, reflecting their love and grief.

As the preparations continued, I couldn't help but feel overwhelmed by the weight of it all. The funeral seemed like a colossal production, a tribute to a life that had been tragically cut short. The anticipation of seeing so many people come to pay their respects was both comforting and heart-wrenching. It was a testament to the impact Chris had on so many lives, but it also amplified the void he had left behind.

From the church, we embarked on a solemn drive, navigating the winding roads that led us to Beechwood Cemetery. The gates of the cemetery welcomed us, and I couldn't help but notice the towering trees that stood as silent guardians of this sacred ground. The staff received us with utmost sensitivity, understanding the pain that brought us here.

They ushered us into a small room adorned with 3D maps and blueprints, giving a tangible form to the vast expanse of the cemetery. Our guide pointed out the different sections, but my mind struggled to focus. It was as if reality had become hazy, blurred by the weight of grief. As I peered at the blueprint-size paper, with its tiny numbers and writings within the boxes, the realization of Chris' imminent resting place hit me like another tidal wave. My throat tightened, and tears welled up in my eyes, threatening to spill over at any moment. The thought of choosing a final resting place for him seemed unbearable—an acknowledgment that he was truly gone.

In the midst of the guide's explanation about how many people could be laid to rest together, my mind started to wander. I could no longer bear to hear such practicalities. My heart ached, and I needed to escape from the painful reality unfolding before me. Leaving the conversation mid-sentence, I walked away, seeking solace by the flagpoles. There, beneath the fluttering flags, I allowed my anguish to flow freely.

In that moment of vulnerability, I found myself voicing my fear of the future, the thought of being laid to rest beside Chris at such a young age was too much to bear. *I am twenty-nine years old. I don't want to think about being buried beside him.* It was as if saying those words out loud made the reality of death too real to bear. A gentle response of reassurance broke through my despair, urging me to focus on the present moment, on the tribute we were paying to Chris.

"You don't have to," they said, their voice understanding and compassionate. "Just think about today and what spot you think he'd like best."

Wiping away the tears, I retraced my steps back to the man with the oversized paper, and there, amid the maze of boxes, I found a spot that felt right. It was a place close to the path, so others could visit easily. Memories of Chris' bald head and fair skin flooded my mind, and I knew this shaded spot would have been his preference, a quiet refuge under the cool shade of a tree.

The weight of the decisions I had to make, the emotional turmoil, and the relentless pace of the day had all taken their toll. I felt my mind and body shutting down, yearning for respite from the overwhelming reality I was facing.

"I just want to go lay down," I murmured, my voice barely audible.

The exhaustion from the day's emotional rollercoaster threatened to engulf me entirely. In that moment, I realized that the process of grief was not linear, nor was it predictable. It was a tumultuous journey through the depths of sorrow, and I was only just beginning to comprehend the magnitude of the loss.

That evening, amidst the heaviness of funeral preparations, a glimmer of relief washed over us. News arrived that the RCMP and Edmonton Police Service had successfully apprehended the shooter in Edmonton. He was now in custody, facing a charge of first-degree murder. For days, my emotions had been tightly wound, like a coiled spring, waiting to be released. The burden of not knowing had been suffocating. The weight of uncertainty had been crushing my heart, and the constant barrage of unanswered questions had left me feeling lost and adrift in an ocean of grief. I yearned for closure, for some understanding of what had happened on that Saturday morning when my life was shattered. The news of the shooter's arrest felt like a small victory against the relentless torment of the unknown.

The prospect of the justice process starting brought a flicker of reassurance. I clung to the hope that the investigation would uncover the full truth behind Chris' tragic death. But I also understood that the journey to healing and closure would be long and unpredictable. This was just the beginning, and I took some solace in knowing that justice had taken its first step. As I prepared for the visitation and the funeral, his killer was behind bars.

7

•••••

IN THE MIDST of my grief and running on autopilot, my appearance was the last thing on my mind. But I knew that the upcoming visitations and the funeral demanded a certain level of respect and dignity. I leaned on my sister Deb, who took on the role of guiding me through the process of selecting appropriate outfits for each occasion. We wanted to honour the memory of Chris by dressing our best, even amidst the overwhelming sorrow.

We started with finding black tights and shiny black shoes to go with the mini Red Serge Alexis would be wearing. This was a manageable task that I found a small amount of success in achieving. For myself, it was much more difficult. I had little appetite, and food was tasteless during those days. It was as if my taste buds had numbed along with my mind. I had lost eight pounds in a week.

Together, Deb and I walked into a store to find the dress I would wear for the funeral. I remember feeling the weight of the world on my shoulders as I told the young sales agent about the sombre occasion.

"I need a dress for a funeral," I said, mustering the strength to convey my need. "We're going for the Jackie O look."

The sales agent, with compassion and professionalism, immediately understood the gravity of the situation. She guided us to the dressing room and brought me dresses to try on. I stood in front of the mirror, the reflection staring back at me showing a face etched with sorrow, exhaustion, and disbelief. Deb offered her opinion, and we collectively worked to find the perfect outfit for the solemn day ahead.

I knew that the funeral would be a public event, with media coverage and photographs capturing the moments of grief and remembrance. These images would become a part of our family's history and something I would later use to help Alexis understand the significance of that day. The weight of this realization added to my already overwhelming emotions.

Dressed in new mourning clothes, the day of the public viewing had arrived, and the anticipation was almost unbearable. I needed to make sure Alexis was cared for while we attended the funeral home. I managed to coordinate the babysitting schedule, and soon, all the adult family members from both sides piled into vehicles for the short drive to the visitation. The sun was shining brightly, which seemed oddly out of place amidst the heaviness of our hearts.

As we walked into the funeral home, we were met with a sense of solemnity. The building had three large viewing rooms, but on this day, it was reserved solely for our family. We were led to the room where Chris' body lay, and my heart tightened as we approached the casket. The sight of the white lining contrasting with his Red Serge was striking, a vivid reminder of the sacrifices he had made as an RCMP officer. His hands were gently placed near his waist, just above his ceremonial belt, and his wedding ring was predominately on display.

In a moment of candour, MaryAnn broke the silence, expressing her thoughts on Chris' appearance. The funeral director assured us that he could adjust the makeup to match his skin tone better and we asked him to do so. Stepping outside the flower-filled room, I was escorted to a smaller one down the hall. Inside were Chris' troopmates, forming a receiving line to greet me. Hugs and tears were exchanged as we came together to pay our respects to a man who had left a mark on all our lives.

I recognized many of these men from my visit to Depot six years earlier when I had attended Chris' graduation. Over the years, we had made time to connect with some of them during our vacations outside the north. Two of them had served in the Honour Guard at our wedding.

In this small room, memories of laughter, camaraderie, and shared experiences mingled with the profound sense of loss. Three of these dear friends would now serve as honorary pallbearers.

As MaryAnn and I reassessed the makeup on Chris' face, we both agreed that the adjustments were an improvement. With a deep breath, we gave the green light for others to come and pay their respects. The troopmates filed in, each offering their own quiet moment with Chris, honouring their fallen comrade.

The extended family was expected to arrive around 2:00 p.m., giving us a brief window of time to take a much-needed break. We made our way downstairs to a room that served as our hideout, a refuge from the overwhelming emotions outside. It reminded me of an old, small-town community multipurpose rec hall, with its cement floors marked with activity lines and long tables set up at the far end. The card table chairs lined along the wall felt oddly comforting.

Despite the sterile environment, this room became my haven during those difficult days. It was the one place in that building where I felt I could catch my breath, where I felt a sense of calm amidst the storm of grief. This room provided a brief respite, a space where I could collect my thoughts and prepare myself to face the world outside again.

The memory of my cousin Chris arriving at the funeral home is etched vividly in my mind. As I emerged from the doorway that led to the downstairs haven room, there he was - a tall figure walking towards me, backlit by the soft glow in the long entrance of the hallway. He was flanked by an older couple, my aunt and uncle, and a young woman. Chris and his brother Jay were my closest cousins on my dad's side of the family, and their parents were my godparents. They had taken time off work and driven six hours to be here for me. In that moment, I felt overwhelmed by the effort people were making to show their support. They could have stayed safely in their homes and sent a card, but they knew the significance of their physical presence, and it meant the world to me. It was the beginning of my understanding of gratitude, a feeling I would need to rely on many times as I navigated the new path that lay ahead of me.

The family visitation was in sharp contrast to the more formal public visitation. We gathered like we were at a wedding reception, mingling and chatting amidst the sombre atmosphere. It was a respite from the grief, a moment where I could temporarily escape the weight of my own emotions and immerse myself in the lives of others. Engaging in conversations about their lives allowed me to be present without fully acknowledging the pain and loss that enveloped my heart. Functioning in survivor mode, my ability to concentrate and recall was limited, but being a part of these exchanges gave me a semblance of normalcy amidst the chaos of the funeral proceedings.

The evening session brought a significant change to the atmosphere. Throughout the day, the room had filled with an overwhelming display of wreaths and flowers. The other rooms had to be utilized as overflow spaces for the flowers, as well as holding areas to accommodate the long line of people waiting to pay their respects, ensuring they wouldn't have to wait outside in the cold.

As visitors entered the front doors, they were greeted by a solemn and thoughtful display. A circular table was adorned with an RCMP saddle blanket, a symbol of the musical ride, and placed on it were Chris' cherished high brown boots and the iconic Sam Browne leather belt he wore with pride. A single, lit candle in a clear glass holder, inscribed with golden letters spelling "Chris Worden," stood amidst a circular bouquet of white roses and carnations, emanating a sense of honour and remembrance. Nearby, an easel displayed Chris' Depot graduation photo. On one side stood a Canada flag, representing his commitment to his country, while on the other side, a red wreath with a sash bearing the words "Constable Chris Worden" in the same golden letters as the candle holder, acknowledging his service and sacrifice.

The funeral home was adorned with a sea of wreaths, predominantly in red and white, the colours of the Canadian flag. Strong floral aromas filled the air, an overwhelming scent that lingers in my senses even now. It brought me back to that moment when I stood beside Chris' casket, trying to maintain composure as I greeted and shook the hands of thousands of people.

In the primary viewing room, the family stood in a sombre line along the far wall. As people entered, their eyes were immediately drawn to Chris' casket, draped in a sea of flowers that seemed to stretch endlessly. Floral arrangements of various sizes adorned the foot and head of the casket, perched on elegant easels, each bouquet a tribute to the love and respect he had garnered.

The order of the family members in line changed occasionally, but I remained at the forefront, closest to Chris, followed by Chris' parents, siblings, my parents, and my own siblings.

For three long hours at each viewing, I stood next to Chris' lifeless body, shaking hands with countless people who came to pay their respects. Inside, my emotions were a whirlwind, but I went into autopilot mode, channeling my inner waitress. I greeted people warmly, thanking them for coming, and providing reassurance to those who seemed lost for words. Those I had a close connection with, I embraced tightly, sometimes sharing a tearful moment.

Occasionally, I would take a brief break from the receiving line and steer close friends to the room where I had met Chris' troopmates to steal a moment of privacy. In these quiet moments, we could express our grief and find solace in shared memories. One particular arrival stands out in my memory.

As the clock approached 9:00 p.m., the scheduled visitation hours had long passed, but the line of people coming to pay their respects still seemed endless. We continued to greet each person with appreciation for their presence. In the midst of this sea of faces, my sister Deb spotted someone familiar—was my high school friend Ed. He was a giant of a man, standing 6'6" tall and weighing over 300 pounds, yet he had the gentlest heart of anyone I knew. He and I had shared many memories together, and he was the one who had introduced Chris to me during football camp.

Seeing Ed was a welcome sight, but as he approached Chris' casket, the weight of the moment became too much for him to bear. My heart ached as I saw him crumble, overwhelmed with grief. Without a second thought, I rushed to his side, and we embraced tightly, seeking comfort in each other's arms. Together, we found our way to that small, quiet room, where we could share our pain in privacy. Sharing moments with those who knew Chris well and carried cherished memories of him that could bring fleeting smiles and tears helped me get through the formalities of the visitations. For the rest of that night, I withdrew from the receiving line. Grief had washed over me, and shaking hands and offering words of thanks were distant concerns.

The evening continued with a mixture of emotions. We gathered back at John and MaryAnn's home. As we settled into the living room, the familiar sound of "Coaches' Corner" filled the air. Saturday is Hockey Night in Canada, a beloved tradition in many Canadian households. During the first intermission, the iconic duo of Don Cherry and Ron MacLean took the stage to discuss the game and share their thoughts.

As the segment began, my heart skipped a beat. Don Cherry's booming voice filled the room, and I watched with a mix of emotions as they showed a picture of Chris holding Alexis. Seeing that image on national television brought a surge of pride, but it was intertwined with profound sadness. Don Cherry, in his signature flamboyant style, paid tribute to Chris, recognizing his service, sacrifice, and dedication to duty. The nation witnessed this moment of remembrance, and I felt both honoured and overwhelmed by the public acknowledgment of Chris' life and dedication to his profession.

Don's words of appreciation and condolence touched my heart, even amidst the deep grief I was experiencing.

In that moment, the sense of community and support that had surrounded us since Chris' passing became even more noticeable. It was a bittersweet moment, knowing that Chris' memory would be forever etched in the hearts of not only those who knew him intimately but also in the hearts of countless strangers who watched Coach's Corner that night.

Sunday afternoon and evening dragged on with a sense of repetition and weariness. The constant stream of mourners offering their condolences felt like an unending marathon of politeness and gratitude. As each person approached, I mustered the strength to say "thank you for coming," over and over again. But inside, I felt drained and overwhelmed by the sheer magnitude of it all. Meeting people I didn't know under these circumstances, feeling like I was on display, was anything but comforting. I longed for a moment of solitude, a chance to escape the flood of sympathetic eyes and the weight of their expectations.

Yet, there was a sense of duty that pushed me forward. I felt an obligation to be the "brave widow," to put on a strong front, and to represent Chris with dignity and grace. It was as if I owed it to him to show the world that I was coping better than expected. But the truth was that every passing day seemed to bring new levels of fatigue, both physically and emotionally. Living in survivor mode took a toll I couldn't have imagined.

Throughout the day, I sought solace in the haven room downstairs. Sitting on the card table chairs, I tried to nibble on the food laid out for us, but my appetite was non-existent. I knew that being downstairs allowed me to be away from the prying eyes and conversations. It was a small refuge among the expectations and formalities.

One thought that weighed heavily on my mind was Alexis. I couldn't help but wonder how she was processing everything.

Was she aware of the heaviness in the air, the sorrow that surrounded us? I desperately hoped that we had shielded her from the full impact of our grief, that she was still blissfully unaware of the tragedy that had befallen us. In my heart, I yearned to preserve her innocence for as long as possible. As a twenty-nine-year-old adult, I had lost much of my own innocence in the face of this tragedy, and I couldn't bear the thought of Alexis experiencing this pain at such a tender age.

The hours between the viewings were a whirlwind of activity. Despite the heaviness in my heart, we had to push forward to finalize the details for tomorrow. There were still so many things to arrange, and time was slipping away. The program for the funeral needed to be completed and sent to the print shop before 3:00 p.m. to have five thousand copies ready in time.

In addition to the program, we had to complete the invitations for the gathering that would take place after the funeral. It was a complex affair, with two separate venues to accommodate the vast number of people who were expected to attend. One venue would host the 2500 police officers who would be marching in the parade, while the other, the RCMP Officers' Mess at National Headquarters, would be reserved for invited friends and family.

The clock was ticking, and time seemed to move both too fast and too slow simultaneously. The emotions were overwhelming, and yet, there was a sense of purpose in all the chaos. The preparations were both a burden and a privilege, a way for us to show our love and respect for Chris.

8

•••••

THE MORNING OF the funeral felt like controlled chaos. The Worden house, usually a place of warmth and comfort, now buzzed with a mixture of emotions. Six adults and a baby all needed to get ready, and the single shower was a hot commodity. My parents' RV parked outside provided extra space, but the electricity draw led to a temporary power outage, adding to the mayhem.

As everyone scrambled to get ready, tension hung in the air. We were all on edge, and even the smallest setbacks seemed amplified. I could hear the frustration in Cathy's voice as she let out an expletive-laden outburst when her hair dryer stopped working due to the power outage.

Amidst the hustle and bustle, Brent, one of the RCMP support staff, stepped in to help feed Alexis, taking on the role of caregiver in a sea of busy adults. It was a moment of both sweetness and significance, as we were reminded of the support and kindness we had from the people around us.

Despite the chaos, we managed to pull ourselves together. The power was restored, and we continued with our preparations. As we all got ready, there was an unspoken understanding that we were doing this not just for ourselves but to honour Chris, to give him the farewell he deserved.

The morning of the funeral was both surreal and heart-breaking. Our transportation arrived on schedule at 10:00 a.m., each of us assigned to specific vehicles. Alexis and I were in the lead car, and I couldn't help but feel a mix of pride and sorrow as I looked at her dressed in her little Red Serge, ready to honour her daddy. Her innocence was a stark contrast to the heaviness of the day.

At the funeral home, we had our private moments with Chris before the ceremony. I brought Alexis with me, unsure of how she would react. As I held her, she playfully touched the edge of the cherry coffin with her tiny hands and feet, her curiosity unaware of the significance of the moment. She reached towards Chris' head, and I watched with a mix of pain and tenderness as she interacted with the man she would never fully know.

As the clock ticked, I knew we had to keep to the schedule. I handed Alexis to my mom and went back in for my own moment.

I gently pried Chris' hands apart, my heart heavy with a mixture of sorrow and determination. They had been glued together during the preparations, as if they wanted to preserve the last touch of warmth he once offered. With a determined jerk, I managed to separate his left hand from his right, feeling the weight of this final gesture. His wedding ring slid off his fourth finger and onto my thumb. The precious gold band felt both familiar and foreign, a reminder of the life we once shared together. Clutching it tightly, I knew that it would now serve as a cherished keepsake, a tangible connection to the man I loved.

With trembling hands, I carefully placed a 4x6 photo of the three of us between Chris' hands. The image captured a moment of pure joy at Alexis' baptism, a snapshot of a time when life was full of promise and hope. The photograph felt like a small lifeline, a reminder of the beautiful life we had created together.

As I looked down at his still form, my heart ached for the dreams and plans we had shared, now shattered by the cruel hand of fate. Tears welled up in my eyes. But amidst the pain, I felt a sense of peace knowing that I had the opportunity to say my farewell in my own way, to offer my love and gratitude one last time.

Taking a deep breath, I let myself be present in that moment, honouring the life we had together and the love he had given me. The funeral director signalled it was time to close the casket, offering me the option to stay if I wished. I chose to stay, needing this closure even if it was heart-wrenching. I watched as Chris' body was slowly lowered to lie flat, and the lid was closed, sealing our final moments together inside. My throat tightened, and I took a deep breath. With steady hands, I congratulated myself on making it through this phase of the process. It was a moment of silent acknowledgment of my strength, a small victory as I endeavoured to make it through the next few hours.

The city made preparations, closing off the streets surrounding Notre Dame Cathedral Basilica. The parade route stretched for 1.2 kilometres. The hearse took the lead, solemnly leading the police procession from Parliament Hill, while the family was taken directly to the church. As we approached the majestic cathedral, its grandeur and history were evident. It was a place of reverence and sacred significance, befitting the occasion.

As we stood at the bottom of the twelve steps that led up to the church doors, the magnitude of the moment became apparent. The sidewalks were thronged with people. They had come to pay their respects, offering their support in this time of grief and loss.

To accommodate the overwhelming crowd, large screens had been erected across the street, outside the National Art Gallery. This thoughtful gesture allowed not only the police officers marching in the procession but also the public, unable to fit inside the church, to witness the service. In a time before live streaming on phones was commonplace, this act of inclusivity brought comfort to those who couldn't be with us physically.

As we stood on the steps of the church, the crisp air of the day embraced us with its chilly touch. The weather, hovering around 10°C (52°F), made me aware of Alexis' well-being. I glanced down at her, bundled up in her doll-sized uniform, little black tights and shiny shoes. Despite the cold, she looked up at me with her innocent eyes, seeking reassurance and warmth.

I had already given her a soother to pacify her in the midst of the crowd. The comfort of the familiar soothe gave her a sense of security amid the sea of unknown faces and emotions swirling around us.

Brent had gone inside the church to see if he could find something to cover Alexis and shield her from the cold. While there, he encountered a friend from our time in Wha Ti, someone who had journeyed all the way from the North to be by our side on this day. This friend offered their blanket for Alexis, a gesture that spoke volumes about the bond formed through shared experiences and the compassion extended during times of need. Wrapped in the Snoopy blanket they gave us, Alexis found comfort throughout the day. It became a soft cocoon of warmth, protecting her from the cold and providing a sense of familiarity amidst the overwhelming events unfolding around her.

As the parade drew nearer, the sounds became more pronounced, echoing through the streets of Ottawa. The combination of engines, horseshoes hitting pavement, and the haunting music of bagpipes filled the air, creating an almost surreal atmosphere. My heart pounded in my chest as I held Alexis in my arms, facing outward so she could witness this sombre yet awe-inspiring procession.

The motorcade led the way. Six flag bearers on horseback followed, their steely determination mirroring the gravity of the occasion. Among the ranks of the RCMP pipe band, I spotted a familiar face—my teacher friend Thea, who had travelled all the way from Yellowknife to be a part of this moment. She had gifted Alexis the tiniest kilt in the tartan of the Yellowknife clan, a cherished keepsake that would forever be treasured.

My chest rose and fell with each breath, and I held Alexis close, her small body pressed against mine. Behind my large black sunglasses, I closed my eyes, seeking a moment of inner calm amidst the whirlwind of emotions. The words of Dr. Schmaltz echoed in my mind, reminding me of the breathing technique she had taught me. Inhale deeply, hold, and exhale slowly—simple, yet profound. In the chaos of grief and survivor mode, it was easy to forget such simple practices, but in that moment, I recalled. With each breath, I sought to regulate my racing heart and calm my mind. I silently repeated a mantra *just breathe, just breathe*—as a way to anchor myself amidst the overwhelming tide of emotions.

As the procession moved closer, I could see the hearse coming into view, and my heart tightened in my chest. Flanking the hearse on both sides were the uniformed RCMP pallbearers and honorary pallbearers. They walked with solemn precision, their faces etched with respect and grief as they accompanied Chris' body towards the church. The headdress bearers and honorary pallbearers were walking directly beside the vehicle, their presence adding to the sense of honour and reverence.

In the outside row, the pallbearers who would carry Chris' casket up the church stairs were resolute in their duty. Their strength and resolve were evident as they prepared to bear the weight of their friend and colleague, offering one last tribute to a man they held in high regard.

Following the hearse and its accompanying honour guard, the members of the Hay River detachment and Chris' troop-mates marched with purpose. They had come to pay their final respects, standing together in unity, a brotherhood and sisterhood forged by shared experiences and camaraderie.

But what struck me the most was the vast sea of red and blue that followed. Over 2500 police and peace officers from forces across Canada and the United States had gathered to march in solidarity and pay their respects. Their presence was a powerful reminder of the incredible community that Chris belonged to, and the impact he had made in his service.

As the procession advanced, I felt a mixture of emotions—pride in Chris' dedication and sacrifice, gratitude for the outpouring of support, and an overwhelming sense of loss. The sight of so many coming together to honour him was both heartwarming and heart-wrenching.

As the casket emerged from the hearse, the pallbearers executed their duties with precision and grace. Two headdress bearers carefully carried the stacked pallbearers' hats on pillows, while James Lang, entrusted with the honour of carrying

Chris' Stetson, followed closely behind. It was a solemn sight, a symbol of the deep respect and tradition that accompanied Chris' service as an RCMP officer.

With a sense of reverence, the pallbearers removed their Stetsons and placed them on the designated pillows. Their faces bore the weight of the moment, a mix of sorrow and determination as they prepared to lift their fallen comrade upon their shoulders.

As they hoisted Chris' casket, their movements were steady and synchronized, a testament to their training and dedication. The weight they bore was not just physical but emotional too, carrying the memory of a dear friend, a colleague, and a beloved family member. I couldn't help but wonder how they felt at that moment, if they shared in the depth of grief and loss that I carried.

As the procession made its way up the steps of Notre Dame Cathedral Basilica, the priest and altar servers were there to receive Chris' body. The music began, filling the air with a haunting melody that added to the solemn atmosphere. The funeral had begun.

The service began with Corporal Mike Carter delivering his eulogy. The air in the cathedral was still. His words held a weight that resonated with every person present. Dressed in his ceremonial uniform, he stood tall and resolute. As he began to share his memories of Chris, his voice carried a mix of sorrow and admiration, a deep sense of loss intertwined with pride for his fallen friend and colleague.

He spoke of the moments they had shared, the laughter and camaraderie that had filled their days on shift and off, the challenges they had overcome together, and the bond that had formed between them as officers. He shared personal anecdotes, inside jokes, and the quirky habits that had made Chris unique and endearing. Each story brought Chris to life once more, a vivid presence in the hearts of those listening.

As he spoke, the emotion in the room was palpable. Tears glistened in the eyes of many, while others fought to hold back their sobs. The respect that Mike held for Chris was evident in every word, telling of the deep friendship they had shared. He spoke of Chris as a dedicated and honourable officer, a man who had served his country and his family with unwavering devotion. And as he concluded his eulogy, his voice softened, filled with a mixture of grief and gratitude.

"Stand easy, Constable Worden. Be proud of the life you lived, the sacrifices you made, and the impact you had on all of us. You have served your family and your country well. Rest in peace, my friend."

It was a Catholic funeral service. My mom, my sisters and Chris' Aunt Molly participate by doing readings. The mass ended with the family eulogy. Cathy stood tall and composed, flanked by her brothers Michael and Peter, as she took the podium to speak on behalf of the entire family. The church fell into a hushed silence, and all eyes were on her, awaiting the heartfelt tribute she was about to share.

With grace and poise, Cathy began to paint a vivid picture of Chris' life, weaving together a tapestry of cherished memories and endearing anecdotes. She spoke of his childhood antics that often left the family in stitches, recounting the times Chris brought laughter and joy to their lives. Cathy's eulogy wasn't just about the playful boy Chris once was. It delved deep into the core of his being, emphasizing his unwavering love for family and his passion for football. She spoke of the countless family gatherings where he was the glue that held everyone together, the one who made sure traditions were kept alive and new memories were created.

As her words flowed, Cathy brought the attendees on a journey through Chris' life, reliving his many accomplishments. From his early days as a young athlete and musician to his devoted service as a member of the RCMP, she captured the essence of his commitment and dedication to his chosen path.

But it was the mention of Chris becoming a father that stirred the most profound emotions. The joy that radiated from him when he held his daughter Alexis for the first time was etched in everyone's memory. Cathy shared anecdotes of Chris' endearing moments as a father—the pride in his eyes, the warmth in his smile, and the gentle touch that enveloped his precious little girl.

Cathy's words touched the hearts of all those present, but for me, they had an even deeper impact. As I listened to her eloquent speech, I felt an overwhelming swell of pride. Pride for the man Chris had become, pride for the love he had showered upon our family, and pride for the father he had become to Alexis. His legacy was one of love, dedication, and selflessness, and it was all beautifully encapsulated in Cathy's heartfelt eulogy. Cathy demonstrated exquisite resolve and represented the family with grace. Her strength and spirit were much the same as her brother's. Her words signalled the final phase of the funeral.

As Chris' casket was gently placed back into the hearse, I took a deep breath and gathered myself for the journey ahead. The cars that had brought us to the church were lined up, forming a sombre procession, each vehicle carrying a piece of our shattered hearts.

I settled into our assigned car, making sure Alexis was comfortable. I took the diaper bag and retrieved the change pad, laying it down in the backseat. With a sense of routine in the midst of the chaos, I gently placed Alexis on the pad and began the familiar movements to change her diaper. In that tender moment, I was reminded of the simple, everyday tasks of parenting that continued even in the face of heartache and grief.

As I focused on attending to Alexis, a gentle voice broke through the silence, calling my name. "Jodie, look up." Startled, I lifted my gaze to find people lining the sidewalks, their faces filled with respect and sorrow. The general members of the public had their hands over their brows in a salute, honouring not only Chris but also his family—Alexis, me, and all those who were left behind.

In that instant, I felt an overwhelming wave of gratitude and awe. Here we were, a grieving widow and her eight-month-old daughter, surrounded by strangers who had taken a moment out of their day to pay their respects. Alexis, lying on her back drinking from her bottle, represented the future, the continuation of Chris' legacy. And in that moment, those nameless faces along the streets became a part of our shared story.

The ceremony at Beechwood Cemetery was an intimate gathering, contrasting with the overwhelming and public nature of the past few days. Under the canopy of a white tent, rows of chairs were neatly arranged, facing the prepared plot where Chris would be laid to rest. The atmosphere was solemn, and a gentle breeze carried the scent of fresh flowers and earth.

We stepped out of the cars, and my eyes fell on the familiar sidewalk where just days ago, I had experienced a moment of vulnerability. Memories of that day washed over me, but I pushed them aside, focusing on the present.

Taking our assigned seats, I gently handed Alexis to my mom, who cradled her in her arms. The soft rocking motion seemed to soothe her, and soon, Alexis was fast asleep, covered in the Snoopy blanket, oblivious to the weight of the moment surrounding her.

The pallbearers, resolute in their duty, made their final march, bearing Chris on their shoulders for the last time. I watched them, each step taken with purpose and dedication, a testament to the bond they shared with him as brothers in service.

The flag folding ceremony commenced, a meticulous and heartfelt process that held deep meaning for all of us. The Canadian flag, which had draped Chris' casket, was now being folded with utmost precision, each fold symbolizing a different aspect of his service and sacrifice.

When the tightly folded triangle was handed to me, I held it with both hands, feeling the weight of its significance. I knew the flag was not just a piece of fabric; it represented the love, bravery, and dedication of the man I had loved and lost. I wanted to honour it with the same reverence and care that had been put into preparing it for me.

During Chris' time at Depot, he joined the band and took up the glockenspiel. It was an instrument he had never played before, but being in the band had its perks. The main one was that he had permission to bypass the long cafeteria lines so he could make morning practice. Nothing stood between Chris and food! I watched Chris perform in the band as the group marched around the parade square carrying what looked like an inverted xylophone.

When it was time to lower Chris into the ground, the distinctive sound of the glockenspiel filled the air. I couldn't help but smile, knowing that somewhere, somehow, someone had listened to my recounting of Chris' band days at Depot during the funeral preparations in Hay River. They had managed to find a glockenspiel player in Ottawa.

The music echoed through the cemetery, a touching tribute. It was a thoughtful gesture that touched my heart.

This remains my final recollection from the day of the funeral. While photographs capture my presence during the evening's events, my mental capacity had peaked. I operated on autopilot, carried unconsciously by the flow. It was as though my survival instincts had activated to shield me.

During the last ten days, I faced an overwhelming array of emotions and responsibilities, but through the fog, I continuously chose to push forward, even when it seemed impossible. Each day presented a myriad of challenges, but I remained committed to enduring whatever came my way. My capacity to process new information might have faltered, but my resolve to keep going never did.

The funeral day had been a test of my endurance and I knew that my journey of grief really was just beginning. I made the conscious decision to keep moving forward, one step at a time.

9

THE NEXT STEP had me in deep contemplation, strategizing about what to discuss with Prime Minister Harper. The Worden family had received a rare invitation to meet with the Prime Minister of Canada, and Michael, Peter, and I decided to accept. It was a significant moment, especially given the recent national election that had concluded with Stephen Harper and his Conservative Party being re-elected.

Politics had never been a prominent topic of discussion in my upbringing. While I understood the importance of voting and exercised my right diligently, I didn't possess the same fervour for politics that the Worden family did. They were well-versed in political science, with five out of the six having obtained or pursuing university degrees in the field. As a result, lively debates about policies and platforms were not uncommon in their household.

Regardless of the differing political affiliations, I recognized the privilege of having an audience with the leader of my country and I was determined to make the most of it.

This was an opportunity to express my concerns about public safety and the justice system. After all, the Prime Minister had campaigned on a platform of being "tough on crime," and I believed it was essential for him to hear the perspectives of citizens directly affected by these issues.

With the meeting on the horizon, I prepared myself mentally, organizing my thoughts and crafting the most impactful message I could deliver. It was both an exciting and daunting prospect, but I felt a sense of duty to advocate for meaningful change in areas that deeply mattered to me and my family.

As the day of the meeting approached, I reminded myself of the importance of speaking from the heart, ensuring my concerns were conveyed with clarity and conviction. It was a unique opportunity to engage with the highest office in the country, and I was determined to make my voice heard in hopes of contributing to a more just and secure society.

Peter, Michael, and I made our way to Parliament Hill, feeling a mix of anticipation and resolve. Passing through security, we were escorted to the Prime Minister's office. The presence of photographers, a constant throughout the past week, signaled the significance of the meeting. They captured the moments as we shook hands, preserving them as mementos of this important encounter.

Stepping into the office, I took in the ambiance. Sunrays streamed through high, narrow windows, adding a touch of brightness to the otherwise dark walls and trim. A large desk stood opposite the doors, and the three of us settled onto a long, plush leather couch. Prime Minister Harper, a figure of authority and responsibility, occupied an armchair to our right. His demeanour was composed, and he began by extending his condolences and gratitude on behalf of all Canadians. The appreciation for Chris' service and ultimate sacrifice was genuine in his words.

"What's on your mind?" he asked us, opening the door for us to address our concerns professionally and candidly. We delved into the pressing issue of repeat offenders and the need for updated laws and legislation to address their actions. My husband's killer, at the time of Chris' murder, had been out on bail despite a firearm prohibition and a charge of breaching conditions. This tragedy underscored a failure within the justice system that we yearned to be rectified.

Regrettably, concrete answers were scarce as the Prime Minister expertly manoeuvred the conversation in typical political fashion. He assured us that his government had plans to address these matters, particularly emphasizing the mandate for his new term to be revealed in the upcoming speech from the throne. This event, a significant occasion in certain constitutional monarchies, marks the opening of a legislative session, where the government's agenda and focus are outlined. The Prime Minister hinted that details of his "tough on crime" plans would be unveiled during that address.

While he emphasized that change was underway, he cautioned that it took time to implement such reforms. As a person living in survivor mode, where every moment felt like an eternity, I knew patience was a luxury I could scarcely afford. The road ahead appeared fraught with frustration as we awaited meaningful action and the tangible realization of the promise for a safer Canadian society.

Leaving the Prime Minister's office, I couldn't help but feel a mix of emotions. Gratitude for the opportunity to be heard mingled with impatience for the pace of change. Nevertheless, we left with a shared determination to continue advocating for meaningful reforms, knowing that the memory of Chris and the many others affected by violent crimes deserved nothing less.

On the evening of October 16, 2007, I found myself seated beside Laureen Harper, the Prime Minister's wife, in the upper gallery of the House of Commons as the throne speech was read aloud. The invitation to attend had come through the RCMP, and I couldn't help but wonder about the reasons behind it. It seemed clear that they wanted my presence to serve as both a symbol of support for our grieving family and a magnet for media attention to promote their agenda.

The previous eleven days had been a whirlwind of national news coverage, as the story of Chris' murder, the manhunt, and the funeral had dominated headlines. Being present at the throne speech would undoubtedly attach a name and a personal story to the government's proposed ideas. While I recognized the potential benefits of using this platform to advocate for positive policy change, Chris' parents were not supportive of my attendance. They expressed strong reservations about bringing more attention to the tragedy and preferred to grieve in private without being further thrust in the public eye.

I was faced with a difficult decision. On one hand, I wanted to respect John and MaryAnn's wishes and provide them the space they needed to cope with their grief. On the other hand, I felt a responsibility to leverage my position as a "new RCMP widow" to contribute to the conversation on crime reform and public safety.

Over breakfast, I shared my opinion with John and MaryAnn and explained that I needed to go. My resolve was met with mixed emotions, but they understood the weight of my choice and respected it.

As I took my seat in the upper gallery, I knew that the media's eyes would be on me, connecting the recent tragedy to the proposed policy changes. The conversation had begun, and I hoped that my presence could help drive meaningful reform. I also knew that it was a waiting game to see how the discourse would unfold from there. I left Parliament Hill that night feeling like I could use what happened to me to support change.

With the intense planning and execution of the funeral and its related events and the meeting with the Prime Minister now behind me, the demands on my family and friends gradually eased, and they needed to return to their regular lives outside of Ottawa. I knew I'd see many of them again soon as a memorial was scheduled in less than two weeks and they would be making arrangements to come up to Hay River for that.

Alexis and I needed to make our way back up north. After leaving the Worden home, our first stop was at the RCMP Divisional Headquarters in Edmonton, where I had some paperwork to sign. I'd been prepped a little about the format of the day. I would be meeting with human resources where they would be discussing compensation and entitlements. After this, I would have time to speak with Kim Gordon. Kim's husband had been killed in Mayerthorpe just over two years earlier. She had a toddler and was pregnant at the time of her husband's murder.

Brent led me through the impressive headquarters building, a place that felt like a second home to him when he wasn't traveling across the country for work. The entrance foyer was adorned with grand displays, including a large buffalo head mounted high on the wall, and the RCMP crest surrounded by flags at eye level. Passing through security, we made our way to the elevator, and as we exited on another floor, I noticed curious glances from people who recognized me. It was a surreal experience, being known to others while they remained strangers to me.

We walked down a long hallway that seemed to stretch forever until we reached a spacious boardroom. Inside, a man and a woman were seated behind a large oval table, surrounded by stacks of papers and file folders. As we entered, they rose from their seats, offering their condolences with sincere expressions of sympathy. We shook hands, and they invited me to take a seat. The gravity of the situation began to sink in once again, and my emotions were a swirling mix of vulnerability and trepidation.

The man's explanation of the requirements after a line-of-duty death felt like a distant echo in my mind. The weight of everything was overwhelming, and my attention drifted in and out as he spoke. I mechanically signed forms, acknowledging things I could hardly comprehend in the haze of the moment. Everything was fine until the woman started speaking.

"This is what we are going to do for you, Julie. We are going to get an advance on the life insurance and encase Chris' badge in acrylic as a memento...."

Without a word, I stood up and walked out of the room. I sought refuge in the nearby washroom, needing a moment to collect myself. In that moment, I moved firmly into the anger stage of the grief cycle.

How dare the shooter put me in this position? Not only to carry on as an only parent but must subject myself to these processes?

How dare they talk to me about money when I've just lost the love of my life?

How dare they say that they are going to encase Chris' badge in acrylic as a memento when I knew full well they encase badges so that they can't be used to impersonate a police officer.

How dare the lady who was trying to help and support me call me Julie? Can't she even get my name right?

How dare anyone.

I'm not sure how much time passed before I exited the washroom. Brent was waiting outside. He listened patiently, allowing me to express my anger and anguish. With his calm and gentle demeanour, he used his negotiation skills to convince me to return to the boardroom and complete the necessary paperwork. Reluctantly, I composed myself and went back inside. My mind was still clouded with anger and sorrow, but Brent's steady support helped me navigate through the remaining paperwork. I signed the forms, feeling like I was signing away a part of my soul. The folder I left the room with was filled with duplicate copies, a tangible reminder of the bureaucratic obligations that now burdened my grief-stricken heart.

The next stop on the agenda was the Mess. As I stepped into the large, empty room, I couldn't help but notice the dark curtains shrouding the windows, casting a darkness over the space. My eyes were drawn to yet another buffalo head mounted on the wall, surrounded by flags that held untold stories of valour and sacrifice.

I found a seat at one of the circular tables, trying to gather my thoughts after my earlier episode. It was then that a young woman made her way towards me, carrying a large box under her arm. Brent, who had accompanied me, introduced us and then discreetly departed, leaving us alone to connect in this unfamiliar territory.

As she sat down, the room seemed to hold its breath. The initial moments were marked by a heavy silence that spoke volumes about the pain we both carried. Kim, the young woman before me, gently broke the hush with heartfelt words.

"I am so sorry you are going through this," she said.

Those words, uttered by others in the past two weeks, had never resonated so deeply until that very moment. It was as if she had a special insight into the depths of my heart, having once walked the path I was now treading.

Kim understood the excruciating process of planning and enduring a regimental service while grappling with the reality of becoming an only mom. She knew what it meant to be on public display while struggling to come to terms with such a life-altering truth—to sign the paperwork, to exchange insurance for a spouse who was no longer there. In her presence, I found a kindred spirit who had weathered the storm and emerged on the other side, two and a half years removed from her own crushing news.

She listened with unwavering attention, her eyes filled with compassion as I shared my fears and uncertainties. Her responses were nothing short of gracious, as if each word was carefully chosen to offer comfort and guidance. In her presence, I discovered a safe space where vulnerability was embraced, and I felt seen and understood like never before.

The two hours that Kim spent with me that afternoon transcended the boundaries of time. They became a transformative experience. It wasn't just what she said—it was the unspoken understanding, the shared pain, and the beacon of hope she represented. Her very presence conveyed a message of resilience and survival, and in that moment, I knew that if she could make it through, so could I.

Kim's empathy and genuine care left an unforgettable mark on my soul. She became a guiding light, illuminating the way through the darkness, reminding me that there was strength in vulnerability and beauty in the process of healing. As I left the Mess that day, I carried with me a newfound sense of hope, and the knowledge that even amidst the most trying circumstances, there were people like Kim who would stand beside me, offering support and showing me that life could go on, even in the face of immense loss.

10

THE DRIVE FROM the Hay River airport to my house felt strangely quick, almost as if time had played a trick on me. Today was the day I had been mentally preparing for—Alexis and I would be alone in this house together for the first time since we received the devastating news about Chris. Many friends offered to come stay with us, but I made the conscious choice that Alexis and I needed to embrace our "new normal" on our own. The last two weeks had been a whirlwind of emotions, filled with constant presence and support from family and friends, leaving very little time for private moments.

As we arrived home, my friends kindly helped carry our belongings into the foyer. I thanked them sincerely and, as they left, I closed and locked the door behind them. Standing in the entrance with Alexis in my arms, I took a deep breath and told myself: *you can do this*. It was time to embrace the reality that Chris was no longer physically with us. As I walked up the stairs, I placed Alexis on her playmat, and began to unpack. The house felt quieter, the absence of Chris painfully apparent, yet being there still offered a sense of comfort.

In every corner of the house, I could vividly "see" him—the way he would sit on the couch, eating peanut butter toast and watching TV, his presence in the gym downstairs, and his eyes scanning the computer screen as he read the international news. It was as though his spirit lingered here, and his memory was still alive within the walls of our home. In Hay River, it was easier to hold onto those memories and to feel his presence in my heart.

I watched Alexis play on the mat, cherishing her innocence and embracing the responsibility of being her sole caretaker now. Though the future held uncertainties, in that moment, I felt a glimmer of hope, knowing that I could face each day with my precious daughter by my side. We would show this united front at the upcoming memorial.

As the days passed after returning to Hay River, I couldn't help but notice the solidarity and support from the tight-knit community. In this small town of only 3500 people, grief had touched everyone, and they were all mourning alongside me. To show their empathy and solidarity, community members crafted black and blue ribbon pins, which I saw proudly displayed on the lapels of people's coats as I walked through town. The ribbons tied to utility poles and trees swayed gently in the late fall breeze, a symbol of the collective sorrow that gripped the town. The date for the Hay River Memorial was set, just a few days away on Saturday, October 27th. I made the choice to speak.

As the family gathered in Hay River, it was a unique experience for many of them, especially those who had never been to the North before. The landscape was covered in a pristine layer of snow, and the freezing temperatures were a sharp contrast to what they were used to. For our parents, this was not their first time visiting Hay River, as they had come to meet Alexis shortly after her birth.

During their stay, the local investigating team, who had been tirelessly working on the case, offered to do a walk-through of the events leading up to Chris' tragic death. It was emotional as they retraced the steps of Chris' final moments. They showed the exact spot where he had the altercation with the accused and the place where his life had been taken from him. Despite the chilly weather, the family stood attentively, trying to comprehend the events that unfolded that fateful day.

As they walked through the town, they saw the heart-warming display of community support. The flower bouquets, placed by the flagpole on the lawn of the detachment building, were covered in fresh snow, a symbol of the love and respect the town had for Chris. The cards written by community members and school children were taped to the public entrance of the detachment, a touching tribute to a fallen hero.

The family also saw the space where Chris and Mike shared an office, a glimpse into Chris' everyday working life and the camaraderie with his fellow officers. It was an opportunity for them to connect with the place where Chris had spent so much of his time, serving and protecting the community he loved.

While the rest of the family was engaging in this walk-through, I found myself at home, sitting in front of my computer, writing my speech for the next day's memorial service. It was an opportunity to honour Chris' memory, to share his remarkable life with the community, and to advocate for the changes needed to prevent such a tragedy from happening again.

In addition to providing some details about Chris and my history as a couple, I expressed my appreciation and gratitude for the support I'd received. I wrote:

To the town council and Mayor Pollard for organizing this service; to Father Black, Reverends Smith, Simms and Steele for speaking today; to Jane Groenewegen and the members of the territorial government for their words of encouragement and the beautiful painting; to the Elks club for their generous donation to the Chris Worden Memorial Fund and Alexis' trust fund.; to all who have dropped food off at the house or at the detachment, or have purchased flowers or made donations, thank you. To those in attendance today I wish to say thank you. Thank you for welcoming us into your community; thank you for giving Chris and I the opportunity to make a difference; thank you for attending today and showing us how he touched your lives in a positive and memorable way.

Remember Chris. Talk about him to others. Tell your stories. If we talk about him, he will continue to live through us. By talking about Chris, you will make it easier for me to help Alexis remember her wonderful daddy.

Help make the jobs of the remaining detachment members in Hay River easier, "If you see something, that's wrong, that looks suspicious or questionable, call them. Every bit of information helps to put pieces of the puzzle together. Drugs are a terrible problem in this town, but the police can't do anything—nothing—without your help. Chris died because of the illegal drug trade. Please don't let his death go without meaningful consequences. We need to do something right as a result of this devastating wrong.

I would like the residents of this town to know that while Hay River is the place where we tragically lost Chris, I will fondly remember it more for its nutritious soil for gardening; the abundance of pickerel in the river; the day trips to the falls; the beautiful northern lights; the friends that we have met and the community that had embraced us. But most of all I will remember Hay River for the place that Chris and I welcomed our beautiful Alexis into the world.

Prayer for the RCMP. Almighty God, who has called men and women to your service for the protection of your people. And for the maintenance of your right, we beseech your blessing upon the Commissioner, Officers, Members and Employees of this Force. Endue them with loyalty and courage, and grant that wherever they may be called to duty or danger they may be under your protection. Amen.

I made this speech to more than twelve hundred people at the Don Stewart Community Arena. Deb stood beside and slightly behind me holding Alexis. When I concluded the final prayer, I took Alexis into my arms and walked off stage to applause. It was my hope that this could be the start of positive change, not only for the community, but also for myself.

So when I learned the news of Constable Doug Scott's death my world was tilted more off its axis. Just over a week had passed since we gathered to mourn Chris in Hay River, and now, another young RCMP officer had been tragically taken from us. One day shy of the one-month anniversary of Chris' passing, this heartbreaking incident unfolded in the remote northern territory of Nunavut.

Constable Scott was responding to a call regarding an impaired driver in the arctic hamlet of Kimmirut when he was shot. Just like Chris, he had faced this danger alone, a practice that needed to change. The loss of two young constables in such a short span of time was a harsh and glaring reminder that the safety protocols for RCMP officers attending calls solo were inadequate.

I was approached by Global News and asked to provide my thoughts about policing in the north and the RCMP backup policy. Once again, I chose to leverage the publicity and have my voice heard. While sitting on the sofa in my living room, staring into a video camera, I answered their questions. The reporter's questions were pointed, and my responses were equally direct. This was not a time for vague answers or diplomatic language. It was time to speak the truth about the challenges faced by RCMP officers in the north and the pressing need for change.

With a mix of sadness and determination in my voice, I conveyed the harsh reality of the situation. The officers in the north were overworked, stretched beyond their limits, and lacked the necessary resources to carry out their duties effectively. The toll this was taking on their mental and emotional well-being was alarming. If the RCMP didn't address these issues promptly, they risked losing dedicated members to sick leave, leaving communities vulnerable and unprotected.

I spoke from my heart, advocating for the well-being of the officers who put their lives on the line daily to keep us safe. I emphasized that supporting these officers was not just an organizational responsibility but a moral imperative. The RCMP needed to do more to ensure the safety and welfare of their members.

One of the critical changes I highlighted was the need to revise the backup policy. The current practice of sending officers to calls alone was dangerous and put their lives at unnecessary risk. The policy had to be amended immediately to prioritize officer safety.

As the interview concluded, the camera shifted from my face to Alexis' crib, where I gently placed her down for a nap. The soft music from the Fisher-Price aquarium played in the background, a stark contrast to the weight of the conversation that had just taken place. It was an emotional moment that captured the duality of my life—the strength and resilience needed to advocate for change, coupled with the tenderness and love required to care for my daughter.

With my family returning to their homes after the memorial and the recent news of another RCMP death, time alone became both a blessing and a burden as I embarked on the process of grieving. On one hand, I craved those moments of solitude because I needed a respite from people, the constant condolences, and the overwhelming support. Yet, on the other hand, being alone meant facing my emotions head-on, and that was daunting. For so long, I had been in survival mode, functioning on autopilot, and numbing myself to the pain. It was easier to go through the daily motions when I was in a state of emotional detachment. Numbness was a cocoon that shielded me from the rawness of my grief.

As I settled back into the familiarity of my home in Hay River, that numbness began to wane. The relentless fight-or-flight response that had gripped me was slowly releasing its hold. I knew I had to confront the hurt and allow myself to feel the pain if I wanted to move forward.

Grief was not something I could escape or suppress forever. It demanded to be felt, acknowledged, and processed. The conflicting emotions surged within me, creating a whirlwind of sorrow, anger, and vulnerability. Each emotion vied for my attention, making me question if I had the strength to face them all.

But somewhere deep within me, I knew that confronting my grief was the only path to healing. Like a criss-crossed web, the pain had to be unravelled and untangled, piece by piece, in order to make sense of the devastation that had been thrust upon me.

So, with determination and trepidation, I allowed myself to really start grieving. I let the tears flow, the anger rise, and the heartache consume me. It was a rollercoaster of emotions, and at times, I felt like I was drowning in the intensity of it all.

I made the decision to acknowledge the weight of reality, to confront the depths of my pain, and to embrace the emptiness as a part of my healing process. It was a difficult path, but I was determined to walk it with courage and resilience.

As time seemed to slow down, I confronted the reality that my life had changed irreversibly. I chose to confront the uncertain future head-on, embracing the challenges ahead with a willingness to adapt and grow. I knew that grief was an individual journey, and I was willing to face it on my own terms.

As the days turned into weeks and the reality of being a young widow settled in, I found myself searching for ways to keep moving forward on this new and unfamiliar path. Time that was once dedicated to being a spouse now stretched before me, open and vast. The routines of cooking for two, making plans for vacations, and having long conversations with my best friend were now memories of a life that was gone.

To cope with the overwhelming emptiness, I sought out a book that could provide some guidance and comfort in navigating grief. I went to the local library, hoping to find a relatable title. However, nothing seemed to fit my unique situation. The lack of resources was exacerbated by the fact that online shopping, especially with overnight delivery, was not commonplace in 2007, especially in the remote northern region where I lived. Amazon and online bookstores were not yet easily accessible.

Nevertheless, I persisted and tried searching the Chapters website. My keywords were "young widow," hoping to find a voice that resonated with my own experience. The results presented a few titles, but as I read the descriptions, I noticed that these women were all in their mid-40s or older. While their stories were undoubtedly valuable, I couldn't help but feel like I didn't quite fit the mould. I was just twenty-nine years old, and my journey as a young widow felt different from those who were further along in life.

In hindsight, I understood that women who lost their husbands at my age often had young children to care for, which could be all-consuming and leave little time for writing books. Still, I longed for a narrative that could mirror my own emotions and struggles.

Feeling like I didn't quite belong in the grief literature available, I chose to turn my focus inward. I started to explore ways to invest my time in new and meaningful ways. I delved into activities that brought me joy and offered an escape from the overwhelming grief.

I attended a playgroup with Alexis a few times a week. It provided a safe space for her to interact with other children while allowing me to connect with other moms. These women knew me both before and after Chris' death, treating me with the same kindness and understanding throughout. However, as much as I appreciated the support, I struggled with the emotions that came with the perception of pity from others. I did not want to see any more pity-faces, as it made me feel uncomfortable and put walls up between myself and those who genuinely cared. While I understood that their intentions were kind, I couldn't help but resent the feeling of needing to appear strong and put-together to comfort them. This internal battle sometimes caused me to withdraw, engaging only with those in my immediate circle of trust.

I learned to cope by staying within that circle, only engaging with those who I felt understood me without the need for pity. Occasionally, I had the energy to step outside that circle for planned events, and I would ask Michèle to tell the group to bring their happy faces. I craved moments of joy, laughter, and normalcy amidst the grief.

One such event was a get-together at a teacher-friend's house. Steve had set up the PlayStation game RockBand in his garage. It was a game I had never played before, but I decided to give it a try. I sat at the drums and learned to follow the colours on the screen, pounding the drumsticks and pressing the foot pedal in time with the music. To my surprise, I found a cathartic release in the energy I put into hitting the drum pads. The rhythm allowed me to release some of the pent-up emotions I had been holding inside, and I felt a sense of relief and empowerment. Steve offered me full access to his garage to come and go as I pleased. It became a place where I could unleash my emotions through play. When I eventually left Hay River to start anew, RockBand became a cherished gift, a reminder of the power of music and friendship in healing.

Establishing new routines became a central focus of my life, especially with a baby like Alexis, whose sleep patterns seemed to change as quickly as she grew. Before Chris' passing, she was sleeping through the night, but the upheaval in our lives disrupted her routine, and she started waking up multiple times during the night. As a result, I found myself constantly waking up as well, contributing to my overwhelming exhaustion.

Towards the end of November 2007, my mom came to stay with us for a week. I took this opportunity to ask for her help in getting Alexis back to sleeping through the night. My mom stayed in my bedroom, just across the hall from Alexis' nursery, while I slept in the spare bed in the basement with earplugs. It was challenging to hear Alexis cry, but we followed a method of letting her settle herself, and after four nights, she started sleeping through the night again. The relief of being able to sleep soundly was immense and had a positive impact on both Alexis and me. With more rest, I found myself with increased energy and mental clarity, and Alexis' nap schedule became more predictable. The predictability brought a sense of control that I deeply craved during those turbulent times.

As the days moved forward, I realized that predictability and control were important coping mechanisms for me in dealing with traumatic grief. Having some sense of order and knowing what to expect offered a small semblance of normalcy in the midst of chaos. It helped me feel more grounded and provided a comforting illusion of stability. Little did I know that these coping strategies, while helpful in the short term, could later become a maladaptive habit.

A few weeks later, I had the opportunity to spend some quality time with my family, seeking warmth and relaxation in the Caribbean. It was a trip that had been planned earlier, with Chris included in the original itinerary. Now, without him, we decided to add his sister Cathy and my sister Deb to the group alongside my parents. We all converged at the airport in St. Maarten, looking forward to a much-needed break from the cold weather and an opportunity to bond together.

The timeshare we booked provided us with a comfortable space to stay. The two-bedroom setup, complete with a full kitchen and living area, allowed us to feel at home. We requested a crib for Alexis, which we rolled into the closet in the room Cathy, Deb, and I shared. Alexis, now ten months old, had reached significant milestones, sitting on her own and crawling. Her excitement and curiosity about the world around her were infectious.

The Caribbean scenery provided a stark contrast to the snowy landscape we had left behind. Alexis enjoyed floating in the pool on a floatie, giggling and splashing around. She was now down to one afternoon nap, and each of us took turns staying back in the suite to accommodate her schedule. We explored the beautiful sights and sounds, putting miles on her stroller as we ventured through the vibrant surroundings.

One of the highlights of the trip was Alexis' first time in the ocean. With just a sunhat on her head, I held her on my hip as we waded deeper into the warm blue waters. She was mesmerized by the waves, playfully slapping at the water, laughing as it bounced up and hit her skin. Yet, in these beautiful moments, my emotions were a mix of joy and sorrow. Each laugh and giggle from Alexis filled me with joy, but an underlying ache remained. As a proud parent, I celebrated her firsts, but it was also a painful reminder that Chris was not there to share these precious moments with us. My sense of excitement and pride was matched with a sense of sadness and longing. It was difficult to reconcile that my best moments were simultaneously my worst.

From St. Maarten, Cathy, Alexis, and I flew back to Ottawa, where we would experience our first Christmas without Chris. As the holiday season approached, a mix of excitement and sorrow filled the air. A baby's first Christmas is usually met with great anticipation, and while we were looking forward to making it special for Alexis, our emotions were still raw from our recent loss.

The Worden's home was adorned with a festive tree surrounded by presents, many of which were for Alexis. The kindness of Chris' friends shone through as packages arrived with heartfelt notes for both Alexis and me. This was another reminder of the incredible kindness of people during challenging times.

On Christmas Eve, I dressed Alexis in red pyjamas adorned with cheerful snowmen and gingerbread houses. The next morning, she woke up with her usual infectious smile. As we gathered around the tree, we placed a framed photo of Chris on a chair nearby, giving him a physical presence in our celebration.

With excitement, I placed Alexis on the floor near the tree, hoping to see her open her presents. To my amusement, she was more fascinated with the ornaments, picking them off the branches, studying them with curious fascination, rolling them in her tiny hands, and shaking them with delight. When it came to unwrapping gifts, she would make a half-hearted effort, often getting the paper stuck to her little hands. It took her nearly two days to finish opening all her presents, each moment filled with wonder and joy.

Her favourite gift turned out to be the Fisher Price Little People barn. She spent hours opening and closing the barn doors, giggling at the farm animal sounds it made. Throughout the day, we felt Chris' presence through cherished memories and the love that still enveloped us.

At dinner, Alexis proudly wore her "baby's first Christmas bib" and enjoyed the delicious feast prepared by MaryAnn. As we sat together, the absence of Chris was deeply felt, but we supported each other without judgment. Each of us needed different things at different times, and we understood and respected those needs.

As the holiday season drew to a close, I couldn't shake the feeling that it was time to make some crucial decisions about the future. Being closer to family, especially her grand-parents, was a priority. I knew that having their support would be invaluable, both for Alexis and for me. The idea of raising my daughter in Ingersoll, Ontario, where I grew up, didn't feel right, especially considering my parents' frequent travels.

In early January 2008, before leaving Ottawa, I enlisted the help of a real-estate agent. Together, we explored numerous homes in the area, but none of them felt like the right fit for us. Then, we came across a model home located just ten minutes from the Worden's place. It was under construction and scheduled for completion in early June. The prospect of being able to personalize the finishes and fixtures to make it my own was incredibly appealing. In my heart, I knew this was where we belonged.

As much as I looked forward to the new journey ahead in Ottawa, I knew there was unfinished business in Hay River that needed my attention first. The preliminary inquiry, a crucial step in the legal process, was scheduled to take place in late spring. I felt a sense of responsibility to be present and involved until that concluded. The inquiry would bring closure to one chapter of this painful journey, and I wanted to see it through before embarking on the next chapter of our lives.

So, for the time being, Alexis and I would remain in the north, facing whatever challenges lay ahead with the strength and resilience we had learned to muster.

11

•••••

NAVIGATING THE CHOPPY sea of emotions that accompany grief can easily derail you. This was not lost on me; I keenly felt the turbulence, but I was determined to resist being swept away by it. My primary objective was to maintain an upbeat energy, especially for the sake of Alexis. I was acutely attuned to the fact that she could pick up on my emotional state, and I was resolute in shielding her from the overwhelming waves of sadness and despair that threatened to engulf us. My priority was safeguarding her, ensuring that she wouldn't bear the weight of any additional pain. This determination became the driving force propelling my efforts forward.

February 6, 2008, marked Alexis' first birthday. To celebrate, I joined forces with one of her close friends, Julianne, who shared a birthday only three days apart. Julianne's mother, Kathleen, had been there for me on the morning Chris passed away, driving me home from the hospital. My house was filled with the joyful presence of friends, creating an atmosphere of warmth and togetherness. To ensure that the focus remained on the cheerful moments, I made it clear to the person operating my video camera that if tears started to flow, those moments were to be left off the recording. My intent was for the camera to capture Alexis' chubby fingers playfully covered in icing and her radiant smile, allowing these images to stand out, rather than showcasing my own emotions, which vividly revealed how deeply I longed for her father's presence. Alexis was a source of comfort and happiness. She had an uncanny ability to bring forth the best within me. Her presence infused my life with a sense of purpose and determination. She was the reason I was able to move forward, both in my daily existence and in my preparations for the impending preliminary inquiry.

I made the deliberate choice to remain in Hay River until this concluded. Despite the fact that the accused had been apprehended and charged with first-degree murder the day before Chris' funeral, it took a span of eight months for the legal process to reach its first formal step. This legal proceeding serves as a crucial assessment in serious criminal cases. Its purpose is to determine whether the evidence presented by the Crown is substantial enough to warrant a trial. While not a full-fledged trial itself, the preliminary inquiry holds significance as witnesses testify under oath, and the accused or their legal representation is granted the opportunity to cross-examine witnesses. The dates for the preliminary inquiry were set for June 16-20, with the decision being rendered on June 30, 2008. Looking ahead to our imminent departure, I booked our flight for July 1st to Edmonton. My plan was to spend Canada Day with my sister Sandy and her family in Red Deer before continuing into Ottawa on July 4th, marking the beginning of our life in a new city.

In the months leading up to the pivotal preliminary inquiry, the relentless efforts of the RCMP continued to peel back the layers of the harrowing events surrounding Chris' untimely death. Each revelation, each discovery, felt like a step closer to uncovering the full truth, and I clung to the hope that justice would ultimately be served. The anticipation weighed heavily on my heart, knowing that this inquiry would mark a critical juncture in our journey towards closure.

The RCMP major crimes unit extended their compassion by crafting a comprehensive timeline of the tragic events. Before this sensitive information could be unveiled in the courtroom, they wanted to offer our family the opportunity to process it privately. It was a gesture of empathy, allowing us to brace ourselves for the emotional rollercoaster that lay ahead.

In Canada, killing a police officer is classified as first-degree murder, carrying with it a sentence of life imprisonment. Eligibility for parole is set at a minimum of twenty-five years. The Worden family arrived in town a few days in advance of the inquiry. Our meeting with the investigators and Crown lawyers at their hotel was a sombre affair. Gathered around a table, we were presented with the comprehensive narrative of the events that led to Chris' tragic death. The evidence, meticulously compiled, painted a haunting picture that was etched into our minds. With each detail revealed, a mix of emotions surged within us—grief, anger, and an unwavering resolve to seek justice for Chris.

With the inquiry imminent, we were granted a glimpse of the courtroom that would soon bear witness to this crucial proceeding. Walking through the doors of the Hay River courthouse, the gravity of the moment was clear. Metal detectors and heightened security measures served as a reminder of the significance of what was to come. The doors to the courtroom were open, revealing the layout within. On both sides of the aisle were four rows of bench seating. The first two rows on the right, situated behind the Crown prosecutors' desk, were reserved for our family. Straight ahead, on a raised platform, stood the judge's bench. To its left was the witness stand; to its right, the court reporter. On the opposite side of the aisle was the defense attorney's desk, and adjacent to it, a specially constructed plexiglass enclosure designated for this case, serving as a barrier between the accused and the public gallery. This partition was a physical reminder of the emotional chasm that had torn our lives apart—the accused, separated from the world by an insurmountable divide.

Every morning, as we stepped into the courthouse, our designated seats awaited us—unchanging reminders of the gravity of the situation. With each instruction to rise or be seated, we complied with the routine, the cadence of court proceedings guiding our movements. Throughout the entire ordeal, the accused never once met our gazes, perhaps a conscious choice to shield himself from the searing intensity of our collective emotions. But if he had dared to look, he would have found himself staring into the eyes of six individuals—eyes ablaze with a mixture of anger, disbelief, and inner turmoil. Our eyes were windows to a storm of emotions that words could never adequately express.

In that courtroom, I sat, bound by the formality of the proceedings, while my heart wrestled with a multitude of feelings. The accused faced justice, but we faced the haunting shadows of a tragedy that had irrevocably altered my life. The sound of legal arguments and witness testimonies filled the room, each syllable cutting through the air like a reminder of what had been lost. Yet, despite the overwhelming urge to speak out, I remained silent, choosing to abide by the rules of the court.

Every passing moment was a challenge in restraint. The desire to question, to demand answers, simmered beneath the surface, threatening to erupt. The courtroom held so many unanswered questions, so many discrepancies that begged to be addressed. In an attempt to preserve my thoughts and concerns, I turned to a journal—a place where I could capture my raw emotions, my observations, and the unspoken inquiries that gnawed at my mind. Each entry served as a record of the anguish, the disbelief, and the overwhelming need for answers.

In the midst of the legal intricacies, there were certain boundaries we had to adhere to—conversations with witnesses prior to their testimonies were off-limits. However, once the formalities were over, I was granted the chance to converse with those who held insights into the heart-wrenching events. Among them, one figure stood out—the coroner. In a dimly lit room adjacent to the main courtroom, the family gathered, seeking answers that only he could provide.

As the questions flowed, we delved into the specifics of his findings. In the courtroom, we learned that Chris stood at 6'4" and weighed 212 lbs. These measurements contrasted with my memory of my husband—standing 6'2" and 220 lbs. The coroner's explanation was sobering: a body's ligaments relax post-mortem, causing a lengthening effect, accounting for the height difference. The weight discrepancy, he explained, was a sombre reflection of the blood loss resulting from the traumatic wounds—the severed jugular vein and the entry and exit points of the bullets. His directness in discussing these details was appreciated, yet it sent my mind spiralling into a tumultuous whirlwind.

With this new information, my mental image of Chris was altered forever. The vivid scenes that now dominated my thoughts were those of my husband, marked by the permanent scars of four bullet wounds and lying in a pool of his own blood. The trauma of those harrowing moments seemed to compound, each layer adding to the weight of my grief. The process was excruciating, and yet I knew I had to confront it. I had to grapple with the agony, the fury, the chaotic mess that had become my emotional landscape. I recognized that moving forward demanded understanding and an immersion in the painful truths of my reality.

The ten days that bridged the gap between the conclusion of the testimony and the impending judgment were a whirlwind of activity. Amidst the intensity of the courtroom proceedings, a ray of warmth and solidarity emerged from the embrace of my friends. They orchestrated a heartfelt 'starting over' shower for both Alexis and me. Their thoughtful gifts resonated with the fresh chapter awaiting us in Ottawa—a new home, a new beginning. Each item was a symbol of their support, a gesture that would forever etch their kindness in my heart. A compilation of their treasured recipes bound into a cookbook was a culinary companion that continues to grace my kitchen to this day. And then there was the unexpected joy of receiving RockBand, a reminder that moments of joy could blossom even in the midst of adversity.

Overwhelmed with gratitude, I returned home with these tokens of care and affection, hesitant to unpack them. The movers were poised to converge upon my belongings in mere days, orchestrating the transition of my life from Hay River to Ottawa. Practical tasks punctuated the countdown—a ski-doo to sell, a boat to be passed along to a friend, and pieces of our life to be carefully handed down.

As the snowmobile found a new owner and the boat was entrusted to Michèle for a symbolic dollar, I realized that these actions were more than just practicalities. They were symbolic gestures of connection and continuity. Much of the free weight equipment and Chris' suits found a new home—with Tyler, a younger member of the watch, who had a similar build as Chris.

The knowledge that these possessions would continue to be treasured and cared for by individuals who understood their significance brought me a sense of peace, a reassurance that pieces of Chris' world would continue to thrive in the hands of those who valued them.

I met the day the movers arrived with a mix of emotions. I had meticulously gone through our belongings, carefully deciding what to bring as we embarked on our new journey. The movers went about their task, wrapping and boxing up the remaining items, their actions serving as a reminder that the chapter of my life in the North was drawing to a close. I stood in the driveway, watching as my belongings and even my car were loaded onto the transport truck. It was a surreal sight, one that solidified the reality of our imminent departure.

As the truck pulled away from the driveway, memories of the day I left Hay River for Ottawa for Chris' funeral flooded back. I took a deep breath and stepped inside the house, a familiar space that had held so many moments of love, laughter, and shared dreams. This time, however, it was different. This time, it was a final farewell to the place that had been our home. Standing there, I felt a mixture of gratitude and sadness, a deep appreciation for the memories we had created within those walls, and a profound ache for the future that Chris and I would never get to experience together.

In that quiet moment, I spoke to the house, expressing my heartfelt thanks for the time we had spent there, for the love that had blossomed there, and for the family we had started for Alexis. I made a silent promise to carry forward his memory and uphold the dreams we had shared for our daughter's upbringing. It was a bittersweet pledge, a commitment to navigate this uncharted path without the person who had been my partner and confidant.

Letting go wasn't easy, and I would be lying if I said I wasn't afraid of what the future held. But I knew that I had to take this next step, not just for myself, but for Alexis. As the transport truck disappeared down the road, I closed the door on that chapter of my life, carrying with me the love, strength, and resilience that Chris had instilled in me. Our journey was far from over, and I was determined to face whatever lay ahead with the same determination and spirit that had brought us this far.

June 30th brought us back to the courthouse, the weight of uncertainty hanging in the air. As the judge's words resonated, confirming that the evidence was indeed sufficient to warrant a criminal trial, a mix of emotions surged within me. A sense of validation mingled with apprehension, for this outcome meant that the path ahead was clear, yet veiled in shadows. The judge's mention of "due course" was a phrase laden with implications. It spoke of a journey that would extend far beyond the horizon of that day, a timeframe that would test our patience and resolve. Those two words encapsulated the essence of the challenge before us—the long, winding road of the legal process that lay ahead, fraught with delays, complexities, and the unknown.

My final evening in Hay River unfolded without any significant moments. I made the choice to depart without drawing attention to myself, preferring a subtle exit rather than a grand farewell. The quietness of my departure aligned with my emotional state, a mixture of relief, anticipation, and a touch of sadness for leaving a chapter behind.

The airport's waiting area stood as a testament to the town's modest size. Memories of that space remain somewhat blurred, whether the need to navigate security checkpoints existed or not seems to fade into the background. Yet, one memory stands out vividly against the backdrop of departure. Cindy, with her genuine warmth, approached me for a hug. Her words, laced with both sincerity and a hint of exasperation, lingered in the air. "I hope you never have to return to this fucking town."

To date, I have not.

12

WE BECAME RESIDENTS of Ottawa on July 4, 2008. In those initial days, Alexis and I stayed with John and MaryAnn as we eagerly awaited the arrival of our belongings from the moving company. As we settled into the new space, it became apparent that the landscaping was still a work in progress. The sod for the backyard wasn't due to be laid until September, leaving it a bit muddy. With a toddler in the house, I was determined to make the most of our outdoor space. With creativity and resourcefulness, I transformed the garage into a spacious play area for Alexis. It was a way to provide her with a play space despite the absence of a complete backyard.

The transition to our new home in Ottawa didn't seem to faze Alexis at all. She embraced the changes with her characteristic enthusiasm and boundless energy. The fact that we were in a different city and in a new house, seemed to hold no significance for her. She was content with having her own room, a dedicated play area, and a flight of stairs to explore. Every little discovery became a source of excitement for her.

One of the things that thrilled Alexis the most was the park just a short distance away from our new home. It quickly became a part of our daily routine. We'd venture there almost every day, basking in the simple joy of swings, slides, and open space. As I chatted with other parents at the park, I learned about local activities and groups tailored for kids and their caregivers. Intrigued, we joined swimming and gymnastics classes. Alexis' natural athleticism and eagerness to learn made her an excellent student. She approached these activities with enthusiasm, making it clear that she was genuinely enjoying herself.

I scheduled these activities around Alexis' nap time. This structure not only benefited her but was equally essential for me. That precious hour and a half or so when she would drift into slumber provided me with a valuable opportunity to recharge and recenter myself. It was during these moments that I could replenish my own energy, preparing to be the best version of myself when she woke up again.

This routine was more than just a schedule; it was a lifeline. As an only parent, my responsibility was immense, and I was determined to rise to the occasion. I understood that in order to be patient, attentive, and loving towards Alexis, I needed to take care of my own well-being. This commitment meant that I strived to offer her my utmost care and affection, especially during those waking hours we spent together.

There were moments when exhaustion and the weight of my responsibilities threatened to dim that version of me. I knew that if I allowed tiredness or overwhelm to take over, I wouldn't be able to provide Alexis with the nurturing environment she deserved. There was no one else to share the responsibilities with or to step in, which made these periods of rest even more critical.

During Alexis' naps, I didn't just catch up on sleep, but I actively worked on refueling my resilience. I engaged in activities that brought me joy, whether it was reading a book, listening to music, or simply sitting in silence. These seemingly small acts were my way of fortifying myself, preparing to be the support and loving presence that Alexis needed as she woke up, ready to explore the world around her. It was a silent commitment to being the best mother I could be.

From the moment we settled into our new Ottawa home, I began to notice a fascinating aspect of Alexis's personality—her innate sense of organization. She had a natural inclination to arrange her toys meticulously, often forming neat lines and patterns that seemed to bring her a sense of order and comfort. Tidying up became an enjoyable activity for her, a way to maintain the sense of structure she seemed to crave.

One constant companion in Alexis's world was "bubba," her cherished "blankie." This simple piece of knitted thread held a special place in her heart, providing a source of security and reassurance wherever we went. Alexis's sensitivity extended to her sense of touch, and she expressed her preferences clearly. There were instances when I would excitedly dress her in a new outfit, only to find her resisting, tugging at the fabric, and communicating her discomfort through crying until I relented and changed her clothes.

One of the most remarkable aspects of Alexis's personality was her commitment to routine. Like a well-choreographed dance, she effortlessly followed our nightly routine without needing any prompts. Every step, from brushing her teeth to getting ready for bed, was executed flawlessly. I couldn't help but be amazed by her consistency and determination, and I made sure to celebrate and praise her for it. These early glimpses into her personality brought both wonder and joy to our everyday interactions, reminding me of the uniqueness and complexity that makes each child's journey through life so special.

Beyond the embrace of the Worden family and a few compassionate RCMP members who had been part of the funeral arrangements, Ottawa was a city of strangers to me. Cathy introduced me to a group of what I fondly call my "insta-friends." These were individuals who were already a part of her social circle, and they were privy to our story—the loss of Chris and the challenges I was navigating. What made these relationships special was the immediate bond and understanding that existed. I didn't need to elaborate or explain my emotions; they knew, and they provided a safe space where I could simply be, without fear of judgment.

For much of that summer my main interactions were with John and MaryAnn and the occasional insta-friend. I would stop by the Worden household often with Alexis, mostly around lunch or dinner time. This allowed time for Alexis to play in their nice yard, as well as allow me to benefit from MaryAnn's culinary skills. I found it difficult to cook for myself. Alexis was seventeen months old and had unrefined taste buds. I did not enjoy investing time in cooking a large, proper meal for myself. I would rather spend that time making the ten-minute drive to Le Café Worden!

These visits also allowed me to have adult conversations. I needed more of this in my life. I would see the odd parent at the park where we would exchange pleasantries, but nothing more than superficial chatter. When I talked to friends on the phone, I craved hearing about their lives. Mine seemed to be running in a continuous loop. Wake up to Alexis' talking. Make us breakfast. Monitor Alexis playing in the living room while doing laundry. Head to the grocery store or run errands. Snack time. Walk/wagon to the park. Eat lunch. Put Alexis down to nap. Do administrative work and housekeeping. Grab Alexis from her nap. Snack time. Play/craft time with Alexis. Dinner time. Play in the garage/driveway. Bath time. Reading time. Bedtime for Alexis, quickly followed by bedtime for me.

Our days settled into this familiar routine, one that lacked the thrill of novelty. My life felt quite contained, with limited inputs and a sense of steady predictability. In my conversations with others, I sought to break away from the monotony by diving into their worlds. I was genuinely interested in learning about their endeavours, passions, and experiences. However, I noticed a tendency among many to hold back on sharing the positive aspects of their lives with me. Perhaps they believed they were shielding me from feelings of longing or sadness—perhaps they wanted to avoid any unintended comparison that might evoke a sense of "this is what I have, and you don't." It seemed as though they were cautious about sharing their own happiness in fear that it might magnify my own perceived lack.

I tried to convey to my friends that this approach wasn't necessary, that their sharing wouldn't disrupt my reality. Each passing day, with or without their conversations, reminded me of Chris' absence. Their happiness didn't make my grief any heavier, nor did it dilute the weight of my emotions. I longed for them to relate to me as they always had—as a friend, not as a friend who had become a widow.

Living in Ottawa gave access to much more shopping than I was used to when living in the north. On rainy days instead of going to the park, I would pop Alexis into the car and head to the mall. We spent hours in bookstores. I would often peruse the grief self-help section hoping something new and relatable would magically appear. It did not. However, in the fiction section, I stumbled across the book "How to Talk to a Widower" by Johnathan Tropper. The book jacket read:

> *Doug Parker is a widower at age twenty-nine, and in his quiet town, that makes him the object of sympathy, curiosity, and in some cases even unbridled desire. But Doug has more urgent things on his mind, such as his sixteen-year-old stepson, Russ, a once-sweet kid who is now getting into increasingly serious trouble. As Doug starts dipping his toes into the shark-infested waters of the second-time-around dating scene, it isn't long before his new life is spinning hopelessly out of control, cutting a harrowing and often humorous swath of sexual missteps and escalating chaos across a suburban landscape.*

This truly captured my interest. I picked it up and delved into its pages that very night, once Alexis was tucked in bed. The characters resonated with me in a profound way. Doug's raw and unfiltered anger struck a chord with me. His inner monologue seemed to echo my own thoughts, as if the author had tapped directly into my mind. The blend of profanity and unapologetic commentary mirrored my own inner dialogue, and I found myself laughing out loud at the shared sentiment. It wasn't just the humour that connected with me; it was the uncanny resemblance between Doug's grief process and mine. While I didn't share his reliance on alcohol, much of the rest seemed eerily familiar.

I devoured the book within days, unable to put it down. Struck by its impact, I returned to the bookstore and purchased ten more copies. With heartfelt notes, I sent them to my parents, sisters, Cathy, Chris' parents, Michèle, and a few other friends from up north, expressing a hope that the book might help them better understand me. I also took the time to email the author, expressing my deep appreciation for his skillful writing and candid exploration of the bitterness and challenges of grief and life. His response was gracious and filled with gratitude. Writing to an author was a first for me, and to this day, I haven't repeated the experience. But that book, more than any self-help guide, became a crucial tool in my journey towards understanding myself and communicating my feelings and needs to those around me. This was especially timely because in September 2008, our lives were consumed by a series of formal memorial events.

The first memorial, held at Wilfrid Laurier University in Waterloo, Ontario, held a bittersweet significance. On a warm, sunny day, just before the opening football game, coach Jeffries presented me with a jersey—number twenty-two, Chris' number. With a mix of pride and sorrow, I donned the jersey, knowing that it was a physical symbol of the impact of Chris' legacy and for the support we had received. The team, standing behind me outfitted in brand new uniforms, was a testament to the generosity of those who donated to the Chris Worden Memorial Fund.

But this was more than just a game. It was a moment of unity and healing, where the community came together to celebrate Chris' life and legacy. As I stood at centre field, surrounded by the team, wearing the team jersey that Chris wore with such pride, I couldn't help but smile through the tears. On the front of the jersey, just above and to the right of the number, were the initials "CW," a small yet powerful reminder of the young man who had touched the hearts of many. As the anthem, "O Canada," resonated through the stadium, I held Alexis in my arms, her tiny figure clad in a purple jersey of her own, symbolizing the bond with her late father. Standing beside the team mascot, "Hawk," I felt a sense of pride knowing that the Chris Worden Memorial Fund had contributed to outfitting the team in new uniforms. It was a small glimmer of hope and a testament to the impact Chris had left behind.

The second event, the annual RCMP Memorial Service held at Depot, was both impactful and sobering. The memories of Chris' graduation from Depot, filled with excitement and anticipation, clashed with the sombre atmosphere of this occasion. As an honoured family, we were given a private tour of the base, including the cemetery and cenotaph. I remembered how Chris would salute the cenotaph every time he passed it during his time at Depot, explaining that it was to honour the fallen officers. Now, others would pay the same tribute to him as his name stood engraved on the cenotaph beyond the eternal flame.

Seeing Chris' name etched in granite on the Memorial Wall in the cemetery was like a sharp blow to the gut. He was so young, and the weight of his sacrifice pressed heavily on my heart. Chris' plaque read:

IN MEMORY OF
 # 49314 CST.
C. J. WORDEN
DIED 07-10-06 ON DUTY
AT HAY RIVER, N.W.T. AGE 30

Alongside MaryAnn and Alexis, I laid a wreath, with Alexis leaving a single pink rose as a loving tribute. She wore the dress Chris had bought for her when she was just three months old, and it was a beautiful reminder of the love he showered upon her. As we stood there, surrounded by the memories of fallen heroes, I couldn't help but marvel at the strength and courage displayed by these brave officers who gave their lives to protect others. It was a humbling experience, a significant reminder of the sacrifices made by law enforcement officers and their families.

The third and final event took place the last Sunday of September. This was the thirty-first Police and Peace Officers' Memorial at Parliament Hill in Ottawa. Again, this is an annual event. My birthday is the last day of September, so there have been many times when this memorial has fallen on it. In 2008, it was held on a grey and cloudy day. The overcast weather mirrored the emotions that filled the air as we gathered once again to honour Chris and all the fallen officers. The Minister of Public Safety, Stockwell Day, delivered a heartfelt address, expressing the nation's gratitude for the ultimate sacrifice made by Chris and his fellow officers.

As the ceremony unfolded, I couldn't help but reflect on the events of the past year. The pain of losing Chris was still raw, but the love and support we had received from friends, family, and even strangers were a source of comfort. The parade of police officers that filled the front lawn, the steps leading to the centre block lined with uniformed officers from a variety of police forces—it was a powerful visual representation of the unity and solidarity that existed within the law enforcement community.

As the minister concluded his speech, the sound of bagpipes filled the air, a haunting melody that echoed through the hearts of those present. One by one, we stepped forward to lay wreaths and flowers, a small yet significant gesture to honour the memory of our fallen heroes. Each of us laid a carnation—Alexis' was once again pink, a sweet reminder of her innocence and resilience.

As I returned home that afternoon, a sense of relief washed over me. The wave of memorials had finally subsided. Engaging in these events demanded an immense amount of energy. It wasn't just about the condensed hour of the ceremony itself. These memorials were all-encompassing, stretching out into weekend-long affairs. They comprised receptions, meetings with other grieving families who had navigated this painful path in years past, and the presentation of commemorative tokens. My collection now included coins, ribbons, framed certificates, and paintings from each event. I carried with me memories of chapel services and photos captured in front of engraved names.

But looming on the horizon was the most significant event, the one-year anniversary of Chris' death. In the days preceding this milestone, I was swept up in a whirlwind of emotions. The approaching anniversary held within it a mix of bitterness and sweetness. It stood as a pivotal marker on my journey of grief, a year of navigating the maze of pain and healing. I eagerly waited for the upcoming weekend to come and go, as if marking the crossing of a finish line. I yearned to celebrate the fact that I had somehow endured an entire year without Chris by my side.

This milestone was layered with significance. It signified the culmination of all the "firsts"—the first birthdays, holidays, and other occasions without him. It marked the completion of the sombre September memorials. It encapsulated the multitude of administrative tasks and paperwork that had consumed my time. With this anniversary, I felt a deep longing to move forward, to take another step towards healing, so I could continue to shape my new life.

I marked this occasion by taking Alexis to Pink Lake in Gatineau Park. Chris' brother Michael came with us, providing a comforting presence in this meaningful journey. The sunny weather that day—October 6, 2008—seemed to mirror the newfound sense of hope and determination in my heart. We hiked the small two-kilometre trail around Pink Lake, Alexis enjoyed her snacks, and Michael and I engaged in heartfelt conversations. The picturesque surroundings served as a gentle reminder that life goes on, even after the deepest tragedies.

13

•••••

WITH THE MEMORIALS finally behind me, I found myself at a turning point, ready to shift my focus towards forging a new path as a working mother. The opportunity emerged in August 2008 when the RCMP approached me to join a committee dedicated to enhancing support for the families of employees. This initiative was a pivotal component of a broader project aimed at reshaping the culture within the RCMP. Without hesitation, I accepted the invitation. If my experiences could contribute to helping other families navigate the challenges they faced and connect with the resources they needed, I was more than willing to participate.

A pivotal moment arrived with a five-day conference, where all project and committee members converged. Introductions were exchanged, presentations were delivered, progress was shared, and collaborative working groups were formed. Beyond the realm of funeral preparations, this was my first professional engagement since commencing my maternity leave. The prospect of being part of a team again stirred a sense of excitement within me. I relished the opportunity to dress up in attire that wasn't confined to mourning black or comfortable leggings. It felt like a chance to rebuild and redefine who I was.

I was slowly coming to believe that I didn't have to let a single moment shape my entire identity. I was a composition of various facets, each contributing to a version of myself that held worth, significance, and genuineness. It was becoming clear that I had a multitude of attributes to rediscover—my talents, my ambitions, my core essence. The journey required me to reestablish my identity and embrace the person I am. The traumatic grip of grief had altered me, but I refused to let it continue to define me. Rather, I sought to incorporate that experience into my life in a way that could drive me forward. And in my involvement with the RCMP, I had found the avenue to achieve just that.

A new unit was taking shape within the RCMP's learning and development directorate. This unit's prime focus was to equip recently promoted supervisors and managers with the essential skills they needed to excel in their roles. Their mission was to design comprehensive learning programs tailored to this purpose. While I was participating in the committee meetings, the director general of learning and development approached me. He inquired whether I'd be interested in becoming a part of this new initiative. Without hesitation, I expressed my keen interest. I promptly updated my resume, went through the interview process, and was thrilled to receive the job offer. After the four month wait for my security clearance to be processed, in early January 2009, I began my employment with the RCMP, stepping into a new professional life.

In the meantime, I needed to find childcare for Alexis. Fortunately, one of the mothers of my insta-friends ran a home daycare and had a spot for Alexis. She started going for morning visits throughout the Fall to help her adjust and become familiar with her new daytime setting. She enjoyed playing with the other children and I enjoyed having a few hours to myself. During her visits, I went to the gym. It was during this time while I was using the cardio equipment that I took the time to actively reflect on the past and make goals for the future. With one year of widowhood under my belt, and starting a new job in a few weeks, I was ready to really start making strides away from the tragedy. It was time to start living again. I didn't know exactly what that would look like, but I was ready to explore possibilities. Joining the gym and putting myself in new public spaces was a start.

At the beginning, I would force myself to smile and say hello to strangers as they walked past me in the parking lot or hallway. With time, the level of effort to do this decreased. There eventually came a time that these morning greetings became natural and genuine. I was able to make eye contact while speaking to strangers. These simple acts of courtesy and kindness started to shift the way I perceived the world and my place in it.

This trend continued as I transitioned into my role at the RCMP. The team I joined was relatively small, which facilitated a quicker integration process. The onboarding was well-organized, and my supervisor, Sean, invested significant time in acquainting me with the building layout and office environment. He walked me through the ongoing projects, highlighting the distinctions between units: "This other unit focuses on operational training, while our unit designs leadership programs." My designated desk was located in an open workspace configuration. The layout featured four workstations arranged in a square, each occupying a corner. I found myself situated by the corner windows, on the outer perimeter of the arrangement.

This setting contrasted significantly with the workspaces I had known as a teacher. With each passing moment, my initial nervousness gradually transformed into genuine excitement. The atmosphere felt reassuringly comfortable and surprisingly familiar, both of which were elements I had deeply longed for in my life.

Sean proposed that the best way for me to understand the programs our team was developing and enhancing was to participate in them as a student. So, with about eight weeks in the position, I was sitting in a classroom with twenty-three other employees participating in the Supervisor Development Program. This program is divided into three phases: pre-class independent study, in-class modules and groupwork, and post-class application of skills and knowledge in the workplace. I spent my first month of work as a learner. I know that there is a learning curve with each new job as you come to understand the expectations and tasks, however, this was actual course work that I was completing. I would drive to the office, log onto the computer, and take online courses or read the required articles. It was a great way to acquire knowledge about policies and to situate myself within an organization which I used to only view from the outside. I was taking the information I had from a spousal perspective and building on it as an employee. It was an eye-opening experience.

Part of the curriculum was to complete the Personal DISCernment Inventory (DISC).[1] The DISC inventory is a behavioural assessment tool that helps individuals gain insight into their preferred communication and behavioural style. It is based on the DISC model, which categorizes a person's tendencies into four primary behaviour styles: Dominance

1 "The Personal DISCernment Inventory," Triaxia Partners, accessed 16 September, 2023, https://triaxiapartners.com/store/the-personal-discernment-inventory/.

(D), Influence (I), Steadiness (S), and Conscientiousness (C). The premise of the DISC inventory is that everyone possesses a unique blend of these four behaviour styles, which influence how they interact with others, approach tasks, and make decisions. By understanding their own behaviour style, individuals can enhance their self-awareness, improve communication skills, and adapt their behaviour to different situations. It helped me recognize characteristics of people whose style differed from my own. After the insights from "How to Talk to a Widower," this was another "aha moment" that helped me better understand myself and those around me.

My DISC results revealed a pattern of cautiousness and a strong desire to prove myself to others. As a relatively new member of the team, both for the project and within the organization, I couldn't shake the feeling that my colleagues might view me as inexperienced or inadequate for the role. I feared I was being viewed as a "pity-hire." This revelation intensified my preoccupation with showcasing my qualifications. I had a perception that others were watching my every move, waiting for any sign of weakness that could confirm their doubts about my suitability for the project. Not only did I yearn to demonstrate my expertise and capability as a project leader, but I also wanted to prove that my personal circumstances as an RCMP widow did not diminish my ability to excel in my profession.

As my role in the project expanded, my cautiousness grew more pronounced. While I had always been meticulous in my work, this new sense of pressure pushed me to double and triple-check every decision I made. The fear of making a mistake haunted me, driving me to spend extra hours conducting research, validating assumptions, and ensuring every detail was in order.

One specific event stands out in my memory. I was tasked with presenting our project's critical findings to a stakeholder group. Though I had done similar presentations in the past, this time, the burden of proving myself felt heavier than ever. I rehearsed my pitch countless times, refining every detail to ensure I covered all the bases. When the day of the presentation arrived, I took a deep breath before stepping into the boardroom. The weight of my self-imposed burden, combined with the knowledge that my late spouse's legacy could be tied to my performance, felt almost overwhelming. As I started speaking, I sensed a subtle shift in my mindset. I realized that the true test was not about proving myself to others or carrying the weight of my personal circumstances, but about delivering results that would benefit the project and the organization as a whole.

Gradually, with each milestone achieved and each positive outcome, my confidence began to grow. I started to let go of the constant need to prove myself, understanding that my value was reflected in the project's success and the contribution I made to the team. Over time, my colleagues began to notice the transformation. They saw a professional who was confident, resourceful, and dedicated.

I had the great fortune to complete the DISC assessment multiple times over the course of my career, including when I received my certification to be a master trainer. With these data points and my understanding of the model, I now had language to support how I was progressing through my healing journey. I also found myself with a greater appreciation for the behaviours of others. Previously I would take things personally. I would create a story in my mind. Often, it would be very elaborate. The themes almost always focused on:

They don't understand.

How could they think that is ok?

What were they thinking?

Why aren't they listening?

This dialogue was not helpful. It kept me in a perpetual loop of negativity. The insights from DISC helped break that cycle. I understood that we all have different preferences and motivations. What was comfortable and second nature for me, was not for others. People were not purposely trying to irritate me. They are being true to themselves. I realized that I needed to adapt and grow up. I acknowledged that I was being a selfish thirty-year-old. Yes, while what happened to me was tragic and unexpected, other people were also carrying hardships. I wanted to be more sensitive and attune to that.

With this newfound clarity, my perspective on the world continued its gradual evolution. Forming friendships at work became a noteworthy accomplishment. In Heidi, LeeAnne, and Chantal, I found my chosen people. Each of these women was distinct, yet together we formed a cohesive gang. They played a pivotal role in coaxing me out of my shell. Despite their diverse backgrounds, we harmoniously coexisted and supported one another. Chantal, being a mother with young children, became a valued source of parenting guidance, and our weekends often included playdates for the kids. Navigating city life was made easier with Heidi, an Ottawa native with strong family ties. Her partner Glen also played a role as a technical and practical support when I needed assistance. LeeAnne, characterized by her intuition and spirituality, engaged me in discussions about serendipity and life's contracts. Her beliefs about our purpose and our alignment with our life's journey broadened my perspective. Interacting with her felt different from a year prior when hearing similar viewpoints would prompt an internal eye-roll from me. Back then, I wasn't quite ready for such insights. Meeting LeeAnne when I did felt like a serendipitous occurrence, and she has remained a grounding influence in my life ever since.

Participating in the workforce and embracing a job also had a transformative effect on my identity as a mother. It introduced a dimension of contentment and purpose that extended beyond the boundaries of my role as a parent. While nurturing and raising a child is undeniably profound, I discovered that cultivating an identity outside of this sphere was an essential facet of my healing journey.

The process of grieving and recovering from the loss of my husband was intricate and multifaceted. Initially, the weight of grief seemed to overshadow everything else, making it challenging to see beyond the immediate sorrow. However, as time progressed and I ventured into the realm of employment, I started to regain a sense of agency and self-worth that went beyond my responsibilities as a mother.

Being a mother is an incredible privilege, but it's just one aspect of who I am. Having a job allowed me to exercise my skills, talents, and expertise in a different context. It allowed me to channel my energy into pursuits that were unrelated to parenting, thus creating a more holistic sense of fulfillment. This was a powerful counterbalance to the grief that had once dominated my emotions.

Equally significant was the social aspect of returning to work. Engaging with colleagues, collaborating on projects, and contributing to a team provided me with a renewed sense of belonging. These interactions fostered connections that extended beyond the realm of parenthood, giving me the opportunity to connect with others on a professional level. This social engagement was a lifeline that offered support, camaraderie, and a sense of normalcy in the midst of profound change.

In many ways, my job became a conduit for growth, healing, and redefining my identity. As I navigated the complexities of my role, I realized that I was not solely defined by my grief. I was a multi-faceted individual with talents, interests, and aspirations that deserved recognition and fulfillment. This realization, in turn, positively impacted my role as a mother. The newfound sense of self-assuredness and accomplishment spilled over into my parenting, allowing me to be a more patient, engaged, and emotionally present mother to Alexis.

Ultimately, embracing work as a vital part of my life journey played a pivotal role in my ability to move forward. It allowed me to integrate my experiences of loss and healing into a process of resilience and growth. While my identity as a mother remains fundamental, being a capable, empowered individual with diverse interests and skills also adds depth and richness to my narrative.

14

LOVE OFTEN HAS a way of finding us when we least expect it.

I wasn't actively seeking out love when Chris and Ed crossed paths with me during football training camp in the late summer of 2000. Love's presence surprised me, catching me off guard, and I willingly opened my heart to its embrace. It wasn't a calculated decision, a deliberate search, or a conscious effort on my part. Love simply found its way into my life, and I allowed it to take root within me.

Following Chris' passing, I didn't experience a specific moment where I felt compelled to re-enter the world of dating. It wasn't a matter of checking off a box on a timeline. My focus wasn't on seeking out a romantic connection; rather, it was on navigating the complex emotions of grief and rebuilding my life. Dating wasn't a priority for me at that point.

During those initial stages of healing, I realized that I wasn't yet ready to venture into a new romantic relationship. There were times when I would interact with men and find myself unintentionally making comparisons. Thoughts like, *he's not as tall as Chris* or *Chris had the most amazing eyes* would cross my mind. This internal assessment highlighted that I was still holding onto the memory of Chris in a way that prevented me from fully engaging with someone new. I recognized that as long as I continued to measure others against Chris' qualities, I wasn't emotionally available for a meaningful relationship.

It was crucial for me to acknowledge this truth and give myself the space to heal without the pressure of seeking companionship. Over time, as I journeyed through my grief and embarked on the process of self-discovery, those comparisons started to fade. My heart began to open up to the possibility of forming a genuine connection based on the unique qualities of the individual rather than a comparison to what I had lost.

Music has a unique and profound way of speaking to our emotions and aiding in the process of healing. In my personal journey of healing, music played an integral role, and among the various songs that accompanied me, Leona Lewis' "Better in Time" held a special place. Its lyrics acted as a guide, helping me navigate the challenging terrain of letting go and embracing a new chapter in my life.

The verses of the song struck a chord with me, echoing the stages of healing much like a physical wound. Just as a wound initially numbs the pain to shield us from its impact, I realized that my initial grief was buffered by a sense of shock and emotional protection. But as time progressed, much like a healing wound, the rawness of my emotions began to surface, causing a range of feelings from swelling sorrow to the tightness of longing.

The lines *Since there's no more you and me, It's time I let you go so I can be free* resonated deeply with the process of releasing my past and embracing the idea of personal freedom. Just like the process of a wound healing, it required removing the stitches and letting go of the protective scab, resulting in a scar that eventually fades with time.

The song's chorus, *And even though I really love you, I'm gonna smile 'cause I deserve to, It'll all get better in time*, became an anthem of hope and renewal for me. Through this chorus, I found the strength to smile despite the pain and acknowledge that I deserved happiness and growth. It became a way to reaffirm that the healing process, while challenging, would eventually lead to a better place.

Singing along to this song, shedding tears, and sharing it with loved ones became my way of expressing the profound transformation taking place within me. It allowed me to declare that I was ready to close one chapter and embrace a new beginning. Just as the scar fades over time, this song became a beacon of light, guiding me towards the realization that healing is not only possible but can lead to a life filled with newfound strength and joy.

"Better in Time" served as a musical companion on my healing journey, echoing the stages of healing and growth that mirrored the physical healing of a wound. It was a reminder that even in the most challenging moments, there is a path towards renewal and transformation, and that embracing this choice enhances our resilience and capacity to heal.

Conversations with my parents about the concept of wasted energy left a lasting impact on my perspective. The idea of investing time and emotional energy into a relationship that couldn't be reciprocated resonated with me. The love I felt for someone who was no longer physically present had become a source of exhaustion rather than fulfillment. It was a sentiment that I needed to acknowledge and internalize. Loving Chris as much as I did was an integral part of my life, but I began to understand that it was essential to recalibrate the focus of that love. It was time to channel that love into ways that supported my own well-being and growth.

Moving forward in my personal life didn't equate to erasing the love and memories I held for Chris. The love we shared, the memories we created, and the family we built remained intact within me. It was about acknowledging the past while opening up space for the future. The decision to explore new relationships wasn't a betrayal of our history; rather, it was a testament to the depth of the love that existed.

Through the lens of Leona Lewis' "Better in Time," I found the permission I needed to let go of the one-sided relationship that was holding me back. The song's message resonated deeply—recognizing that healing doesn't mean forgetting, that moving forward doesn't mean letting go of cherished memories. Instead, it signified embracing personal growth, acknowledging my own needs, and allowing new connections to flourish. It served as a reminder that love can take on different forms throughout life, and that growth and happiness are attainable even after experiencing profound loss. Through its lyrics, I found the courage to let go of what was no longer serving me, and to embrace the possibilities that lay ahead while still holding a cherished place for the past.

Shortly after Alexis' second birthday, Brent paid us a visit in Ottawa. His role as a Staff Relations Representative for the RCMP often brought him from Edmonton to Ottawa for meetings with senior leaders. Our interaction began through email when I reached out to him regarding an issue I was having with an insurance provider. He was actively working on resolving the matter and needed me to sign a form. Kindly, he offered to swing by our home after his meeting concluded.

As Brent arrived, his thoughtful gesture of bringing a small gift for Alexis highlighted the warmth and genuine care he held for our family. Alexis' eyes sparkled with excitement as she unwrapped the tissue paper and pulled out a magnetic wooden fishing puzzle game. Each puzzle piece was designed with a silver metal circle at its centre, and a fishing rod equipped with a magnet offered a delightful challenge of picking up the pieces and placing them into the puzzle. Adding to the joy, there was a charming turtle that, when its shell was pressed, played the enchanting melodies of Beethoven. Both toys captured Alexis' attention and brought smiles to our faces as we sat on the floor together, engrossed in play.

During our time together, the conversation flowed effortlessly. We discussed my experiences transitioning into work at the RCMP, the connections I was building with new friends, Alexis' adaptation to daycare, and my overall impressions of life in Ottawa. Brent also shared a significant piece of his own life—his recent separation from his wife. He opened up about the challenges he faced in making the difficult decision to leave, despite his concerns for his two children. Drawing from his own experiences of growing up in a broken home, he was resolute in his determination to create a healthier environment for his own children. Our discussions revealed that we were both navigating periods of deep introspection and profound change.

As the evening approached, the aroma of homemade lasagna filled the air, and I extended an invitation for Brent to join us for dinner. It seemed like a simple gesture, a way to share a comforting meal and continue our engaging conversation. Knowing that he was staying at a hotel, I thought a home-cooked meal might offer a welcome change from the routine of restaurant dining.

As we sat down to enjoy the meal together, the atmosphere was relaxed, and the conversation flowed effortlessly. It was a refreshing departure from our previous interactions, which had been centred around formal matters. This was the first time we engaged in a dialogue that revealed more about our personal lives and thoughts, allowing me to glimpse the person behind the title. In those moments, he wasn't just Sergeant Baulkham; he was simply Brent—a man who was navigating his own challenges and transitions.

Throughout our conversation, it became increasingly clear that Brent was not only compassionate and empathetic, but also a genuine and authentic individual. I reflected on how he had been a steady presence during the difficult times, offering a safe space for vulnerability and understanding. This evening, I was witnessing the evolution of our relationship from an initial professional contact to something more profound—a true friendship built on shared experiences and mutual concern.

The sense of familiarity and connection I felt with Brent was both comforting and intimidating. It brought back memories of the early days with Chris, when a connection had sparked and blossomed into love. Yet, this time, it was different. Questions swirled in my mind: *Was this appropriate? Was I ready for this? What would others think?*

In the midst of this internal debate, a resolute inner voice emerged, silencing the doubts and uncertainties. It reminded me that life is meant to be lived and explored, that taking a chance on connection is an essential part of healing and growth.

In that moment, I made a decision guided by intuition and courage. I chose to embrace the opportunity to get to know Brent on a deeper level, to nurture the budding friendship that was forming between us. It was a step into the unknown, a willingness to open my heart to the possibility of new beginnings. And as we shared that dinner together, I realized that the journey of healing and moving forward often requires us to be bold, to follow our instincts, and to welcome the unexpected connections that come our way.

In the days following our initial dinner, Brent's presence lingered in my thoughts. His visit to Ottawa was drawing to a close, but I was eager to continue our conversations and explore this new connection further. With a surge of courage, I reached out and suggested meeting for a coffee during one of his breaks. We settled on a Starbucks nestled within a Chapters bookstore, providing a cozy and relaxed setting.

As I sat across from Brent, sipping on my latte, I found myself captivated by the smallest details of his being. His expressions as he spoke, the shifting hues of his eyes reflecting the changing topics, the rhythmic tapping of his foot in sync with his head nods—each nuance held my attention. It was as if I was seeing him for the first time, noticing the subtleties that make a person unique and fascinating.

Our conversation flowed effortlessly, much like our previous interactions. We delved into various subjects, sharing anecdotes and insights that revealed more about our lives, thoughts, and aspirations. With every exchange, I felt a growing sense of connection and intrigue. It was during this coffee date that we made plans to meet again, this time on the evening before his departure back to Edmonton.

In anticipation of our next encounter, I made arrangements for Alexis to stay with the Wordens overnight. While I didn't provide elaborate details about my plans, I simply mentioned going out with friends. The prospect of spending more time with Brent felt simultaneously exhilarating and nerve-wracking. I realized that it had been years since I had experienced anything resembling a first date, and yet, this situation was unique. We had known each other for over a year and a half, and he had witnessed my journey through grief—from the lowest moments to the gradual healing.

As the evening approached, I stood before my wardrobe, considering my outfit with newfound attention. It had been eight years since I had been in this position, contemplating what to wear to make a good impression. The question of whether this was truly a "first date" hung in the air. We had an existing connection, shaped by shared experiences and a genuine history. Still, I couldn't deny the desire to present myself in a way that exuded confidence and attractiveness.

After thoughtful consideration, I settled on a fitted shirt paired with jeans. I straightened my hair and applied a touch of makeup, not to mask who I was, but to enhance my features and exude self-assuredness. As I stood before the mirror, I acknowledged the significance of this moment. It was an opportunity to show Brent a different facet of my identity—not just a widow he had helped in his professional capacity, but a woman who was embracing life, exploring connections, and stepping into the realm of new beginnings.

Our plans were set—an evening of casual fun, shared stories, and hopefully some laughter. We had agreed that discretion was key, wanting to enjoy each other's company without the eyes of familiar faces upon us. With this in mind, we chose MacArthur Bowling Lanes as our destination. It was a place where we could blend in, away from prying eyes.

As the designated time approached, I eagerly awaited Brent's arrival at the front door. When he arrived, I couldn't help but notice his appearance—a navy-blue v-neck sweater paired with jeans, a combination that exuded casual charm. The scent of his cologne lingered in the air, its alluring fragrance heightening my anticipation. With a slight spring in my step, I joined him as we headed to his car.

Arriving at the bowling alley, we checked in and exchanged our regular shoes for bowling shoes. Brent's eyes scanned the room, assessing the surroundings and perhaps ensuring our privacy. Our assigned lane was tucked away at the far right, offering us the seclusion we had hoped for. As we selected bowling balls that fit our hands, I couldn't help but notice the subtle touch of our hands brushing against each other—a fleeting yet charged moment of contact.

With our chosen pseudonyms entered into the computer scoring system, we began our game. I had grown up in a small town where bowling was a popular pastime, and my parents had been part of a bowling league during my childhood. So, while I wasn't a pro, I was comfortable with the game's basics. Brent, on the other hand, confessed to having less experience. As we started playing, it became clear who had the upper hand in terms of skill and familiarity. Our shared laughter and the occasional "accidental" physical contact—hands brushing against each other or playful nudges—added an element of flirtation to the evening.

We played two rounds, the sound of clattering pins and our cheerful banter filling the air. As the games concluded, we swapped our bowling shoes for our street shoes and made our way back to my place. The ride back was filled with easy conversation, the comfortable flow of words reaffirming the connection that was growing between us.

A sense of anticipation hung in the air. With a gentle smile, Brent walked me to my front door. Standing on the step, I became acutely aware of our proximity—our heights nearly aligned. Standing face to face, our eyes met in a silent exchange that spoke volumes. It was as if time momentarily stood still, our surroundings fading into the background.

With unspoken understanding, we leaned in, our lips meeting in a tender kiss. The sensation was electrifying, sending bright flashes of light behind my closed eyelids. The warmth of his lips against mine was accompanied by a rush of feelings that seemed to transcend the moment. As we parted briefly, our foreheads gently touched, a shared breath of anticipation passing between us.

Emboldened by our connection, we leaned in once more, our lips meeting with a newfound confidence. My hand found its way to the back of his head, fingers intertwining with his hair before tracing down his neck and resting gently between his shoulder blades. Drawing him closer, I could feel the reassuring strength of his embrace. It was a beautiful collision of vulnerability and desire, a silent acknowledgment of the budding emotions that had been quietly growing between us.

Before parting ways, he promised to call me in the morning before his flight, a gesture that added a touch of sweetness to the moment. He walked back to his car, the sound of his departure echoing in the quiet of the night. As I closed the door behind him, I found myself mirroring scenes from romantic movies. Leaning my head back against the door, I let out a sigh of contentment, my heart racing and my cheeks flushed.

It was a perfect first kiss. As I closed my eyes and let the memory of that kiss linger, I couldn't help but feel a bit weak in the knees—not from physical weakness, but from the overwhelming rush of emotion that comes with a moment of connection, vulnerability, and the promise of something beautiful unfolding.

15

•••••

BRENT AND I effortlessly bridged the two-hour time difference, using technology to keep our connection alive. Our days consisted of multiple phone conversations, each call bringing us closer and revealing new layers of our personalities, allowing us to share our thoughts, feelings, and stories across the miles.

In those hours of conversation, I felt like I was opening up the pages of a book about myself, while Brent was already well-acquainted with the words written inside. There was a certain vulnerability in this, a willingness to expose my thoughts and experiences to someone who was becoming an important presence in my life. I felt a sense of urgency to catch up, to understand him as deeply as he already seemed to understand me.

Questions flowed freely from my lips, each one an attempt to bridge the gap between our pasts, our experiences, and our dreams for the future. It was as if I was on a quest to uncover the intricacies of his personality, to understand the nuances that had shaped his worldview. At times, I wondered if my barrage of inquiries was overwhelming, if I was diving too deep too quickly. But there was an undeniable curiosity within me, a thirst for knowledge about this person who had entered my life.

Through our conversations, I discovered that communication had not always been a cornerstone in Brent's life. Growing up, open dialogue was not a common practice in his household. And in his marriage, healthy communication had been elusive. It was an eye-opening revelation that helped me understand his perspective and appreciate his willingness to engage in such meaningful conversations with me.

Our connection was built on more than just words; it was a bridge that connected our pasts, our struggles, and our aspirations. With each conversation, we were forging a bond that transcended the physical distance between us. And in those late-night talks and early-morning exchanges, I found myself falling deeper into a connection that felt both genuine and profound.

We were both aware that our relationship would be questioned by several players in our lives, primarily Chris' parents and RCMP management. We'd talked at length during our coffee meeting at Starbucks about the barriers to us being in a personal relationship. Brent raised a number of concerns, to which I made counter points:

"I'm too old for you."

"I married a man my age and look what happened."

"I live in Alberta."

"I'm experienced with long-distance relationships. Being separated provides us the opportunity to honestly and openly communicate and really get to know each other."

"This is career suicide. The perception of a member of the support team dating a widow is not good."

"We will be honest. Disclose our relationship to your boss. Have them speak with me. When they hear how I respond, they'll understand that this is not a situation of a woman being taken advantage of. They'll hear a woman who is moving forward after a sad event in her past. A woman who now works for the RCMP. A woman who is thinking clearly and coherently and can make her own informed decisions."

"Chris' parents won't accept me."

"They will have a hard time accepting anyone. Leave that with me. You talk with your boss; I'll talk to John and Mary Ann."

I was so aligned during our conversation. I exuded a confidence I hadn't displayed in years. I felt so assured that these obstacles could and would be overcome. I knew we could survive together.

In the wake of Brent's visit to Ottawa, a series of pivotal conversations were set into motion, bringing our developing connection to the forefront of our lives. Brent, feeling a sense of responsibility and transparency, took the initiative to engage in a candid discussion with his superior—the Commanding Officer (CO) of his Division. This conversation would have far-reaching implications for both of us.

During this conversation, Brent conveyed the reality of his personal circumstances, explaining that he was in the process of a formal separation from his wife and that we had developed personal feelings for each other. In a display of his characteristic integrity, Brent even offered to step down from his role as a staff relations representative if it was deemed necessary due to our connection. This act demonstrated his commitment to maintaining professionalism and ensuring that there were no conflicts of interest.

In response, the CO listened attentively and acknowledged Brent's honesty and forthrightness. Recognizing that Brent and I were both adults capable of making our own decisions, the CO emphasized that our personal lives were our own to navigate. In essence, he extended his support for us to continue pursuing our connection and to determine for ourselves how we wished to proceed.

This stance was a testament to the CO's understanding of the complexity of human relationships and his recognition that, while our connection may have begun in the context of professional interactions, it had grown into something deeper and more personal. His decision not to accept Brent's offer to step down from his position indicated a willingness to respect our autonomy and choices. However, it became clear that not everyone shared the CO's perspective.

Some of Chris' former coworkers were not supportive. Our relationship generated gossip and judgement, which was especially disheartening because none of the people involved ever reached out to me to have an open conversation. These rumours created a challenging atmosphere and added a layer of complexity to an already sensitive situation. The anger and disappointment I felt were valid, yet I also recognized that I had a choice in how I directed my energy.

Ultimately, I made a deliberate choice not to engage with those who seemed unwilling to see my happiness and growth beyond the confines of their preconceived notions. I knew that investing my time and effort into proving my worthiness and explaining my choices would be draining and likely futile. Instead, I chose to channel my energy into my relationship with Brent and our shared journey forward. I understood that the perceptions others had of my happiness was not my responsibility; my focus needed to be on building a future, not dwelling on the past.

This decision to prioritize my relationship with Brent and to invest in our shared goals allowed me to maintain a sense of agency over my own narrative. It also reinforced the importance of surrounding myself with individuals who supported and respected my choices, as well as those who were willing to engage in open and honest dialogue. The experience highlighted the power of taking control over where I directed my energy, choosing growth, positivity, and love over the negativity of gossip and judgment.

Conveying the news of my budding romantic relationship with Brent to Chris' parents was undoubtedly one of the most challenging conversations I have faced. It's a conversation that involved a delicate balance of empathy, honesty, and understanding, while navigating their emotions and fears. I had prepared for this moment meticulously, rehearsing my words and anticipating their potential questions and reactions. Yet, even with all the preparation, the actual conversation was emotionally charged and filled with unexpected twists.

Choosing the setting of John and MaryAnn's living room, a place filled with memories of our shared family moments, felt symbolic and grounding. I began the conversation with the words I had carefully crafted, aiming to approach the topic with sensitivity and respect for their feelings. The initial response was as I had anticipated—dismissal and fear tinged with anger and disbelief. Their faces reflected a mixture of emotions—skepticism, hurt, and perhaps a touch of denial. It was as if my attempt to move forward had ignited a storm of emotions that they had long held beneath the surface.

MaryAnn's skepticism hit me like a wall, and John's fears seemed to echo in the room like a distant thunderstorm growing ever closer. The weight of their concerns pressed upon me, and I struggled to maintain my composure. The living room, once a sanctuary of shared memories, now felt like a battlefield of emotions colliding.

As their concerns were voiced, my rehearsed responses seemed inadequate in the face of their raw emotions. The room grew louder, filled with raised voices and overlapping words. Despite my best intentions, my carefully chosen words faltered, and I found myself caught in the whirlwind of emotions that surrounded me. In that moment, I realized the impossibility of fully preparing for a conversation so deeply entwined with grief, loss, and personal growth. The emotions in the room, fueled by years of pain and longing, had taken on a life of their own. I felt a knot forming in my throat as the weight of the conversation bore down on me.

Feeling both emotionally overwhelmed and outnumbered by their collective response, I knew that stepping away was the only way to regain my own equilibrium. With a heavy heart, I rose from the sofa, a mix of frustration and sadness swirling within me. As I walked out the front door, I held onto the hope that time and reflection might pave the way for a more open and understanding conversation in the future.

As I drove away from their house, the weight of the conversation lingered in the air around me. My hands gripped the steering wheel tightly, the tremors a reflection of processing the emotions that had just transpired. Adrenaline pulsed through my veins, leaving my heart racing and my thoughts in disarray. The living room confrontation had left me shaken and vulnerable.

My trembling hands reached for my phone, and I dialled Brent's number with a mixture of relief and uncertainty. As his voice came through the line, I felt emotions bubbling to the surface. My voice wavered as I recounted the conversation to Brent, the experience still fresh and raw. He listened patiently, providing a steady presence. The release of sharing the news, long kept beneath the surface, was cathartic in a way, but it also carried a sense of apprehension. I could almost see the uncertain path ahead, paved with potential awkwardness and challenging conversations that loomed on the horizon.

In the days that followed, I continued to process the conversation, each moment dissected and analyzed in my mind. It was an emotional rollercoaster, but amid the turmoil, there was also a glimmer of gratitude. Gratitude for the courage to open up the conversation, for taking a step towards authenticity and vulnerability. It was a messy, raw, and imperfect step, but it was a step forward nonetheless.

Brent and I had been quietly building a connection, nurturing something that felt special and real. Now, with the conversations behind us, we were standing at the threshold of something new. We were committed to moving forward together. As I looked ahead, I knew that navigating this new chapter wouldn't be easy, but we were facing it head-on, hand in hand, ready to embrace whatever challenges and joys lay ahead.

16

IT WAS BOTH exhilarating and nerve-wracking as Alexis and I stepped off the plane in Edmonton. The anticipation of reuniting with Brent, coupled with the knowledge that I was about to meet his sixteen-year-old son Keegan, added a layer of excitement to our day. Meeting Keegan was a significant step, one that carried its own set of emotions and uncertainties. As we settled into a cozy booth at Boston Pizza, I observed Alexis sitting in her booster seat, happily engrossed in playing with her favourite Toy Story figurines. At that moment, her adorable innocence eased my nerves, and I found myself smiling with delight.

Then came the moment to meet Keegan. He arrived in a flurry, and I couldn't help but feel a mixture of excitement and apprehension. Keegan proved to be warm and welcoming, effortlessly engaging with Alexis, asking her about her favourite characters and games. His easy going nature put me at ease, and I soon realized that this was going to be an enjoyable meeting. We engaged in light conversation, discussing school, hobbies, and common interests. It was evident that Keegan had a strong bond with his father, and their interactions revealed a close and supportive relationship.

Throughout the meal, I observed the dynamic between father and son. It was heartwarming to witness their easy rapport, the way they shared jokes and stories, and the mutual respect they showed each other. It was clear that Brent had worked hard to create a supportive and nurturing environment for his son, even in the midst of personal challenges. As the lunch progressed, my nerves began to subside, replaced by a sense of comfort and connection. Keegan's presence felt like a natural extension of Brent's life, and I appreciated the opportunity to get to know him better. It was a reminder that our lives were intricately woven with our roles as parents, and the merging of our families was a significant step.

With lunch behind us, Brent suggested we go golfing, and the afternoon continued.

On our way Keegan, eager to test out his car's recent repairs, led the way, kicking up a cloud of dust on the gravel backroads. Suddenly, the red and blue lights of a police car came into view, and my heart skipped a beat. As we pulled into the golf club's parking lot, the police officer approached Keegan. Brent calmly parked the car, instructing us to wait inside. We watched in silence as Brent skillfully navigated the situation, engaging in a conversation with the officer. Though I couldn't hear their words, it was evident that Brent's charm, experience, and wit were at play. After a few minutes, the officer returned to his cruiser, and with a nod of his head, he drove off. A sigh of relief washed over us as Brent rejoined us, a hint of victory in his eyes.

With the speeding ticket escapade behind us, we continued our golfing adventure. Bent Stick Golf Club was a rustic course that had recently changed ownership and entered a rebuilding phase. The course might not have been in its prime condition, but that didn't deter Brent and Keegan from enjoying their game, their laughter echoing amidst the dry and crunchy grass. As Alexis and I followed along in the golf cart, I couldn't help but feel a sense of contentment. There was something special about watching a father and son bond over their shared love for the sport. For Alexis, driving around in the golf cart was a dream come true, and with the help of Keegan, she even tried her hand at putting. She held his hand and walked alongside him on the ninth hole, the image imprinted on my heart forever.

In the evening, we reached Hay Lakes, in rural Alberta where Brent was renting a small bungalow. The house belonged to the mother of one of his colleagues, and stepping inside felt like taking a time machine back to the '70s. The gold and brown colour scheme, and vintage appliances and furniture, gave the place a nostalgic charm. As the night grew darker, exhaustion from the day's adventures set in, and we were all eager to rest our heads. Alexis, always the trooper, dozed off effortlessly in her own cozy bedroom. Yet, for Brent and me, the supposed comfort of the primary bedroom turned into a rather hilarious predicament.

The bed, which was meant to provide a good night's sleep, turned out to be less of a refuge and more of an amusement park ride. Unbeknownst to us when we first laid down, the mattress seemed to have a mind of its own, sloping down in the centre and creating a rather uncomfortable ridge. As we lay side by side, trying to find a comfortable position, we couldn't help but burst into laughter at the absurdity of the situation.

In the darkness of the room, we tried shifting and adjusting, but it felt as if we were sleeping on different elevations, somehow trapped in an optical illusion. The irony was not lost on us, as we had just spent the day careening through rough golf course terrain in a golf cart, only to find that our sleeping arrangements were the ones providing the real adventure.

But amid the laughter, we found joy in each other's company, eventually finding some semblance of comfort amidst the mattress's quirks. As we lay side by side, sharing stories and tender moments, the uncomfortable bed became an unexpected source of amusement, leaving us with yet another unforgettable memory to cherish.

The following day, we continued our journey westward, and as a kid from Ontario, I couldn't help but marvel at the majestic Rocky Mountains that rose before us. The beauty of the landscapes was awe-inspiring, and as we stopped in Banff for a picturesque picnic, I felt a great sense of gratitude. As we ventured on, we reached Revelstoke, exhausted but filled with joy of being together. A simple walk around downtown and a quick pizza dinner capped off the day, and we all turned in early.

Arriving in Vernon the next day, we were embraced by the tranquil lakeside community where Glenna and Gord, or "G&G," resided. There was an undeniable charm to the neighbourhood, with the sparkling lake beckoning to visitors and locals alike. G&G's house, a cozy and inviting haven, reflected their warmth and love for life. They welcomed us with open arms, revealing their kind and loving nature. Glenna's angelic voice, accompanied by her guitar and piano playing, charmed Alexis and left us all captivated. Her voice seemed to bring an extra sparkle to Alexis's eyes, as if they had formed a special connection through the universal language of music. Gord was a drummer, and as he shared stories of travelling with bands and performing gigs, I saw a glimpse of the adventurous spirit that had clearly been passed down to Brent.

As they shared anecdotes about Brent's upbringing and past, I gained a deeper understanding of the man I was falling for. Brent's early years were marked by confusion and a longing for the mother he barely knew. His mother lived with undiagnosed bipolar disorder, making her unable to provide the stable love and care a child needs. As a result, Brent and his brother only saw their mom for two weeks a year, leaving them to wonder why she'd left and why she couldn't love them.

Glenna came into Brent's world when he was five, bringing with her the stability and nurturing he so desperately needed. She took on the role of the loving and caring female figure in his life, filling the void left by his mother's absence. It was evident that G&G had played a crucial role in shaping Brent into the kind and compassionate person he was today. I couldn't help but admire the strength and resilience he had shown throughout his life.

When Brent was thirteen, Gord had an opportunity to purchase and manage an Imperial Oil bulk fuel franchise in Creston, which required the family to move an hour and a half from Castlegar. This was a pivotal moment in Brent's life. Being uprooted from his comfort zone, feeling like a stranger in a new town, and coping with emotions that were rarely acknowledged. Brent spoke about the challenges of adapting to life in Creston as an angry teenager, struggling in school, isolating himself from others, and growing more stubborn by the day. Feeling unsettled and displaced, he spent many of his high school summers working in fruit orchards and on construction sites while living with his aunt in Kelowna. These experiences, though challenging, helped shape his character and instilled in him a strong work ethic and resourcefulness. As he shared these intimate details of his past, I realized how those early years had deeply influenced the person he had become.

Brent's journey of self-discovery was not without its challenges. He vividly recounted one winter night when, after seeing the movie "Kramer vs. Kramer" with a friend shortly after his sixteenth birthday, he experienced an emotional tidal wave that overwhelmed him. The emotional turmoil depicted in the movie resonated deeply with Brent, stirring emotions that had long been suppressed in a household that rarely discussed feelings. The film's narrative of a mother leaving her husband and son struck a nerve, and he couldn't bear to watch the ending. Without saying a word to his friend, he bolted out of the theatre and started running for miles in denim jeans, tears streaming down his face. The night ended with Brent returning home, emotionally drained. His father was sitting in the living room, a smoke in one hand and a drink in the other. They looked at each other and didn't say a word.

In the Baulkham household, discussing feelings was not encouraged, and time was not made for heartfelt conversations. Brent learned early on to avoid emotion, to push it down, and not address it. But that night, his emotions broke free, and he could no longer contain them. His body took over and to release pent up trauma, he ran. This would not be the last time his body would make difficult choices for him in the absence of his mind being able to do so.

As I listened to Brent share these deeply personal experiences, my heart swelled with compassion and admiration for the man he had become despite the hardships he endured. Our time with G&G was a revelation, not just about Brent's past but about the love and understanding that could be found within a family, even in the face of challenges.

Looking back, that trip to Vernon held great significance for both of us. We were opening our hearts to each other, allowing ourselves to be vulnerable, and sharing our hopes and dreams. Beyond the romance, the trip was an opportunity for self-discovery. We were learning more about ourselves individually and as a couple. We were discovering how our past experiences had shaped us, and how we were evolving together. It was a chance to redefine our identities, aspirations, and priorities in the context of this budding relationship.

Resilience was also a key theme. Our experiences leading up to that point had tested our strength and courage. We had both faced challenges, loss, and heartache, yet here we were, forging ahead with a determination to find happiness and love once again. The adventures enroute and in Vernon highlighted our ability to overcome adversity and find joy in new beginnings.

As we returned from Vernon, the memories we had created lingered in our minds and hearts. The trip marked a turning point, solidifying the bond we shared and inspiring us to embrace the journey ahead with enthusiasm. We knew that challenges and uncertainties would arise, but we were committed to facing them together, drawing strength from the love and connection we had nurtured.

This was especially true as the trial was approaching.

17

SEPTEMBER BROUGHT A new and exciting chapter for Alexis as she embarked on her journey into Montessori school. Anticipation and eagerness radiated from her as she eagerly embraced the idea of learning and making new friends. Her innate sociability and love for structured environments made this transition a natural and joyful one.

The school's location conveniently fit into our daily routine, situated on my way to work. Mornings began with a delightful routine of dropping Alexis off at school. As we arrived, the schoolyard buzzed with the energy of children ready to explore, learn, and play. With a quick kiss and a warm goodbye, Alexis was off to join her peers, ready to dive into a world of discovery.

The afternoons were equally heartwarming. As I arrived to pick her up, I could hardly contain my excitement to see her. And then, it would happen—the moment that never failed to warm my heart. Alexis would spot me, her face would light up with a radiant smile, and she would start running towards me with open arms, eager to embrace the end of the day together.

In that precious moment, her joyful squeal of "mamma" became the soundtrack of my heart. It was a reminder of the immense love and connection we shared, a bond that grew stronger with each passing day.

As we walked hand in hand, Alexis would eagerly share stories of her day—the friends she played with, the things she learned, and the adventures she had. It was during these moments that I felt an overwhelming sense of gratitude and contentment. Alexis, with her boundless enthusiasm and unwavering affection, became my beacon of hope and happiness. She was my constant reminder that even amidst life's challenges and uncertainties, love and joy were always within reach. I would need to draw on this a great deal in the upcoming months.

As we were settling into the new routine, we needed to shift gears again, as the Fall of 2009 brought with it the trial of the accused. In Canada, the trial typically occurs in the courthouse nearest to the place where the crime was committed. There are exceptions granted when it is feared that a jury may not be able to remain impartial. This was the case in the first-degree murder charge of the accused who killed Chris. The trial venue was changed from Hay River to Yellowknife, the capital city of the Northwest Territories. The trial was scheduled to take place over seven weeks in October-November.

Attending the trial was a conscious decision I made, one driven by a mixture of determination, a thirst for justice, and a need for closure. It was a way for me to face the painful details of Chris' passing head-on, to bear witness to the legal process, and to ensure that my voice and the impact of his actions were heard loud and clear.

As the trial date approached, I found myself navigating a delicate balance between my new life in Ottawa and the impending proceedings that would bring the events of the past back to the forefront of my consciousness. The various aspects of my life—work, parenting, dating, and the upcoming trial—were intertwined in a complex web of emotions and priorities.

In the past year, I had managed to create a semblance of normalcy in my new surroundings. The move to Ottawa, the new job, forming new friendships, and entering into a relationship with Brent had offered me a chance to focus on the present and distance myself from the traumatic events that had occurred in Hay River. It was a coping mechanism, a way to compartmentalize my emotions and create a sense of stability.

As the trial date neared, the compartmentalization became more challenging. Meetings with lawyers and the investigation team brought the impending trial back into sharp focus. They laid out their plans, discussed witnesses, and prepared me for what was to come. I had to confront the reality that I would need to revisit the painful details of Chris' shooting, something I had largely managed to avoid in my day-to-day life.

Recognizing the emotional toll that a seven-week trial could take, I made a strategic decision to only be present in the courtroom for specific witness testimonies—those scheduled during the initial and final two weeks of the trial. This allowed me to fulfill my desire for closure and justice while also taking care of my emotional well-being. Additionally, I had arranged a work-related event in Edmonton to provide a productive distraction during the middle portion of the trial.

Heading back up north, returning to a place that held painful memories, was undoubtedly a challenging experience. It was a step into the past, a confrontation with the reality of the trial, and a reminder of the emotional journey that lay ahead. Yet, it was also a necessary part of seeking justice and closure, and I was determined to face it head-on, just as I had done throughout my entire healing journey.

Returning to Yellowknife for the trial was an emotional rollercoaster, a mix of heartache, strength, and unexpected moments of solace. As Alexis and I touched down in the familiar city, a rush of memories flooded my mind—memories of Chris, of our time here together, and of the life we had built. It was as if the streets and buildings held echoes of our laughter, our dreams, and our love.

Former co-workers of Chris' and friends of ours, Paul and Rachel Mounsey were a lifeline. Their open hearts and welcoming home enveloped us in a cocoon of comfort, reminding me of the kindness that still existed in the world. Rachel's mother stepped in to care for Alexis, a gesture of support that resonated deeply. It was a reminder that we were not alone and that others were invested in our well-being as we braced ourselves for the trial.

The Worden family were staying in a local hotel, and together, we navigated this difficult phase of seeking justice for Chris.

Walking through the familiar streets of Yellowknife was a mix of heartache and comfort. The city that had once been a backdrop for our shared dreams now held a different significance—the place where the trial would unfold, where painful testimonies would be heard, where wounds would be reopened. Yet, amidst the tension and apprehension, there was also a glimmer of connection. People who had known Chris, who had shared moments with him, approached me with stories that painted him as the vibrant, caring person he had been. Their words were like precious gems, offering a glimpse of the Chris I knew and loved, a reminder that his spirit endured.

As I stepped into the courthouse, the air was heavy. The echoes of my footsteps seemed to reverberate through the halls, a reminder of the weight of the trial that awaited us. The security procedures were evidence of the gravity of the situation—metal detectors, bag checks, a tangible reminder that we were about to delve into a world where justice and pain intersected.

The accused, a stranger to the community he had invaded, stood at the centre of the courtroom. His presence was in contrast to the unity and solidarity that radiated from those who had gathered to witness the trial. People from the community filled the gallery, their presence a testament to their determination to see this through. Their eyes burned with a mix of anger and grief, their collective presence a powerful force, demanding accountability.

I found my seat in the second row, behind the prosecutors, a vantage point that allowed me to hold the accused in my peripheral vision. It was a deliberate choice, a silent assertion of my presence, a reminder that the lives he had impacted were not forgotten. As the trial began, I couldn't help but notice the emptiness behind the accused—a marked contrast to the crowded gallery on the other side of the room. Only a few people sat in the area designated for his supporters, and even those numbers dwindled as the days went on.

The courtroom was charged with an air of anticipation as the trial commenced. The most seasoned legal minds in the Northwest Territories had assembled a collective force determined to ensure that justice would be served. As the first day dawned, there was a formality in the air, a recognition that we were about to embark on a journey of profound significance. The charges were read aloud, each word a reminder of the tragedy that had brought us here. And then came the moment of truth, the accused standing before the court, his plea a pivotal moment that would set the tone for the days to come.

In a voice that did not seem to carry the weight of his actions, the accused uttered his plea to the charge of first-degree murder.

"Not guilty."

The words hung in the air, an assertion that would be tested rigorously in the days ahead. And yet, there was an offer, a hint of concession—a guilty plea for manslaughter. It was a moment pregnant with possibility, a fleeting opportunity for resolution. But the Crown would not yield, rejecting the plea for manslaughter and forging ahead with the charge of first-degree murder.

With this pivotal decision, the trial pressed forward, the room a battleground of legal arguments, evidence, and testimonies. Opening arguments began, each side weaving a narrative that sought to shape the jury's perception. As the evidence began to unfold, it was as if a quilt of truth was being sewn, each piece adding depth and complexity to the unfolding story.

Amid the ebb and flow of the trial, as the courtroom atmosphere shifted with the weight of evidence and testimony, there was one constant that provided a comforting reprieve—the lunch recesses. In a schedule that often felt unpredictable, the break for lunch offered a predictable moment of respite, a pause in the midst of the storm.

It was during these breaks that the community's support for our family manifested in a truly heartwarming manner. The members of the Yellowknife detachment, our extended family of law enforcement, stepped forward with a gesture of compassion that would touch our hearts deeply. With meticulous organization, they orchestrated our lunches.

Exiting the courthouse, we would walk the short distance to the detachment. There, at the side door of the building, we would be met by the warm embrace of the law enforcement family. Led into the Mess, we would find a spread of homemade food waiting for us. Volunteers had come together to make it happen, their efforts a testament to the power of community and solidarity.

In that space, away from the public eye and the probing lenses of the media, we found a sense of normalcy. We were able to share a home-cooked meal, a simple yet profound act that reminded us of the joys of life. As we savoured the flavours, we were enveloped in a sense of belonging, a feeling that our community was standing with us, offering sustenance not just for our bodies but for our spirits as well. These acts of kindness, these tangible expressions of support, were a lifeline amid the emotional turmoil of the trial.

As I passed through the security checkpoint on the second morning of the trial, there stood Constable Tyler Reid, a striking figure in a well-fitted black suit. A professional aura surrounded him as he prepared to testify. As I approached Tyler, my heart carried a mix of emotions. Seeing him standing there, dressed immaculately in Chris' suit, evoked a sense of nostalgia and longing. I couldn't help but comment on his appearance.

"Oh, don't you look dapper," I quipped, an attempt at lightening the weight of the situation. Tyler's response was a warm smile, a silent acknowledgment of the connection we shared and the significance of the moment.

The trial continued with each testimony adding to the intricate puzzle of that fateful day. Among the witnesses,

Constable Karla George took the stand, recounting the moment when she had come to my door to receive Chris' portable radio. Her words became a part of the timeline the Crown was carefully constructing for the jury. Yet, as much as her testimony was important, my focus remained on the unknown witnesses, those who had observed the events from different perspectives, shedding light on the truth of what happened on that tragic day.

Of these witnesses, two young teenage indigenous girls emerged with a story that carried a weight too heavy for their years. Through their testimony, they transported the courtroom back to the early morning of the shooting. Their voices tinged with uncertainty and a mixture of fear and courage, they recounted their experience of witnessing the events unfold. Walking from one house to another, they had unexpectedly found themselves on the fringes of a scene that would forever alter their lives.

They described the sounds of shouting, the sight of two figures engaged in a desperate foot chase, gunshots piercing the air, and muzzle fire. They saw one figure fleeing from the scene, a shadow etched into their memories. These young girls bore witness to a moment that would haunt them, but shared it knowing that their testimony could help to illuminate the truth.

Their presence on the stand, and their vulnerability as they shared their story, was a testament to their courage. Their journey through the trial was a delicate one, their voices revealing the emotional toll of being witnesses to such a harrowing event. To protect these young witnesses, a special request was made and granted, allowing them to testify from a separate room, away from the prying eyes of the accused. It was a compassionate decision, recognizing the immense challenge they faced in revisiting their memories in such a public and intimidating setting.

Though I had never taught these girls while they were students at DJSS, their actions touched my heart deeply. On the one-year anniversary of Chris' passing, I had written a letter that was read aloud during a school assembly. In that letter, I had praised their bravery and resilience, commending them for standing up and doing the right thing, even when it was undeniably difficult. Their willingness to share their truth resonated with me on a profound level, and I hoped their example would inspire others to do the same.

As the trial unfolded, these young witnesses represented the crossroads of innocence and harsh reality, their courage a testament to the strength that resides within even the most unexpected of heroes. Their presence in the trial was a reminder that justice is not just about the law, but about the willingness of individuals to come forward and uphold the truth, even in the face of adversity. I needed to be reminded of this as more witnesses gave evidence.

As the trial continued to unveil the layers of the underground world of drug dealing and drug use, I found myself grappling with a reality that was far removed from the circles I had ever known. To some, I might have seemed like a "goodie two shoes," but my avoidance of criminal activities was born from a genuine desire to live a life of integrity and responsibility. I had steered clear of anything that could lead down a path of wrongdoing, opting instead to adhere to the law and embrace a life of morality.

Yet, as the witnesses recounted their experiences and provided insights into the criminal underbelly of society, I couldn't help but feel a sense of shock and disbelief. The world they described was alien to me, a world of illicit dealings in drugs and firearms, dangerous encounters, and a disregard for the safety and well-being of others. It was a world that starkly contrasted with the values I held dear, and it was disheartening to hear about the lives that were being torn apart by drugs and violence.

Listening to the testimonies, I came face to face with the harsh reality of the environment my daughter, Alexis, was growing up in. The accused, in addition to taking my husband's life, had played a role in the destruction of countless lives through drug distribution. The people I was hearing about were the very individuals that Chris had dedicated himself to removing from the streets during his service as a police officer. It was a painful realization that the accused's actions had far-reaching consequences that extended beyond that tragic day.

My emotions were in turmoil as I listened to the witnesses describe their involvement in these activities. I had to grapple with a conflicting mix of feelings—anger, frustration, and an overwhelming sense of injustice. The idea of staying silent while these individuals openly discussed their dealings and interactions with the accused was infuriating. The prosecutors assured me that their testimonies were essential in building a comprehensive case against the accused. Their honesty was crucial in demonstrating his guilt to the jury.

On a rational level, I understood the necessity of their testimonies in the pursuit of justice. They were adding to the bigger picture that needed to be painted for the jury. However, emotionally, I was struggling with the fact that these individuals were free to roam the streets, while their actions had contributed to a web of destruction that had ultimately claimed Chris' life.

Through the course of the trial, I was forced to confront the uncomfortable truth that the world isn't always as black and white as I had once believed. It was a lesson in the complexities of human behaviour, the intricacies of justice, and the overwhelming emotions that can arise when confronted with a reality that challenges our core beliefs.

After the conclusion of the intense second week of the trial, I found myself in need of a change of scenery and a momentary reprieve from the courtroom's heavy atmosphere. It was then I decided to take Alexis with me to Edmonton for a few days. This trip served as both an escape and an opportunity to reconnect with Brent.

Brent's unwavering support and his ability to empathize with my rollercoaster of emotions had become a source of solace. He knew the details of the investigation, the tangled threads of the underground drug trade, and the nuances of our legal system. His understanding allowed me to share my thoughts and feelings without judgment or pressure. He listened with a patience that mirrored the approach he had taken in the early days of our connection, allowing me to set the pace and direction of our conversations.

If I wanted to discuss the trial, its details, or the impact it was having on me, Brent was there to offer insights, provide perspective, and lend a supportive ear. If, on the other hand, I yearned for a reprieve from the weight of it all and desired a more lighthearted conversation, he was equally willing to shift gears and engage in other topics. His adaptability and willingness to meet me where I was emotionally provided me with a deep sense of comfort and safety.

In the hours before our departure, Alexis and I found a brief moment of lightheartedness and joy as we embarked on a memorable adventure. Just before catching our flight to Edmonton, we stopped by the high school where I had previously worked as a substitute teacher to participate in their Halloween parade. Dressed as princesses, with Alexis in a borrowed Cinderella dress and me adorned in Rachel's Snow White costume, we joined the festivities and shared smiles and laughter with the students. Little did I know that this day would hold even more heartwarming surprises.

As we boarded the flight to Edmonton, the enchantment of our costumes still lingering, Brent awaited our arrival at the airport. What I hadn't anticipated was the presence of Jordan, Brent's youngest son, who had chosen this moment to take a significant step forward in our relationship. Emerging from the arrival doors, Alexis released my hand and darted straight toward Brent, as her joyous enthusiasm could not be contained. Brent effortlessly scooped her up into his arms, her princess dress cascading gracefully over his arm.

As I approached Brent and Alexis, my attention was drawn to the two figures standing nearby, Jordan and Keegan. My heart swelled with a mixture of emotions, recognizing the significance of this moment. I greeted Brent with a quick, sideways hug, mindful of the presence of the boys.

Brent's understanding and sensitivity in orchestrating this meeting were evident. Jordan's presence at the airport spoke volumes. It was a gesture of courage and a willingness to take a step forward, despite any apprehensions he may have felt. Brent's patient approach had created a space where Jordan could make this choice on his terms. As we stood there, our costumes breaking the ice and setting a playful tone, Brent introduced us as "Snow White and Cinderella." The costumes not only brought smiles but also provided a bridge for connection, easing the initial awkwardness and allowing us to engage in conversation more freely.

This unexpected encounter, with its blend of whimsy and significance, added another layer of depth to our relationship. In the midst of the trial's gravity, it was a reminder that life continued to unfold with its moments of beauty and growth, even in the face of challenges.

Our Halloween trip to Hay Lakes brought a touch of festive joy and laughter. We eagerly anticipated an evening of trick-or-treating, excited to see Alexis' reaction to this new adventure. This marked her first Halloween where she could walk from door to door, and her innocence and curiosity were on full display.

As we approached the first house, excitement radiated from Alexis. However, her enthusiasm took an unexpected turn when Brent's neighbours opened the door. In her innocence, she stepped right into their home, ready for a visit as she started to take off her jacket. Chuckles filled the air as we gently guided her back outside, explaining that we were there to collect candy. With each subsequent house, her understanding grew, and she soon embraced the concept with a newfound determination. It was a heartwarming sight to witness her joy and curiosity as she eagerly collected her Halloween treats.

After a delightful evening, we returned to Brent's home, where the sense of togetherness and warmth settled over us. The following day, we embarked on another outing, this time to the iconic West Edmonton Mall. With Brent's birthday approaching, I had a practical gift for him in mind—a new bed. Recognizing the importance of comfort for quality sleep, I wanted to ensure that he had a restful place to lay his head. Our trio ventured into a furniture store, where we tested various mattresses. Brent's humble nature and reluctance to accept gifts were evident as he hesitantly selected a mattress that suited his preferences.

Brent was a man accustomed to giving, fixing, and offering his support. Receiving kindness and generosity wasn't something that came naturally to him. This role reversal, where he was the recipient of care, posed a challenge. As I observed his interactions and hesitations, I gained a deeper understanding of the complexities that made up his character. Despite his reservations, I was determined to show him the same care and consideration that he had extended to us.

That evening, a heartwarming scene unfolded as Jordan and Keegan joined us. In a gesture that exemplified their openness and willingness to embrace change, Jordan downloaded a colouring app onto his phone and took the time to show Alexis how to use it. This simple act of sharing technology led to a delightful bonding experience. Sitting together on the retro-themed couch, the two of them immersed themselves in colouring and played with Polly Pocket figurines. Their interactions were a testament to their genuine effort to connect with Alexis, a young girl who had become a part of their father's life.

It was clear that the boys were making an earnest attempt to bridge the gap and engage with Alexis despite any initial reservations they may have had. Adjusting to a new dynamic, especially one involving a young child, can be a complex experience for anyone, let alone teenagers. Yet, they demonstrated maturity and adaptability by embracing these interactions without showing any visible signs of discomfort.

This time together, filled with lighthearted moments and meaningful connections, added another layer of depth to our growing relationship. As we continued to navigate our journey, these shared experiences became the building blocks of a bond that was steadily evolving, grounded in understanding, patience, and a shared willingness to embrace the changes life had brought our way.

Returning to Yellowknife after our brief respite, I slipped back into the rhythm of attending the trial. As the court proceedings continued, I found myself more at ease when listening to the police officers' testimonies. They represented a sense of order and justice in my mind—individuals dedicated to making our community safer. The testimony of other witnesses, particularly those involved in criminal activities, stirred a different kind of emotion.

One individual, in particular, stood out—the man who had accompanied the accused to Hay River, participated in selling drugs, and assisted in hiding the accused during the subsequent manhunt. He faced charges of "Accessory to murder after the fact."

Listening to these accounts triggered a shift in me. As each new detail of the case emerged, I felt a growing panic, a fear that somehow the jury might not deliver the outcome I hoped for. The fate of the accused rested in their hands, guided by the intricacies of the Canadian justice system that, in my eyes, had already let me down by allowing the accused to be out on bail when he committed the murder.

My faith in the system was shaken, and my faith about the trial's outcome began to slip. The carefully compartmentalized box in my mind, which held the traumatic events and emotions related to Chris' murder, burst open. The contents, once contained, now flooded my thoughts and emotions, and I struggled to regain control and seal the lid shut once more.

The trial had not only exposed the details of the crime but had also unearthed my inner turmoil, leaving me grappling with fear, anger, and a deep-seated desire for justice.

Only in hindsight do I realize that I had unknowingly slipped back into survivor mode during the trial. As I had gone through the preliminary inquiry, and had a certain expectation that I would be prepared for the full trial. I had convinced myself that it would be an extended version of what I had already experienced—a process of listening, understanding, finding closure, and finally, allowing myself to heal. But the reality was far more complex and challenging than I had anticipated.

After a few days of grappling with my emotions and attempting to contain the flood of memories and feelings that the trial had unearthed, I came to a realization. I decided that it was time to let go of the struggle, to stop forcing myself to compartmentalize and suppress. Instead, I chose honesty—with myself and those around me. In search of rediscovering my own identity and gaining a deeper understanding of myself, I made the decision to temporarily step away.

The timing coincided with my work in Edmonton leading focus groups. I saw this as a chance to create some distance and give myself the space I needed. While I engaged actively with the group during the day, I intentionally chose to spend my evenings alone. I refrained from seeing Brent during this time, not out of avoidance, but as an act of self-care. Those solitary nights in the hotel became my sanctuary for reflection, a place where I could confront my emotions head-on and begin processing what I was going through.

Recognizing that I had slipped into autopilot mode, I was determined to break free from its grasp. I used those three nights as an opportunity to reassess where I stood and where I wanted to go from there. It was a period of self-discovery and reconnection with my own desires, needs, and aspirations. By taking this step back and allowing myself the space to breathe and think, I began to chart a course towards a healthier, more intentional path forward.

In those moments of introspection during my stay in Edmonton, I faced some hard truths. I confronted the fact that I had actively grieved for an entire year—a year of mourning, of grappling with the painful reality that Chris was gone from my life. I came to terms with the undeniable truth that my life had been irreversibly altered, and living without Chris was an immense and ongoing struggle. His absence was a constant ache that I couldn't escape.

I also acknowledged the weight I had placed on the outcome of the trial—a culmination of years of anticipation and expectation. The trial had become a symbol of closure, a finish line that I believed would signify the end of a particularly painful chapter. I had invested so much emotional energy in the legal process, hoping that once it was over, I would finally find the relief I longed for. I had tied my hopes of feeling lighter, happier, and freer to the conclusion of the trial. I yearned for the day when I could take a deep breath without its shadow hanging over me, and I could embrace life's joys with renewed optimism.

I realized that I had drafted a narrative for myself, a story where the trial's resolution would usher in a new era of my life. I eagerly awaited the moment when the accused would be convicted, expecting that this milestone would bring a sense of closure and healing. In my mind, it would be the final step in a long journey towards moving forward.

As I reflected on these expectations, I understood that while the trial was a significant chapter in my journey, it wasn't a guaranteed catalyst for the emotional transformation I so desperately desired. It was a pivotal moment, but it wasn't the definitive endpoint I had envisioned. It was time for me to accept that real healing wouldn't come solely from the conclusion of the trial. It would require ongoing effort, self-compassion, and a commitment to rebuilding my life in a way that honoured both Chris' memory and my own well-being. I would need to anchor into this over the next week and beyond.

18

•••••

AS THE TRIAL entered its final week, my attention shifted towards finalizing the victim impact statements that I was preparing for both myself and Alexis. I sought guidance from the staff at Yellowknife Victim Services, who provided me with the necessary information and guidelines for crafting these statements. It was a vivid reminder that even in the aftermath of unimaginable loss, I was still navigating a system that sometimes felt indifferent to the rawness of my pain.

The frustration I felt at being told what I could and couldn't say was accompanied by a surge of indignation. *How could anyone dictate the words I could use to convey the depth of my grief, the void left by Chris' absence, and the ways in which our lives had been forever altered?* It wasn't just about relaying facts; it was about pouring my heart onto paper, sharing the intimate details of how my world had shattered.

The limitations imposed on discussing the accused's criminal history or the systemic failures that allowed this tragedy to unfold further fueled my determination. These were crucial elements that had contributed to the ordeal my family had endured, and yet, I was constrained from speaking about them directly. It felt like an injustice within an already profound injustice.

But amidst the frustration and anger, I found a way to channel my emotions. The prospect of standing before the accused, knowing that he had to listen, compelled me to find the most powerful and potent words possible. Every sentence, every phrase, carried a piece of my heart, a testament to the love that was lost and the pain that followed.

As I wrote and rewrote, I couldn't help but reflect on the journey I had undertaken since that fateful day. The resilience that had carried me through, the love that had sustained me, and the deep well of strength that I had discovered within myself—all of these emotions swirled and intertwined as I carefully crafted each line of the victim impact statements.

With each word, I aimed to pierce through the limitations, to convey the essence of my pain, and to ensure that the accused truly understood the magnitude of his actions.

As the trial drew to a close, the weight of the moment pressed heavily on all of us who had been involved—the witnesses, the lawyers, the judge, the jury, and me, sitting in that courtroom, heart pounding, waiting for the final chapter of this painful journey to unfold. Fifty-three witnesses had testified, revealing the intricate details of that tragic day and manhunt that followed. The stories shared had painted a vivid picture of the events leading up to and following Chris' senseless murder.

On that November day in 2009, as the closing arguments echoed in the courtroom, the tension was unmistakable. The defence's argument—that the accused's intention was not to kill Chris, but merely to slow him down—was met with a mix of anger, frustration, and disbelief. *How could anyone claim such a thing, given the evidence that had been presented?*

The judge's instructions to the jury became the crux of our collective anticipation. The fate of the accused rested upon their interpretation of his intent when he pulled the trigger those final two times. The gravity of that decision was overwhelming. A life taken, a family shattered, a community forever changed—all hinged on this pivotal moment of judgment.

The potential sentences loomed like shadows, both holding the promise of life behind bars, yet differing in the possibility of parole. Manslaughter, with its four-year parole eligibility, seemed to undermine the magnitude of the crime committed. First-degree murder, with its mandatory twenty-five-year parole ineligibility, carried a more fitting consequence, given the deliberate and heinous nature of the act.

As the jury was sequestered, a tense hush settled over the courtroom. It was now up to twelve individuals to decide the fate of a man who had shattered so many lives.

The afternoon following the closing arguments brought with it a sense of unease that I had not experienced before. As I left the courthouse, the weight of uncertainty settled heavily upon me, making each step feel burdensome. The lack of control over the situation was suffocating, and the stakes felt higher than ever. The outcome of the trial, the justice we sought, all hinged on the jury's decision. The possibility that they might come back with a verdict of manslaughter, with its lighter consequences, seemed to loom larger with every passing moment.

That night, sleep eluded me as my thoughts raced and my heart pounded with anxiety. I tried to envision different scenarios, different verdicts, but the uncertainty was paralyzing. The weight of the past two years, the pain of loss, and the hope for justice collided within me, creating a storm of emotions that I struggled to contain.

The morning of the verdict arrived with a cold bite in the air, and a blanket of snow covered the ground, a reflection of the tension and chill in my heart. Our family gathered at the detachment Mess, clinging to each other for support. As the call came for us to return to the courthouse, we walked together, united by our shared anticipation.

The atmosphere at the courthouse was charged with an undeniable energy. The space was filled with a mixture of people—members of the public, law enforcement officers, teachers—all anxiously waiting for the verdict that would shape the course of justice. Passing through security, I took my seat in the courtroom, my hands tightly clasped together as if in prayer. Michèle sat beside me, a comforting presence amid the rising tension.

My leg bounced uncontrollably as I awaited the jury's entrance. As the jury members filed in, a wave of anticipation washed over the room. My heart raced, and my mind echoed with a single question that threatened to drown out all else: *What if they get it wrong?* Standing, my hands pressed together in an unconscious plea, I fixed my gaze on the jurors as the judge entered and assumed his position. He asked the head juror to stand. My heart pounding, my breath held, as the words spilled forth from the juror's lips, carrying the weight of a verdict that would determine the fate of the accused.

"We the jury find the accused guilty of first-degree murder."

In that moment, a flood of emotions rushed over me—relief, validation, a mix of grief and triumph. It was a verdict that acknowledged the gravity of the crime, the intention behind it, and the impact it had on all of our lives. The weight that had burdened me for so long began to lift, replaced by the gravity of the truth spoken aloud. Tears blurred my vision, and as I turned to Michèle, our eyes met in a shared understanding of the significance of this moment.

In those moments following the verdict, time seemed to stand still. The collective exhale of the gallery mingled with the quiet sobs and whispers that filled the space. With the jury dismissed and the weight of the verdict hanging in the air, a brief recess was called to prepare for the reading of the victim impact statements. The courtroom remained packed, standing room only, a testament to the significance of this moment for all those present. And in the midst of it all, I stood ready to share my words, my feelings, and my experience.

When it came time for me to read my victim impact statement, this is what I said:

Your Honour,

My name is Jodie Worden. I was Chris' wife for four and a half wonderful years. On October 6, 2007, one week after my 29th birthday, I was no longer his wife. I was now Christopher Worden's widow and the single mother to his eight-month-old daughter.

To truly understand all that I have lost, one must hear the story of how Chris and I came to be a couple and all of the plans we made for our long future together.

Chris and I began a friendship in September 2000 and started dating in March 2001, while both still in university.

Chris graduated from Wilfrid Laurier University with a major in Political Science and a minor in history. From the moment I met him, I knew he wanted to be an RCMP officer. He wanted to be a part of the history and heritage of Canada's National Police force. He wanted to serve in the red serge.

Now he is part of RCMP history as the 219th member to have been killed in the line of duty. His name is permanently marked on cenotaphs in Yellowknife, Regina, and Ottawa.

Chris attended Depot the day before 9-11. We wrote each other emails daily and he spoke to me on the payphone outside of barracks each night. I went out to visit him one weekend in October and he flew home to Ontario for Christmas break and proposed to me while wearing High Browns after eight months of being together. I flew out for his graduation in February, six weeks later. On the day he flew back to Ontario to pack his belongings for his posting in Yellowknife, I flew to Australia to begin my post-graduate degree in education at the University of Western Sydney. After four months of school I flew from Sydney to Yellowknife for a 6 week visit with Chris. He was so proud to show me what would be our first rental home together and helped me to experience first-hand what I had only heard about on the phone.

Now I own a home in my name only because I had life insurance money as a result of Chris' death.

I returned to school for 4 more months and upon graduation in November 2002, returned to Canada. I began teaching in Yellowknife and really enjoyed it.

Now I have had to change my career as I do not have the tolerance for high school students experimenting with drugs. Five years of post-secondary education to become a teacher has been wasted.

In February 2003, Chris and I were married. It was one of the happiest days of my life. Now I need to call on that memory to help me through the days where I don't want to get out of bed in the morning because I know he won't be there with me.

Our relationship was based on trust, respect, open communication, valuing one another's careers, appreciating each other and a desire to be the best team we could. Now our relationship is based on fading memories, photos, old cards, newspaper clippings and news reports about his murder.

We lived happily in Yellowknife until January 2004 when Chris was posted to Wha Ti. In an isolated community of less than five hundred people, we were able to spend more quality time together; hunting, fishing, cooking, drives to the falls, campfires, even working as a guard in cells on occasion. We loved each other and we loved spending time with each other.

Now I live as a single mother in Ottawa in a house that always feels it has a void. I don't have local friends as it is difficult to open up to people. The friendships that we made while living up north still carry on, but they are not the same. Chris was always a part of the stories. A part of our group is missing.

In October 2005 we moved to Hay River and decided to start our family. Chris always said he wanted a van full of kids. Alexis was born in February 2007. She was a miniature version of her dad. We had so much fun being parents. He was so supportive and involved in her life. His favourite time with her was reading stories to her in the rocking chair in the nursery.

Now I have to do everything myself for Alexis; feed her, get her ready for daycare, pack her lunch, get her spare clothes ready, drop her off at daycare, go to work so that I can provide financially for us, pick her up from daycare, make dinner, go to the park, play puzzles, bath her, sit in the rocking chair and look at the picture of Chris while I tell her stories about her daddy, put her to bed and tell her that everything is going to be alright while knowing full well that it can't be.

We were living the life we had dreamt of when we first got together. We had the goal of returning to work in Yellowknife and when the kids were in Grade 4 moving to Ottawa to be closer to our families. We would move to an acreage in the country and spend our summers touring around in the motorhome. It was our version of a perfect life. Now when I travel with my daughter I have to carry Chris' death certificate so I can prove that I am not a kidnapper. Our story was one that fairytales are made of, except mine doesn't have a happy ending.

My daughter and I have been away from our home since October 16th because of my attendance at this trial. We have been put through over two years of legal proceedings because the person responsible took no accountability for Chris' death when it happened. For years to come we will have to anticipate his parole hearings and once again relive all of this as we prepare statements for consideration at that time. This will never be behind us.

We have sat here quietly day after day biting our tongues and listening to the testimony of drug dealers, drug users, alcoholics, criminals and the general low lives of society. They have all had their say. The convicted has had his say. Chris will never get a chance again to have his say. I have made the decision to stand in front of you today because I have a choice to have my voice heard, even though the choice to be in this situation was made for me by someone else.

I was worried about writing and then reading this statement because how can I adequately put into words what was taken from me and my daughter through the murder of Chris. There are no words that I have been able to find to describe the amount of hurt, pain, anguish, anger, and utter despair that I have felt over the last two plus years. The thing I have the most difficulty with is that there was no reason that this had to happen. There is no reason that you had to pull the trigger four times. There was nothing to gain from the actions taken that night but hurt and pain for everyone involved. And as a result I have had to live every day since October 6, 2007, with a feeling that I am not complete. There is a hole in my soul that can never be filled because of the selfish actions of a cowardly criminal. Every day since this happened and every day for the rest of my life I will have to live with the fact that you took my best friend and the person I chose to be with and raise a family with. Every day I have to look at my daughter and try to compensate for the fact that she no longer has her father who can play with her or read her bedtime stories or throw her up in the air or tell her that he loves her. She was so young when this happened that she will never remember the feel of his touch or hear the sound of his voice or see how much her mom and dad really loved each other. She will never experience the life she was meant to have with siblings and being the oldest child in a large family. You took that from her.

I continuously doubt my ability as her only parent and wonder if I am giving her what she needs, knowing full well what she is missing out on by not having her dad alive to positively influence her life. I have to worry about when she is older and starts asking questions such as "why don't I have a daddy like my friends?" and then sitting down with her when she is ready and looking through all of the boxes of her dad's things and reading articles that were written surrounding his murder and worrying about how she is going to handle it all. I am scared that I won't be able to adequately paint the picture of Alexis' father to her. How can I describe him in a way that she can understand what kind of person he was? What amazing qualities he possessed and how he loved life. One can't accurately describe these things. They need to be experienced and Alexis will never have that opportunity. She will only know her father through photographs and conjured memories from stories she hears from Chris' family and me.

I live with the guilt that I can't remember Chris' touch and often need a physical picture to remind me of the curves of his frame and the details of his face. It makes me doubt my place as his wife. A great wife wouldn't forget these things. But because of you, I have and it frightens me everyday. I started writing a journal in February 2008 to try and express and release some of my feelings. I feel that sharing a few of my entries from the months following Chris' murder may help Your Honour understand more of the impact that has had on me:

Saturday February 9, 2008 @ 12:44am

I've just checked in on Alexis. She looks so peaceful. It's such a different emotion compared to what I've been doing since 9:30 preparing for tomorrow's debriefing. Michael and Peter arrived today. The three of us sat in the living room talking about how Chris was murdered and how his killer was on the run for six days. It is so surreal. I need to believe that Chris didn't suffer. I really want to believe that he had no idea and so that he couldn't think a last thought about leaving us behind or letting us down.

This Wednesday and Thursday Global Edmonton and National aired another story about Alexis and I. It was really nicely done. I see myself on TV and hear what the reporter is saying about the 'grieving, mourning widow' and while I know it is my life, it still is unbelievable that I am left here with Alexis without Chris. I know he is not coming back, but just because my mind knows it, it doesn't stop every other part of me from wishing that things were the way they used to be. That a few more minutes either way that night that I would still have my husband and best friend and Alexis would have her daddy to play with instead of her two uncles.

Sunday February 10, 2008 @ 10:26pm

I'm sitting in my bed crying because I am upset with the fact that every time I look at a picture of Chris I focus on his neck and picture holes in it from the bullet. How can I get past this? I look at myself in the mirror and picture on me where the bullets passed through Chris. It's like he was shot five times because the chest shot exited and reentered to break his arm. My poor Chris. I know he would have hated dying the way he did; being so close to catching him. I just need to focus on the fact that he died quickly and since he led such a good life he is in heaven watching over us and that when the trial is over, He will be in jail forever. As much as I want to believe that that will make me feel better, right now it doesn't provide me with much comfort.

Sunday April 13, 2008 @ 10:37pm

I was finally able to put into words how I was feeling with regard to my feelings for Chris. I was feeling guilty about not loving him the way I did when he was alive. Right after it happened I couldn't imagine how people could go on to love someone else. While I am so not ready to even consider dating, I understand how widows and widowers do it. It is like how I decided to take my wedding rings off. I am no longer in a committed, active relationship. I am no longer married. Yes, I will always love Chris, but the love has changed because mine is not being reciprocated. What we had, while so great and wonderful while it was happening, is all in the past. It is so difficult to hold onto these feelings when you get nothing back day after day. I find I need to look at the pictures to remember the small features of his face. This is a frightening realization. To admit to yourself that you have a hard time picturing him in your mind, to me, was like I was a bad wife and friend. How could I forget?

Monday April 14, 2008 @ 11:55pm

I started wearing my medical alert bracelet again today. I have had a few moments this week where I have thought: if something happened to me, how long would it take for someone to come looking? I took off the bracelet initially because it was too loose, and I thought: well. Chris is always with me or nearby to tell the doctors about my allergy. Since he isn't here anymore, I will have to rely on the paramedics to look at the bracelet and figure it out. I am alone.

Thursday April 29, 2008 @12:06am

The more I write the more I realize that one of the most frustrating parts of this process is the never-ending questions and knowing that I will likely never get the answers. I need to put my faith in something, but it is so difficult when your faith has been shattered. What keeps me from having absolutely no faith is that I need to believe in heaven so that each night as I put our daughter to bed I can tell her "that mommy and daddy love you and daddy is looking down from heaven while you have sweet dreams" and it not be a lie. I can't lie to her so I have to believe.

Thursday May 15, 2008 @8:56pm

I am writing this and look over at my nightstand and look at the family picture of us taken in May last year. Chris' hand is so big on Alexis' body. He was our protector. I can't believe this is my life. I know he is gone, but to have a journal specifically for expressing my feelings as a result of my husband's murder is something I never ever thought would happen to me, and here I am meeting with lawyers to prepare to see my husband's killer. This should have been a happy day when Chris and I would celebrate the ownership of our new house. Instead, I have purchased a house using his life insurance money. It doesn't feel right in my heart. It wasn't supposed to be like this. I shouldn't be mortgage-free. I shouldn't be buying a house in Ottawa; I shouldn't be sitting through my husband's killer's preliminary inquiry; I shouldn't have to be moving at the end of June; I shouldn't be raising our daughter by myself; I shouldn't have to talk to air because I am trying to communicate with my deceased husband; I shouldn't have to contemplate the future without Chris in it; I shouldn't have to be doing ANY of this!

Your Honour, these entries were made over a year and a half ago, but they are just as accurate today as they were when I wrote them and I don't see it changing in the future. I shouldn't have to be doing ANY of this. I shouldn't be living without Chris.

The trials, the emotions, the struggles—they were an integral part of my story, but not the entirety. Looking ahead, I saw a path of possibilities and the potential for connection. The future was not solely shaped by the past; it was influenced by my choices, my resilience, and my determination to reshape my narrative.

I was no longer trapped in the past or burdened by the present. I was embracing the idea of reshaping my future, of carving out a new chapter that held space for healing, growth, and transformation. It was a realization that came with a mixture of relief, anticipation, and a hint of trepidation. But it was a realization that was undeniably empowering, reminding me that I had the strength to rebuild my life on my own terms, no matter what challenges lay ahead.

October 2000, Wilfrid Laurier University Golden Hawks football

November 2001, Depot Training Academy

February 2002, Graduation from RCMP Depot Training Academy

February 2002, Graduation from RCMP Depot Training Academy

February 2002, Graduation from RCMP Depot Training Academy

February 2003, Ingersoll, Ontario

Winter 2003, South Slave Lake, Northwest Territories

Winter 2003, South Slave Lake, Northwest Territories

Summer 2004, Wha Ti RCMP detachment

Spring 2003, Wha Ti visit with John and MaryAnn

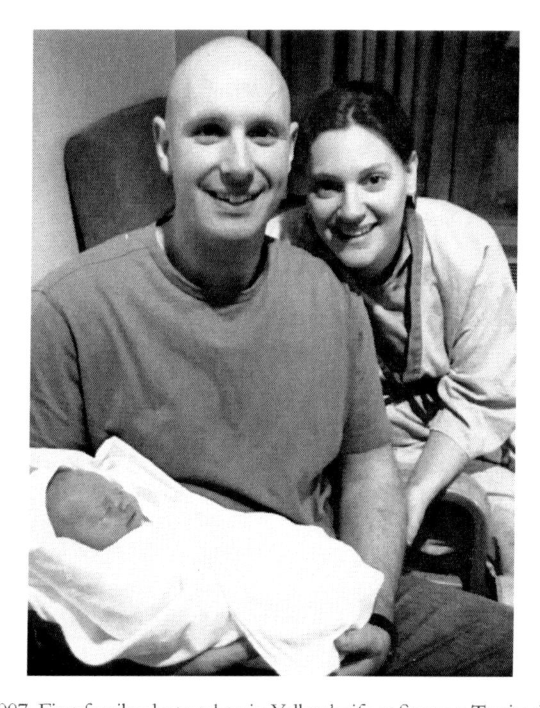

February 2007, First family photo taken in Yellowknife at Stanton Territorial Hospital

May 2007, Ingersoll Ontario at Alexis' baptism

July 2007, Hay River, Northwest Territories on Canada day

October 6, 2007 outside Notre Dame Basilica, Ottawa, Ontario, courtesy of Steve Gerecke

Office of the Prime Minister   Cabinet du Premier ministre

October 2007, Ottawa Ontario, meeting Prime Minister Harper

September 2008, Regina Saskatchewan at the RCMP Memorial

January 2009, Hay River, Northwest Territories

Spring 2008, Hay River, Northwest Territories at the memorial hockey game

June 2021, Beechwood Cemetery, Ottawa Ontario

Part 2: The Wife

19

RETURNING HOME WITH Alexis, my heart felt both heavy and light, a mix of emotions swirling within me. The trial had cast a shadow over my life for so long. The constant stream of legal proceedings, the anxiety of court appearances, and the emotional toll of reliving painful memories had taken their toll on both my psyche and my physical well-being. But now, as I looked around at the familiar surroundings of our home, I felt like I could finally exhale. The weight that had pressed down on me for so long was diminished, replaced by a renewed sense of freedom.

The pressure that had gripped me seemed to dissipate with every step I took. The walls of our home seemed to exude a comforting warmth and held a different energy. There was a calmness in the air, a stillness that whispered promises of a brighter future. Looking at Alexis, her innocent eyes reflecting the simplicity and wonder of childhood, I felt profound gratitude for the chance to provide her with a fresh start. As I held my daughter's hand and walked through our home, I embraced the positive outlook that lay ahead. I felt a surge of optimism and was ignited with a fire to protect and nurture her, to ensure that her life was defined by love and joy, where new memories were created in an environment where she could grow and thrive.

The rhythm of our routine welcomed us back like an old friend. Alexis' laughter and excitement filled the air as she reunited with her friends from Montessori school. Seeing her joyous interactions reminded me of the resilience children possess—their ability to adapt and embrace the present moment with an open heart. I was reconnecting with colleagues and diving into the initiatives that had been put on hold during the trial. There was a renewed sense of purpose in my steps, a determination to contribute and make a positive impact.

My work was finally hitting its stride, and a newfound sense of confidence enveloped me, both in my professional capabilities and my relationships with colleagues. However, amidst this positive momentum, there loomed a significant challenge: my office was relocating to the far side of the city, nearly doubling my daily commute. The mere thought of the impending commute sent shivers down my spine, as it threatened to swallow up precious time I could spend with Alexis.

As I pondered the implications of this move, I realized with a heavy heart that my time with Alexis would be drastically reduced to just two precious waking hours each day. The majority of my days would be swallowed up by lengthy hours spent on the road and immersed in work. Determined to protect the quality of our time together, I diligently assessed our situation and came to the resolute decision that it was in our best interest to relocate closer to my new office.

In pursuit of a solution, my mind became fixated on the idea of moving. The notion crystallized during an unforgettable Christmas visit by Brent and his boys. The conversation meandered toward my predicament, and Brent enthusiastically proposed that we explore potential neighbourhoods together. We set out, driving through various areas until fate led us to stumble upon an open house sign.

The date was December 23rd, and curiosity pulled us inside this inviting home. Our little entourage—Brent, Keegan, Jordan, Alexis, and myself—wandered through the house like adventurers uncovering a hidden treasure. As we explored upstairs, we found a charming room painted in the most endearing shade of pink. Instantly captivated by its charm, Alexis found herself drawn to it, delighting in how pretty and cozy it felt. This room, in particular, shared a jack and jill bathroom with an adjoining space, adding to the house's allure.

What truly captivated me, was the home's open concept layout that invited a seamless flow of energy and light. Every corner held the promise of future memories, and the potential of the backyard was nothing short of spectacular. A manmade lake gracefully extended to meet the back property line, its beauty subdued under the winter's snowy blanket. Yet, even in its dormant state, I could envision the enchanting mornings, waking up to the mesmerizing vista of the water, a sight that could rejuvenate the soul.

Though the house seemed quite spacious for just Alexis and me, I couldn't ignore the intuition that whispered in my heart—this place was destined for more than just the two of us. Bolstered by this deep-seated feeling, Brent and I embarked on a second viewing on December 27th, which only confirmed my longing for this place. Every detail that had enchanted me earlier confirmed its rightful place in my heart. Without hesitation, I made the decision and submitted an offer the very next day. The countdown began, and with great anticipation and excitement, Alexis and I eagerly awaited the day of our big move—February 10th!

The timing of the closing date could not have been more challenging; it coincided precisely with Brent's work commitment at the Olympics, leaving him unable to lend a hand. Our farewell was bittersweet, just after the New Year, knowing we wouldn't reunite until mid-March. Facing this significant move alone wasn't entirely new to me, but the thought of navigating it without Brent's support was disheartening.

Determined to make this transition a smooth one, I leaned on the support of my friends, who came forward with great dedication. The day of the move dawned, brimming with anticipation and a dash of nervous energy. There was much to do, but my focus remained on Alexis and her precious pink room. It was crucial that she could sleep soundly in her "big-girl" bed, marking her first night away from her crib—a milestone that meant a great deal to both of us.

As the memories of our final days in the old house flooded my mind, I couldn't help but reminisce about Alexis's third birthday party—a delightful affair filled with pirate and princess magic. The joy in her eyes as Cinderella graced the occasion with her presence was unforgettable. But as the festivities subsided, and the day's excitement fell away, she lay in her crib, wearing adorable pink onesie pyjamas, looking both endearing and exhausted. The sight of her feet poking through the crib's rails served as a clear reminder that my little girl was quickly outgrowing her baby days.

In the lead-up to the move, Alexis and I had shared countless conversations about her transition to a "big bed" in our new home, and she had expressed genuine excitement about this new adventure. I was determined not to let her down, to make this transition as enchanting as she hoped it would be.

The day of the move arrived, bringing with it a flurry of boxes and tasks to tackle. Despite the whirlwind, when John and MaryAnn arrived with Alexis that night, her room stood calm amid the organized chaos. The love and effort I poured into creating her space was met with delighted squeals that were like music to my ears.

With her "big-girl" bed ready to embrace her dreams and her pink room becoming a haven of comfort and magic, I knew we had achieved the goal set out for that day. That night, I slept on a mattress on the floor and didn't mind one bit. Witnessing the sheer joy in Alexis's face as she explored her room made it all worthwhile.

Our bedtime routine had become a cherished ritual. After bath time and storytime, I would tuck Alexis into bed, leaving the door ajar and the night light glowing softly. As I went about the house attending to my chores, I could hear her sweet voice reading aloud to herself. However, within twenty minutes, she would often come looking for me, admitting that she was scared. In those moments, I would gently guide her back to bed, tuck her in again, and assure her that I would stay close by, banishing any fears that lurked in the darkness.

Sometimes, this meant sitting in the rocking chair nestled in the corner of her room until she fell asleep. Other times, I would be in my own bedroom, just across the hall, but she found reassurance in knowing I was nearby. As Alexis grew and her vocabulary blossomed, she began to articulate more about what troubled her. At the age of four and five, her fear was centred around the worry that she wouldn't fall asleep.

Desperate to help my precious girl find peace, I confided in my friend Heidi about Alexis' struggle. To my relief, Heidi shared a method that had worked for her in childhood. Her mother had given her a box and asked her to put all her worries into it before getting into bed. This simple act of surrendering her fears to the box allowed her to drift into slumber peacefully.

I decided to adapt this concept for Alexis, hoping it would bring her comfort. The following night, as she came to me once again, I led her back to her bedroom. I didn't have a box, but I cupped my hands together and told Alexis to place her worries in my hands. At first, she looked puzzled, unsure of what to do. But with gentle guidance, she mirrored my actions, holding her small hands like mine.

I shared one of my worries and touched my hand to hers, symbolically transferring the burden of the fear into her hands. Encouraging her to close her hands tightly over the worry, we blew softly on our hands and opened them and imagined the wind carrying it far away, freeing us from its weight. The magic of this simple action sparked joy in her eyes.

We began to call this ritual "worry hands," and from that night onward, during our bedtime routine, we performed this act of letting go together. As Alexis was tucked into bed, worry hands became a comforting and empowering tradition, reminding us that love and imagination could conquer any fear that threatened to disturb our peaceful nights. And with each passing night, I could see her worries diminishing, replaced by the tranquility that comes from knowing you are safe and loved.

I, too, was beginning to take comfort in my own sense of tranquility as Brent and I continued developing our relationship. In contemplating the significance of "choice" within the context of my early relationship with Brent, I firmly argued that a long-distance relationship not only allows a couple to prolong the honeymoon phase but also emphasizes the profound impact of conscious decisions.

By actively choosing to be in a long-distance relationship, we opened ourselves up to a unique set of challenges and opportunities. We made a conscious choice to navigate the complexities of distance, building trust and communication in a way that may not have been necessary in a geographically closer relationship. This deliberate decision compelled us to find innovative ways to nurture our connection, constantly seeking to deepen our understanding of each other without the crutch of physical proximity.

Through these conscious choices, we learned to cherish the little moments of connection that others might take for granted. Simple phone calls turned into cherished occasions where we could truly focus on each other, immersing ourselves in the subtleties of our conversations. The choice to be apart reinforced the value of every interaction, making us cherish the time we did have together and fostering an unyielding desire to make the most of it. These choices strengthened our relationship enough that we were confident in making the decision to live together when the time came in August 2010 when Brent accepted a transfer to Ottawa.

This was more than just a career transfer; it symbolized the beginning of a new chapter in our lives—a chapter we eagerly embraced with open hearts and beaming smiles. I remember feeling a profound sense of excitement and happiness as Brent made the heartfelt choice to move from Edmonton to be with Alexis and me in Ottawa. It was a decision that spoke volumes about his commitment to our family and his belief in the potential that lay ahead.

With each passing day leading up to his arrival, anticipation coursed through our veins. We couldn't wait for him to be a part of our daily lives, to share in the laughter and adventures that awaited us. His presence brought a sense of security and warmth that enveloped us like a comforting embrace. Having him by our side in Ottawa brought a sense of completeness and contentment. Each day felt like a treasure, cherished and embraced with gratitude. We relished the simple moments of togetherness—the shared meals, the bedtime stories, the laughter that echoed through the hallways.

As Brent settled into his new role, our lives felt complete. Our modern family grew stronger. As we looked ahead, our hearts overflowed with hope, knowing that no matter what life had in store for us, we were blessed to face it together—united, resilient, and deeply in love.

Keegan had recently graduated high school and had been exploring opportunities to play junior hockey. After trying out for teams in Alberta and British Columbia, he ventured to Ottawa to try out for teams in the east. To our delight, he earned a spot on a team with a home rink just fifteen minutes away from our house. This turn of events meant that Keegan would also be moving in with us, sharing the jack and jill bathroom with Alexis. Our family was coming together, and we began establishing new routines to accommodate our busy lives.

Our days settled into a rhythm. Alexis continued attending preschool, while Keegan attended a city school during the day to upgrade his marks for future post-secondary aspirations. Meanwhile, Brent and I worked out of the same office building, making our mornings a synchronized dance of coordinating school drop-offs and getting ready for work. Brent usually left the house early, and I managed the mornings with Alexis, ensuring everyone was ready for the day. Because I dropped Alexis off at school on my way to work, Brent would leave work earlier to pick her up and start dinner. Evenings were filled with the joyous chatter of our shared experiences over mealtime, followed by tidying up and spending quality time together through play, reading, or watching TV. The energy in our home was brimming with positivity.

With each passing day, Brent and I felt our love grow stronger, and we openly discussed our future together. We knew we were meant for each other, and the idea of spending our lives as a family brought immense joy to our hearts. Our commitment to each other deepened, and we decided to plan a special date night on September 17th—a night that would become a significant milestone in our journey.

With a bit of nervousness in the air, we took a stroll along the picturesque Rideau Canal, enjoying the beautiful sunny evening. It was there, on a green space bench, that Brent handed me a card and revealed his heartwarming proposal. Without hesitation, I embraced him with a hug and kiss and happily exclaimed, "Yes!" The ring sparkled on my finger, and we took pictures to share our joy with close family and friends.

The excitement continued when we returned home, and I found our ensuite bath adorned with rose petals, a touching gesture orchestrated by Keegan before he left for his hockey game. It was heartwarming to see how Brent had involved Keegan in his engagement plans, and it reaffirmed the support and love that we all shared as a family.

Two weeks later, we combined an already planned birthday celebration with our engagement party. With an added reason to celebrate, it turned into an even more meaningful and joyous event. Surrounded by friends from work and the neighbourhood, we felt incredibly supported and cherished. Our journey of growth, healing, and love had been witnessed by those around us, and their encouragement became the foundation of our newfound circle of trust.

20

SHORTLY AFTER OUR engagement, I began noticing changes in Brent's behaviour that raised concerns. Sleep became a challenge for him, as he had difficulty falling and staying asleep. He would often jerk and exhibit signs of distress during his restless nights. Throughout the day, he became quieter and more distracted, frequently forgetting things. His appetite changed, and he started eating less. When I gently broached the subject, he attributed these issues to the demanding workload and frequent travel he was undertaking. But deep down, I knew there was more to it. My intuition told me there was something beyond the surface explanation. I recalled that Brent had visited a psychologist while he was working in Edmonton, which was part of the regular assessments required for police officers. However, I later learned that this visit was not a routine evaluation. His colleagues had noticed changes in his mood and behaviour, and they suggested he might benefit from seeing a psychologist. Reluctantly, he went, but with a predetermined mindset. He merely answered questions to "pass" the assessment rather than engaging fully to seek help. He harboured a strong self-stigma, believing that showing any vulnerability would jeopardize his success as a police officer. In his eyes, revealing his own mental health challenges was not acceptable, given the negative association that society placed on such issues.

As his loving partner, I encouraged him to reconsider seeking help from someone else who might be able to provide the support he needed. I knew that breaking down the barriers of self-stigma and seeking help was not an easy path, but I also understood the importance of addressing these issues before they worsened. I wanted him to know that seeking help was not a sign of weakness. On the contrary, it took immense courage to confront one's own struggles and seek assistance. I hoped he would come to realize that acknowledging and addressing his mental health was an essential step in maintaining his well-being and overall happiness. He deserved the same compassion and support he so generously offered to others.

The stigma surrounding mental illness is a significant challenge, affecting both how others perceive those with mental health difficulties and how individuals with mental illness view themselves. In the context of police professionals, this stigma can have severe consequences on their personal well-being and the communities they serve. Startling statistics from a national survey in Canada[2] revealed alarming rates of mental health disorders among police officers, with a significant percentage screening positive for conditions like depression, PTSD, generalized anxiety disorder, and hazardous drinking. These issues can lead to impairments in attention, self-regulation, and interpersonal interactions, ultimately hindering their ability to provide empathetic and fair support to community members.

---

2 RN Carleton et al. "Mental disorder symptoms among police safety personnel in Canada," The *Canadian Journal of Psychiatry,* 2018 Jan; 63(1):54-64. doi: 10.1177/0706743717723825.

The root of this mental health crisis among police officers can be traced back to the very culture within the force. Law enforcement professionals are often conditioned to suppress their emotions, fearing that expressing vulnerability might interfere with their decision-making, performance, or career advancement. In adhering to the traditional ideals of masculinity prevalent in the police culture, seeking emotional support or acknowledging emotional challenges is perceived as a sign of weakness. Consequently, many officers struggle with feelings of shame and fear being stigmatized if they express their emotional struggles. The fear of undermining their own professional competence by seeking help for mental health issues further reinforces this avoidance of support.[3]

This internalized self-stigma creates what is known as the "help-seeking pathway." Public stigma, driven by society's negative views on seeking mental health assistance, can become internalized as self-stigma, leading individuals to believe that seeking help is socially unacceptable and could damage their self-worth. This negative self-perception influences attitudes toward seeking help, ultimately discouraging police officers from reaching out for the support they need. Numerous studies have highlighted the significant impact of public stigma and self-stigma as barriers to officers seeking help for their mental health challenges.

In a striking contradiction, Brent was actively working on a peer-support program to reduce stigma and provide an outlet for those struggling with mental health issues within the police force. He encouraged members to engage in open conversations with each other and to seek professional help when necessary. However, despite his dedication to breaking

---

3 Grupe, D. W.. Mental health stigma and help-seeking intentions in police employees. *Journal of Community Safety and Well-Being, 8* (Suppl_1) (2023): S32-S39. https://doi.org/10.35502/jcswb.290

down stigma for others, Brent was grappling with significant self-stigma, finding it difficult to acknowledge that he too could benefit from following the same advice he advocated.

The paradox of his situation highlighted the complexity of confronting self-stigma. It was a reminder that even those working to make a difference in the mental health landscape can face their own internal barriers when seeking help. Nevertheless, this realization emphasized the importance of promoting a culture that fosters openness, understanding, and compassion, empowering individuals to reach out for help without fear of judgment or negative repercussions. By acknowledging and addressing self-stigma within the police force, we can create a supportive environment that allows officers to prioritize their well-being, ultimately benefiting both the individuals and the communities they serve.

Brent's journey towards healing and understanding began with his sessions with Dr. Andre. Their rapport was established quickly, and they met every two to three weeks. Early on, much of their focus was on formal assessments, aiming to determine a baseline of Brent's condition to inform the course of treatment. It was during these assessments that Brent received his diagnosis of post-traumatic stress disorder (PTSD) and Major Depressive Disorder.

For Brent, this diagnosis didn't come as a complete surprise. He had been grappling with a sense of inner unease for quite some time, though he had learned to mask it and adapt to this new, muted reality. He believed that starting a new life with me and Alexis, along with the meaningful job he had taken, would help shift his mindset. However, the opposite seemed to be happening, and the changes in his life were exacerbating his symptoms. The stress of the move, the demands of his new job, and the change of pace were all taking a toll on his well-being. His brain was struggling to cope with the mounting pressure.

Dr. Andre, seeking a comprehensive understanding of Brent's situation, invited me to attend a session with them. As I sat beside Brent, I was asked to describe his behaviour, the things I had noticed about his way of being, his reactions to events at work and home, and his patterns. It was evident from Dr. Andre's probing questions and Brent's demeanour that this was the first time some of these observations had been shared. With my input, Dr. Andre was able to paint a more complete picture of the situation.

The latter half of the session was dedicated to explaining the intricacies of PTSD—how it develops and its impact on the brain. This part of the conversation intrigued me, tapping into my science degree. I felt that delving into the biological and physiological aspects of Brent's condition would provide me with a clearer understanding of the behaviours I was witnessing. Fueled by a desire to support Brent fully, I threw myself into learning about his diagnosis and the challenges faced by individuals living with mental health issues.

As I delved into the intricacies of PTSD, I discovered the profound impact it can have on the brain's structures and functions. The consequences of this condition extend to various areas, influencing emotional regulation, memory, and decision-making.

One of the key regions affected by PTSD is the amygdala, a vital player in emotional processing and fear responses. In individuals with PTSD, the amygdala tends to become overactive, resulting in heightened feelings of anxiety and fear, even in seemingly safe situations. The hippocampus, responsible for memory and learning, can also be impacted by PTSD.

It may experience shrinkage, making it challenging for those affected to effectively process and retain new information.

Alterations in the prefrontal cortex, another crucial area of the brain, can further compound the challenges faced by individuals with PTSD. This region is responsible for decision-making and regulating emotions. In those with PTSD, the prefrontal cortex may exhibit decreased activity, leading to difficulties with emotional regulation and impulse control.

PTSD can disrupt the delicate balance of neurotransmitters in the brain—chemicals that play a pivotal role in regulating mood and other brain functions. Imbalances in neurotransmitters, such as serotonin and norepinephrine, are often associated with PTSD and can contribute to symptoms like depression and anxiety.

Overall, the impact of PTSD on the brain is far-reaching, affecting critical areas necessary for emotional regulation, memory consolidation, and decision-making processes. Understanding these neurological changes is crucial, as it can pave the way for more effective treatments and interventions to help individuals struggling with this disorder. Armed with this knowledge, I was better equipped to support Brent on his journey towards healing and recovery.

With a deep sense of empathy and commitment, I chose to stand by Brent's side as he navigated the complexities of the diagnosis. Witnessing the impact this condition had on his brain and emotions only strengthened my resolve to support him wholeheartedly. I knew that the journey towards healing would not be easy, but I was determined to be a source of unwavering support. Together, we faced the challenges of PTSD head-on, armed with understanding, compassion, and a shared determination to emerge stronger and more resilient.

Our love and partnership became the bedrock on which we built a future filled with hope, courage, and the realization that our commitment to one another was not just about embracing the joyful moments but also about facing life's challenges as a united front. Supporting Brent in his battle against PTSD became a journey of growth for both of us, as we learned to lean on each other, break down barriers, and embrace the vulnerability that comes with facing mental health challenges together.

Dr. Andre's suggestion for Brent to consider medication to help with his symptoms was met with strong resistance. Brent had reservations about taking "head meds," believing they were meant for people in more dire circumstances than his own. Witnessing the impact on his mother of the overuse of prescription drugs fueled his reluctance. He had a deep-seated resentment towards his mother, as he believed her mental health issues contributed to the severity of his own struggles from both a biological and historical perspective. The genetic link between them only added to his frustration and anger, which was prominently observed in the early days of his diagnosis.

Understanding the underlying emotions beneath Brent's anger was an important step in his healing. Dr. Andre explained that anger often masks other feelings that are causing individuals to act out with frustration. For Brent, the stigma surrounding mental health and unresolved emotions were significant factors contributing to his resistance towards seeking help and accepting medication.

In an effort to persuade Brent of the potential benefits of medication, I took a practical approach focused on the physical symptoms he experienced. I emphasized that improved sleep would lead to better engagement and performance at work—an essential aspect of his life he was determined not to compromise. Highlighting how his work could be negatively impacted if his sleep and concentration did not improve struck a chord with him, leading him to consider trying medication in the Spring of 2011.

The wait for the medication to take effect was difficult for all of us. Antidepressants often take six to eight weeks to show results, leaving patients grappling with feelings of impatience and uncertainty. We hoped for a positive shift in Brent's condition, not only for his sake but also for all of us living with him. However, as the weeks passed, it became apparent that the medication did not have a significant impact. Brent continued to be symptomatic, struggling to maintain a facade at work while feeling exhausted and unmotivated once he returned home.

Despite this setback, I remained steadfast in my commitment to supporting Brent through this challenging time. I understood that finding the right course of treatment could be a trial-and-error process, but I was determined to stand by him, providing the understanding and love he needed as we continued together.

Dr. Andre's guidance led Brent to consider applying to Veteran Affairs Canada (VAC) for a duty-related pension due to injury or illness. However, this process was far from easy. To make his claim, Brent had to delve into memories of difficult calls and files he had actively tried to forget and suppress for years. Recounting these traumatic incidents in writing was a challenge, especially for someone battling mental illness and struggling to concentrate and focus. Over the course of four months, I worked closely with Brent, helping him articulate each event and its impact. In total, he described twenty-seven traumatic events in his application.

Listening to Brent recount these stories granted me a profound understanding of the man he was. It was reminiscent of the insights I gained when Gord and Glenna shared tales of Brent's childhood, revealing glimpses into the history of the man I had fallen in love with. These stories provided me with a deeper lens of compassion and empathy, fueling my desire to support Brent in the best way possible. As we embarked on this journey together, I realized that my role as a fiancée and future wife would expand to include that of a project manager and administrative assistant. I recognized that I could have a direct impact on creating an environment where Brent, Keegan, and Alexis could thrive as their best selves, despite the challenges posed by mental illness. I embraced this responsibility wholeheartedly, knowing that it would strengthen our bond and bring us even closer together. I was all in.

With this newfound understanding, it became my mission to foster a space where they could feel safe, understood, and loved unconditionally. I knew that navigating the challenges of mental illness and the complexities of family life would require patience, resilience, and a deep commitment to each other's well-being. I took on the responsibility of learning as much as I could about mental health, attending workshops, and seeking guidance from mental health professionals. Armed with this knowledge, I was better equipped to recognize the signs of distress and provide the necessary support.

Communication became the cornerstone of our family dynamics, encouraging open dialogues about feelings, emotions, and coping strategies. As we continued to face the ups and downs of Brent's journey towards healing, I remained steadfast in my unwavering support. I celebrated every milestone, no matter how small, acknowledging the immense strength and courage it took for Brent to confront his past and work towards a better future. Through it all, I never lost sight of the love and admiration I had for him—a love that grew even stronger as I witnessed his resilience and determination.

In my efforts to create a harmonious home, I made it a point to incorporate self-care practices into our daily routine. We embraced activities that brought joy and relaxation, whether it was spending time in nature, pursuing hobbies, or simply sharing laughter together. By prioritizing self-care, we cultivated a sense of balance in our lives.

After much effort and dedication, the VAC application was finally submitted in August 2011. This allowed us to shift our focus to preparing for our upcoming wedding, just three months away. With the application completed, we felt a sense of relief and excitement as we eagerly anticipated the next chapter in our lives. We knew that, regardless of the challenges that lay ahead, we were in it together, ready to face whatever life had in store, as husband and wife.

21

THE PICTURESQUE TOWN of Banff, Alberta, served as the enchanting backdrop for our wedding on a crisp November day in 2011. The decision to choose this destination was driven by two significant factors that held special meaning for our family. Firstly, Glenna's ongoing cancer treatments made air travel impossible for her, prompting us to select a location within a manageable distance. Secondly, the boys were granted a day off school to observe Remembrance Day, perfectly aligning with our wedding date.

Our intimate wedding was a heartfelt gathering of only our closest family and friends, totaling thirty-one cherished guests. Alexis, Brent, and I embarked on our trip to Banff from Ottawa. Our luggage consisted of not only clothes and shoes to accommodate both winter and summer temperatures as we were headed to Hawaii for our honeymoon, but also carefully packed plastic totes filled with decorations, as well as garment bags housing my and Alexis' dresses and Brent's suit. Amid the bustling airport, Brent playfully joked that he felt like a sherpa, carrying all of our supplies.

Our arrival in Calgary marked the beginning of a joyous adventure, as we picked up our rental car and set off to meet

Chris' youngest brother, Peter, for lunch. It had been nearly a year since Peter had seen us, and the reunion was filled with warm embraces and fond memories. While tensions lingered between John, MaryAnn, and me regarding the pace of my relationship with Brent, the love and support from the Worden children remained steadfast.

With a heart full of anticipation and excitement, we continued our journey to the charming mountain village of Banff. Before checking into the hotel, we paused at the Banff Bureau to obtain our marriage licence, a tangible symbol of the commitment we were about to make. Reading the affidavits together, we affirmed that our love was genuine, and we were of sound mind, unswayed by any substances. From there we met with the Commissioner of Oaths, the individual who would officiate our ceremony, and our photographer, who would capture the precious moments of our special day. These preparations added to our sense of excitement.

As the Ontario crowd arrived on a Thursday evening, the anticipation of our upcoming wedding filled the air with excitement and joy. We gathered together, ordered pizza, and shared heartfelt conversations, retiring to bed early due to the time change. The following morning, Jordan, Keegan, and Keegan's girlfriend Jessica, joined us, adding to the sense of togetherness and celebration. Brent was thrilled to have all of us together, but I could sense he also felt the weight of nervousness and stress that naturally accompanied such a significant event. For someone living with a stress disorder, the prospect of a wedding and the influx of people and stimuli could be overwhelming, making the occasion more challenging for him.

In the lead-up to the wedding, I took on most of the preparations, with Brent actively involved in decisions while I executed the plans. My passion for project management made me well-suited for the task, and I embraced it gladly to take pressure off Brent. Throughout the gathering, I remained vigilant, keeping an eye on Brent for any physical signs of stress. Whenever I sensed him becoming overwhelmed, I would step in and find a way to give him a moment of respite. I also made sure to carry Tylenol and Advil, aware of his frequent and intense headaches. Being attentive to the early signs allowed us to address discomfort before it escalated.

As Friday evening approached, Brent and I opened the door to our suite, greeted by a stunning view of the mountains and the Bow River through large windows and a balcony. The atmosphere was joyous, with Alexis and my nephews playfully throwing snowballs over the railings. The adults mingled, toasting to the upcoming celebration. Eventually, the younger crowd headed to a local restaurant and lounge to continue the festivities, while the grandparents lovingly volunteered to babysit.

In the dimly lit and bustling lounge, emotions ran high, and heartfelt conversations ensued. Among the guests was my friend, Michèle. Tearfully, I expressed my gratitude for her support over the years and the significance of her presence at my wedding. I shared with her my joy at finding love twice in my lifetime. These tears were a reflection of the effort and resilience I had put into reaching this point in my life. A journey of survival, grief, and ultimately choosing happiness.

In less than eighteen hours, I would become Mrs. Baulkham, dedicating myself as a loving, loyal, and faithful wife to Brent. Through sickness and in health, I was committed to standing by his side, and I felt a profound sense of readiness and anticipation for the lifelong journey we were about to embark on together.

The wedding day was nothing short of exquisite, filled with excitement and a few anxious jitters. The boys did an excellent job supporting Brent in the hours we were apart on the morning of the wedding. They shared that it took Brent seven tries to get his tie just right! Having our children play a part in the wedding made it all the more special. Alexis looked absolutely adorable in her dress, while Keegan and Jordan looked dapper in their matching shirts and ties.

For Alexis and my nephew Cohen, the roles of flower girl and boy were an adorable addition to the ceremony. Together they held a basket, joyfully tossing purple fabric petals onto the short aisle runner adorned with our purple, pink, and grey wedding logo. Although I couldn't see them from where I waited outside, I could hear the loving sounds of family members oohing and awing over their cuteness.

As the time came for me to walk down the aisle, I made the choice to do so on my own. In my previous wedding, both of my parents had given me away. However, this time, I wanted to present myself as an independent woman, making a deliberate choice to be with Brent. The music changed, and the officiant's voice rang out, inviting everyone to stand and welcome the bride. As I rounded the corner, I saw Brent standing just a short distance away, his face beaming with a huge smile and a touch of mist in his eyes. To my right were Keegan and Jordan, and to my left, my sister Deb, my maid of honour, stood alongside Alexis and Cohen. Our family and friends filled the room, their faces radiating delight as they stood facing me. Beyond the windows, majestic snow-capped mountains served as a breathtaking backdrop to our special moment. It was nothing short of perfect.

The civil service was concise yet deeply personal. We had written our own vows, expressing them with honesty and sincerity, promising to cherish each other's friendship and love forever. We vowed to trust and respect one another, to share both laughter and tears, and to love each other faithfully through the highs and lows that life would bring. As I signed the registry, gratitude and excitement welled up within me. I was surrounded by new, supportive, and loving family members, and I cherished the authentic friendships that allowed me to be my true self. With Brent by my side, I felt empowered to continue evolving into the best version of myself.

Our intimate guest list allowed Brent and me to truly engage with each person, basking in the love and support they had for us. The celebration was a beautiful testament to our journey together, a moment of joy as we embraced the future hand in hand. Our wedding song, "Marry Me" by Train, provided the perfect soundtrack to the beginning of our life together as husband and wife. Halfway through the song, Alexis ran up to us and hugged our legs. Her little face was buried in the fabric of my dress. Brent effortlessly picked her up and the three of us finished the dance together. It is a most cherished memory. To this day, when this song comes on the radio, Brent and I stop what we are doing and dance together. It brings us back to these happy moments and reminds us of our celebration of love.

One of the highlights of the day was the sand ceremony. After Brent and I exchanged vows, Alexis, Keegan, and Jordan joined us. I had purchased purple sand for Alexis and I and brown sand for Brent, Keegan, and Jordan. The officiant read the following:

> *We will now celebrate the creation of this new Baulkham family. The five vases of sand represent Jodie, Brent, Keegan, Jordan, and Alexis. As we joined Jodie and Brent in marriage, we are reminded of the significant role that Keegan, Jordan, and Alexis play in their lives. As each pours in their sand, a visual representation of love and mutual respect is created. Just as the grains of sand are forever intermixed, so are the lives of the people being celebrated today.*

On the day that we poured the sand into the vase, the delineation between purple and brown was very evident. There was some overlap, but it was clear where one ended and the next began. Each time the vase was repositioned or was placed in a suitcase or moving box to travel to its next destination, the grains of sand mixed more and settled into new positions. With each touchpoint, the delineation became less noticeable. There was no way to see where the purple ended and the brown began.

Over time it had become a new colour, created from the cycle of turbulence and rest it experienced over the years. The new colour is more intriguing and artful than the original. I didn't know then how this visual representation of love and mutual respect would mirror the path that our lives would take. The vase holds a predominant place in our living room décor. It is a daily reminder of how far we've come and how the effects of turbulence can be beautiful.

22

EARLY INTO OUR marriage, we encountered a formidable emotional hurdle. Both of us working on the same floor of our office building, Brent and I found ourselves entangled in the web of rumours and formal communications from the Human Resources leadership team. The shadow of the 2008 recession loomed large, with the federal government demanding departmental budget cuts. Efficiencies were sought, programs were slashed, and the peer-support program Brent had tirelessly worked on became a casualty. The news hit him like a tidal wave, leaving his mind, body, and soul in turmoil. Adding to the storm, Keegan's return to Alberta coincided with the loss of Brent's position. As if caught in an emotional whirlwind, Brent's symptoms intensified, becoming more severe and persistent.

Constant headaches tormented him, like relentless drum beats in the background of his daily struggle. They became an unwelcome companion, a shadow that refused to leave his side. Forced into an impenetrable shell of silence, he withdrew from the world, retreating to the inner chambers of his mind where even his family couldn't reach him. His silence echoed through the house like a haunting melody, leaving everyone around him yearning for just a word, a sign, anything to break through the wall he had erected.

Seclusion became his solace, and he cocooned himself within the walls of our home. It was as if he had become a hermit in his own dwelling, shutting out the outside world. The vibrant sounds of laughter and joy that once filled our home were replaced by an eerie silence that weighed heavily on our hearts. It was like living on a deserted island of emotions, where the tides of despair constantly threatened to engulf us.

Within this gloomy landscape, there was a glimmer of hope named Alexis. She was like a radiant beam of sunlight breaking through the thick, dark clouds that shrouded our lives. Despite Brent's emotional retreat, he found solace in her presence. Her laughter became a lifeline, and her infectious enthusiasm brought brief moments of respite to his troubled soul.

However, when it came to Keegan and Jordan, he merely listened, avoiding any revelations about his inner struggles. He resembled a vault, carefully guarding its secrets from prying eyes. It was like watching a magician skillfully distract the audience, performing an illusion while concealing the true source of his pain.

As for me, Brent was often emotionally distant, his heart guarded by the traumas. Despite understanding the medical aspects of his condition, I felt like a helpless spectator witnessing a tragedy unfold before my eyes.

Acknowledging the toll it was taking on him, with the support of his family doctor and Dr. Andre, he made the difficult decision to go Off Duty Sick (ODS). Yet, self-stigma gnawed at him, and he grappled with fears of being perceived as someone taking advantage of the system.

With hope and uncertainty mingling in our hearts, we set out to find help in the form of a psychiatrist, recommended by Brent's family doctor. The anticipation built as the day of his appointment neared. Together, we entered the office of Dr. Arora, a calming presence in a small medical building down the road from the hospital. The room exuded an aura of tranquility, with soft instrumental music playing, inspirational quotes adorning the walls, and the lingering scent of incense. It was unlike any medical setting we had encountered before—more like stepping into a peaceful sanctuary, offering relief from the turbulence of our lives.

Dr. Arora, a gentle and wise man of East Indian descent, provided a safe space for Brent to open up about his struggles. During the appointment, I took on a supportive role, letting Brent take the lead in sharing his story with the doctor. To my surprise, the session was nothing like the hurried encounters I had feared, with a doctor pushing a prescription at us and then rushing us out the door. Dr. Arora genuinely listened, asked thoughtful questions, and guided Brent through a transformative meditation.

Brent's recovery took on multiple dimensions, involving regular medical appointments that became a staple in our lives. Despite these efforts, Brent's emotional struggles persisted, and it was clear that more intervention was necessary. A sleep test revealed the presence of obstructive sleep apnea, prompting the prescription of a CPAP machine to help him achieve much-needed restful sleep.

In our quest to better understand Brent's emotional state, we implemented the number system. Each day, I would gently inquire, "What's your number?"

On a scale from one to ten, with ten being the best and one being the worst, Brent would rate his mood. Keeping track of these daily assessments became crucial, and we used a small calendar as a visual aid to help us identify patterns and potential triggers in his fluctuating emotions.

Admittedly, some days were met with resistance. I would encounter eye rolls, frustrated facial expressions, and the occasional grunt or unpleasant word. But despite the challenges, Brent always provided me with an answer. On those difficult days, the number he gave was typically low, a clear reminder of the battles he was fighting within himself. Yet, as his partner, I was determined to stay by his side, supporting him in every way I could as we navigated this path together.

While the pieces were falling into place, and our efforts were aligned, progress remained elusive. I continued my full-time job, and Brent took on the responsibility of driving Alexis to school. Although the morning routine provided a sense of structure, the rest of the day proved challenging for Brent to navigate.

Brent's longing to return to work was obvious; being Staff Sergeant Brent Baulkham was an integral part of his identity. His connection to the RCMP defined him, and the thought of not being an active member left him feeling adrift, unsure of who he truly was. As fate would have it, an opportunity arose when a specialized unit was formed to update the grievance and harassment processes within the organization. Given his expertise and experience, Brent was a natural fit for this role, and he was accepted into the unit with open arms. This marked the beginning of his gradual return to work. Despite my concerns about his readiness, he remained insistent that this would be a positive step forward.

To ensure a smooth transition after months of being Off Duty Sick, Brent's family doctor prescribed a carefully designed schedule for him. The process began with a cautious approach, where he would work three days a week, with each day limited to a three-hour duration. Over the course of the following weeks, the weekly hours would gradually increase, with the ultimate goal of returning to full-time hours within six weeks.

Filled with a renewed sense of purpose, Brent's first day back at the office saw him energetically working for eight hours, eager to make a meaningful impact in his new role. The following day, he repeated the feat, dedicating himself wholeheartedly to his responsibilities. However, despite his determination and the support surrounding him, the challenges of his return began to manifest.

As the days wore on, the pressure of his role and the stress of being back in the work environment started to take a toll on Brent's well-being. The weight of expectations, both self-imposed and external, bore down on him, exacerbating his existing symptoms. The emotional turmoil and strain on his ego became evident, leading to a reemergence of his distressing symptoms.

The impact of this relapse was even more profound than his first bout with being ODS, leaving Brent to grapple with a deep sense of disappointment and frustration and forcing him to confront not only his symptoms but also his identity and self-worth.

During those sombre days, I found myself gripped by an unsettling fear, dreading the possibility that Brent might succumb to the darkness within him. It was like watching a candle flicker in a strong gust of wind, uncertain if it would remain lit or be snuffed out. Week after week, he casually rated his torment as a mere two or three, but his vacant eyes betrayed a deeper anguish. It was as if his eyes were windows to an abandoned house, void of any signs of life.

Attempting different approaches to break through his emotional fortress, I experimented with silence, allowing days to pass with minimal communication beyond the necessities of parenting. It was like walking on a tightrope, balancing between giving him space and yearning for a connection. I desperately wanted to be his anchor, but it felt like I was clinging to a ghost, reaching out to something that slipped through my fingers like sand.

I met his perceived anger with my own, hoping to elicit any response. It was like sparks colliding, waiting for a flame to ignite, but all he offered was a blank stare as he walked away, seemingly impervious to my animated outbursts. It was like standing in the pouring rain, hoping to be noticed, yet only feeling the cold droplets on my skin.

Tearfully, I poured my heart out to him, only to receive an embrace that felt distant and hollow. It was like holding onto a fragile piece of glass, where the harder I tried to grip it, the more it seemed to slip away from me.

Later, in moments of clarity and improved health, Brent confessed that anger was the sole emotion he could access during those trying times. It was like a torrential river that swept him away, leaving no room for empathy or compassion. My distress, my tears—none of it could evoke empathy from him. It was like trying to warm oneself by a fire that had long extinguished.

Our journey as a newly married couple was met with an unexpected emotional distance, leaving each day fraught with the struggle to understand and connect. It was like walking through a maze with no clear path, constantly searching for an exit that remained elusive. But amidst the shadows and complexities, I clung to hope, knowing that every maze has its exit, and every storm subsides.

Eventually.

23

SHORTLY AFTER LEAVING Toronto, where we visited Deb and her family for the weekend, Brent's emotional turmoil reached a tipping point. As we drove back to Ottawa, he suddenly pulled over on the highway and asked me to take the wheel. His distress was obvious as tears streamed down his face behind his dark sunglasses and he trembled in discomfort. Upon reaching home, Brent hastily exited the vehicle and disappeared into the house without a word. Alexis and I followed, entering the house together. I began calling out his name. Brent was unresponsive to my calls. Worried, I searched the entire house, checking everywhere until I found him in the spare room, lying on his side, rolling back and forth and groaning in distress. I tried to assess the situation, asking if he was experiencing chest pains or possibly having a heart attack, but his response was a faint "no."

Swiftly, I ensured Alexis was settled in the living room, trying to maintain an air of calm for her. Returning to Brent, I laid down beside him, gently cradling him in an attempt to provide comfort and reassurance.

Softly speaking to him, I said, "You are safe. We are here together. It's going to be okay." Gradually, he settled a bit, and I stayed by his side, offering comfort and support. Over the next two days, he remained mostly in our bedroom.

I reached out to Dr. Andre that night, and he promptly contacted me the next morning. He suspected that Brent might have experienced a transient ischaemic attack (TIA), but only an MRI could confirm this. With the RCMP's help, I secured an appointment within 24 hours, and the results came back as "unremarkable," thankfully ruling that out.

Despite this positive outcome, it was evident that Brent's nervous system was under tremendous strain. His prolonged distress had taken its toll, leaving his body and mind in a state of exhaustion. Dr. Arora prescribed a new medication to help regulate his system, and Brent continued to seek support from Dr. Andre, as well as chiropractors and massage therapists to address his physical symptoms.

Alongside his frequent headaches, Brent also struggled with chronic pain, as if his body was storing all the stress in his lower back. This discomfort made it challenging for him to perform simple tasks like getting up from a seated position or walking up and down stairs. The persistent pain contributed to his irritability, compounding the difficulties he faced.

In the midst of Brent's struggles, I felt compelled to step up and infuse our home with positivity and energy. Recognizing that he was unable to find joy during this challenging time, I made it my mission to fill our household with as much positivity as possible, not just for him but for all of us.

Following this central nervous system breakdown, I made the decision to take a few weeks off work to be at home with him. It was crucial for me to show Brent that he was not alone, that I cared deeply, and that I was there to support him through this challenging time. My concern for his well-being was at an all-time high, and I wanted to be by his side to ensure he didn't have the opportunity to act on any suicidal thoughts he might be experiencing.

During this period, I took a step back and reassessed our daily routines and activities. I carefully examined all the tasks that needed to be done in a day, from cooking and cleaning to laundry, school driving, and work commitments. I even included things like grocery shopping, Alexis' after-school activities, socializing with friends, medical appointments, landscaping, and phone calls with family. It was an exercise I had done before, in times of upheaval, to gain a sense of control over our circumstances and identify areas that needed attention.

Through this life activity audit, I could see where we were spending our time and which activities were contributing positively or negatively to our family's ability to cope with the current struggles. By pinpointing our priorities, I was able to create plans and structures to ensure our needs were met during these tough days.

The most significant change I made was choosing to reduce my work hours in half. With the support and guidance of my colleague LeeAnne, I proposed a job-sharing arrangement to my management, and thankfully, they were understanding and accommodating. This adjustment allowed me to spend more time at home, taking on more of the daily responsibilities, and offering Brent the space and support he needed to focus on his health and recovery. It was a challenging decision, but it proved to be a pivotal step in providing the care and attention our family required during this difficult period.

As Brent needed a few days to process his appointments with Dr. Andre or Dr. Arora before he could talk to me about them, I learned to give him the necessary space to be in control of what he wanted to share. Initially, I would eagerly inquire about his sessions right after he returned, but I soon realized that this approach was not helpful. His memory and mental acuity couldn't provide the level of conversation recall I desired, and I had to be patient and understanding as he shared generalities, jumping around based on what he could remember.

Periodically, we attended sessions together, either with Dr. Andre or Dr. Arora. These sessions served as opportunities for me to learn the tools and strategies that Brent was encouraged to integrate and practice at home. They included methods to counter negative thoughts, acknowledging uncomfortable emotions without actively avoiding them, focusing on breathwork, practicing mindfulness, engaging in physical exercise, maintaining a healthy diet, and spending time in nature. While these suggestions were valuable, I noticed that he was not putting many of them into practice, and so wasn't forming new healthy habits.

The doctors explained that creating and implementing new habits was especially difficult for individuals like Brent, who had been suffering from chronic pain and avoidance, and who were experiencing acute, intense symptoms. Unfortunately, allowing the condition to progress to the point of breakdown meant that the journey towards healing and regulation would be long and challenging. We all agreed that a coordinated effort was required to support Brent in the best way possible. The doctors would provide the professional health perspective, employing techniques and medication to serve Brent's needs. Meanwhile, my role was to ensure that Brent followed their prescriptions and advice at home.

This responsibility presented challenges for both Brent and me. He wasn't always the most compliant patient, and my patience was often tested. Some days, our dynamic wasn't ideal, as he would get frustrated by what he perceived as "nagging," leading to more resistance on his part. On my end, I found myself getting frustrated because he wasn't listening or doing what he was "supposed" to do. It felt like I was parenting both Alexis and Brent, and the parenting strategies that had worked with Alexis as a young child were not as effective in dealing with Brent's situation. I knew I had to learn a new approach and do so quickly, but it wasn't an easy task.

Once again, I found myself slipping into my project manager frame of mind. I knew that to support Brent effectively, we needed to address the tools and strategies offered to him, but finding the right time for this conversation was a challenge. Brent's emotional state could fluctuate, making it difficult to engage in a productive way when his number was below four. To tackle this obstacle, I devised a plan and created a document outlining the options for him. This way, we could focus on one option at a time and discuss how to implement it into his daily life.

Drawing from a teaching technique I learned while working with elementary students, I used a sheet of paper to cover the lines of the document we weren't discussing, keeping our focus on one sentence at a time. We delved into each choice, discussing how it would fit into Brent's daily life, setting up reminders, and tracking progress. Brent took the lead in suggesting how he wanted to implement the techniques, while I played the role of asking questions and taking notes. This approach empowered him, giving him more control in deciding how he wanted to be supported. It was a significant step forward for us, reducing tension and fostering a deeper understanding of his needs.

After a few days of going through the options, Brent chose to start with exercise and diet. As he established habits and routines centred around daily exercise and healthier eating and became more consistent, he added another technique, one step at a time. This gradual approach made it more manageable, and although he wasn't always 100% successful in practicing everything every day, it made a noticeable difference. The best part was that we were no longer arguing about the strategies; instead, our frustrations with each other began to subside.

A significant decision we made together to support Brent's treatment plan was to get a mini-goldendoodle puppy named Jak—the first initial of each of the kid's names, Jordan, Alexis, and Keegan. As a means to encourage daily activity and reconnect with nature, we welcomed this adorable red-haired fur-baby into our lives filling our days with newfound joy. Initially, the plan was to train Jak as a service dog, and I worked diligently with the trainer to prepare him for public spaces. We ventured together to hospitals, grocery stores, playgrounds, and friends' homes, with Jak wearing his "service dog in training " vest. However, Brent found himself uncomfortable with the idea of having a service dog accompany him in public. He preferred not to draw attention to himself and felt he could manage daily tasks without such support.

We adjusted our approach, and Jak no longer wore the training vest. Instead, we focused on providing him with the love, care, and attention he deserved. Jak became a cherished addition to our family, especially for Alexis, who, at the age of seven, adored her new puppy companion. Jak's presence in our lives proved to be a perfect match, and he played a significant role in further strengthening our family unit. Jak's arrival in our family had incredible benefits for Brent's mental health, offering a bond that required no expectations or pressures.

As a loyal and affectionate companion, Jak intuitively sensed Brent's emotions and offered nonjudgmental support during challenging moments. When Brent was feeling anxious or overwhelmed, Jak would instinctively nuzzle up against him, providing a comforting presence that eased his tension. The simple act of petting Jak or taking him for a walk helped Brent ground himself, bringing a sense of calm and peace to his troubled mind. Jak's playful and joyful nature served as a gentle reminder of life's simple pleasures. Watching him frolic and play brought smiles to all of our faces, and Brent found solace in this carefree display of happiness. Having Jak by his side also encouraged Brent to engage in more outdoor activities, as taking him for walks became a daily routine that provided much-needed physical exercise and fresh air. Week by week, Brent's numbers improved, and I finally felt a positive trend in his treatment efforts.

However, even as Brent was making progress, the symbols and structures associated with the RCMP continued to be major triggers for him. It broke my heart to see him suffer. The thought of stepping into the headquarters building made him feel nauseous, and news stories about efforts to change the organization's culture and management would send him into a tailspin. I couldn't help but worry about the impact this had on him and on our family dynamics. It was difficult for me to work at the RCMP knowing it added to the tension in our lives. I wanted to support him in every way possible, but I also wanted to respect my needs to continue working in an area where I felt like I was making a difference. Contributing to leadership development was my way of changing the culture.

About two years after Brent first went ODS, in the Spring of 2014, he decided to break employee protocol and speak with the media, critiquing how the RCMP supports its members with mental health issues. With his mental well-being improving, Brent wanted to assist others and believed that speaking out publicly could raise awareness and apply pressure for positive change. It took immense courage for him to share his story publicly, and I couldn't have been prouder of his bravery. Yet, I also felt the weight of this decision on our shoulders. I worried about the potential consequences for him, but I also saw how it was a turning point in his recovery. Witnessing his vulnerability and determination to help others in similar situations made me feel closer to him than ever before.

As I witnessed Brent's mental well-being improve and saw how his willingness to share his struggles started lifting the burden of self-stigma and sparked conversations about mental health within our circles, it deeply impacted me as his wife. It was a rollercoaster of emotions for me, filled with hope, pride, and an overwhelming sense of responsibility.

I had to learn a new approach, be patient, and give him the space to share his thoughts and feelings in his own time. It was a delicate balance of being present without being intrusive, offering comfort without pushing too hard. I cherished the moments of progress and hope, but I also learned to be patient and understanding during the more difficult times. As I watched him navigate the complexities of his recovery, I had to dig deep within myself to find the strength and resilience to stand by his side, no matter how challenging it became.

Brent's journey was not just his; it became ours, intertwining our lives in ways that shaped who we were as individuals and as a couple.

During this period of reflection and self-discovery, Brent made the brave and crucial decision to prioritize his well-being by medically discharging from the RCMP in May 2015. It wasn't an easy choice, but it was the right one for his health. In a private ceremony hosted by the Commanding Officer of National Headquarters, Brent's dedicated service was honoured and recognized. It was a bittersweet occasion witnessing this pivotal moment in his life filled with mixed emotions swirling in the air. On one hand, I was proud of him for putting his health first and making a difficult decision that would lead to a new chapter in his life. On the other hand, I felt a pang of uncertainty and concern about what this would mean for our future as a family. The path ahead remained unknown, and it was both exhilarating and frightening to consider and anticipate.

24

WE TOOK THE plunge and purchased the adjacent lot to build our dream bungalow, seeking to eliminate the challenging stairs in our current home. The idea of staying in the neighbourhood we loved and overseeing the construction excited me, and I thought it would be a perfect project for Brent. My hope was that it would serve as a positive distraction, steering his focus away from not working in the RCMP and giving him a renewed sense of purpose.

As the construction of our house progressed, I found myself caught in a delicate balancing act. On one hand, I was thrilled about the prospect of having a beautiful new home, designed exactly the way we wanted it. The excitement of collaborating with Brent on every detail, from the layout to the decor, was invigorating. I felt a surge of pride in the decisions we made together, knowing they would shape our lives for years to come.

However, alongside the excitement, there was an undercurrent of concern and stress. I couldn't ignore the toll the building process was taking on Brent, especially considering his ongoing struggles with a stress disorder and emotional regulation. Dr. Andre's words echoed in my mind, reminding me that this experience could be exceptionally stressful for most people, let alone someone like Brent, who needed careful support and understanding.

Every day, as I watched Brent navigate the complexities of construction, I was acutely aware of his emotional roller coaster. There were moments when he seemed overwhelmed by the activity and progress, and I could see how it heightened his anxiety. On other occasions, he became frustrated and irritable when things didn't move as quickly as he hoped. Witnessing these fluctuations in his emotional state weighed heavily on me, and I felt an immense responsibility to be his anchor through it all.

The pressure of making swift decisions about various aspects of the house also posed challenges. Brent struggled with the demands of timeliness, and I would often receive calls at work, where his voice betrayed the mounting stress he was under. It became apparent that I needed to be available to provide support, even while juggling my own responsibilities.

In response to Brent's emotional strain, we tried to create a buffer between him and the construction manager, asking them to contact me first before presenting any issues. This small adjustment provided some relief, but there were still days when I returned home to find Brent visibly tense and overwhelmed by the process.

Despite the difficulties, the experience allowed us to grow as a couple. It forced us to improve our communication and collaboration skills, finding ways to navigate challenges together. We faced moments of tension, but also found moments of joy when we saw our collective efforts come to fruition in the design.

After selling our house, we found ourselves with a six-week gap before we could move into our new home. During this time, we decided to live in our motorhome at a local campground. Alexis absolutely loved this living arrangement, but Brent and I quickly grew weary of it. Fortunately, we had a trip to London, England, planned during this time, which provided a welcome escape. We were away for ten days, leaving Alexis in the care of John and MaryAnn while Brent and I explored a potential business venture.

The creator of the program that Brent was eager to introduce into the RCMP for peer support offered us both an opportunity to become trained instructors. We saw the possibility of working together as a team for this company and bringing the program to Canada's context, providing consultancy to support first responder communities. The idea of these new possibilities filled us with excitement and anticipation.

However, as thrilling as the prospect was, traveling through crowded areas posed significant challenges for Brent. His anxiety levels were heightened, and he was always on high alert, scanning for potential threats. Standing in security lines at airports was particularly difficult for him. Thankfully, my project management skills had come in handy once again, as I had obtained Nexus cards to expedite our processing through security, alleviating some of Brent's concerns.

While traveling, I tried my best to minimize our time spent in crowded spaces, but it became more challenging when we arrived at Heathrow, one of the busiest airports in the world. We took our time navigating to the car rental booth, and I had everything arranged in advance to ease the process.

The training course we attended was located in the serene English countryside, providing a welcome contrast to the bustling airport. It was a fantastic week, filled with exploring the countryside, networking with other participants from the UK, and enjoying some tourist attractions. As I watched Brent during the training, I couldn't help but feel a mixture of pride and concern. I admired his determination to push forward despite the challenges posed by his PTSD. It wasn't easy for him, and I knew that being a student in such an intensive program while dealing with his condition was draining both physically and mentally. Yet, he never let his struggles define him, and he always presented himself with professionalism and grace.

I took detailed notes throughout the course, which we would review together in the evenings. His focus and concentration were tested to the limit, and he often expressed his frustration at not being able to absorb the information as he once could. I could see the toll it was taking on him. As his partner, it was heart-wrenching to witness his struggles, but I knew that he was doing his best, and that was all that mattered to me. Only a few days later did I fully realize the toll this intensive training had taken on Brent.

As we arranged to meet the program creator in London after the course, my heart brimmed with excitement about exploring the city and taking in iconic sights like Buckingham Palace and Big Ben. The thought of riding open-air double-decker buses and seeing the Princess Diana memorial fountain, and walking through Hyde Park filled me with joy and wonder. But amidst all the anticipation, there was a constant thread of concern woven within me: *how would Brent handle the crowded and overwhelming environments?*

As we ventured out that morning, I could sense Brent becoming increasingly anxious as the crowds grew around us. The police warnings about thieves in the crowd only added to his unease. I noticed his cheek begin to twitch, a telltale sign of his high stress response. We decided to change our plans and take a sightseeing bus to avoid the overwhelming crowds. I was enjoying the scenery from the upper level, including watching helicopters fly up and down the Thames River but noticed the blare of sirens as police, fire and ambulance personnel went about their daily work. Even our visit to Hyde Park, with its tranquil beauty, had its challenges, as the presence of homeless and intoxicated individuals added to the sensory overload for Brent.

It was time to make our way to a subway station to catch the Tube to Waterloo Station for our meeting. I purchased our tickets on the street and we entered the stairwell. I was slightly in front of him, but when I reached the platform and looked behind me, Brent was not in sight. I walked back up the stairs to find him sitting on a step, tears streaming down his face. My heart broke. The week's sensory onslaught had caught up with him, and the prospect of being in a metal tube underground, traveling at high speed, was simply too much for his frazzled nervous system. I sat beside him and took his trembling hand in mine, trying to be a source of comfort and strength. Encouraging him to stand, I suggested we take a cab to our meeting spot. Brent followed my lead without uttering a word.

In the cab, I did my best to soothe Brent and gave him Tylenol to alleviate any physical discomfort. We had forty minutes before our meeting was to begin. Waterloo Station is Britain's largest and busiest train station. With sunglasses on, Brent entered it with me. I quickly scanned and found that the upper level was less busy than the ground floor we were on. We took the escalator up and entered a pub. I asked for a private table. The hostess accommodated us and we sat away from other patrons. Brent put his head in his hands. I took his hands away from his face and held them in mine. Together we breathed. I guided him through the inhale-hold-exhale-hold process to help regulate his nervous system. We must have done this for at least fifteen minutes. He was able to stop crying and started talking quietly. He was so worried about not being able to participate in the meeting and appearing ill and unstable. I did my best to reassure him, emphasizing the meeting's informal nature and the understanding nature of the program creator. We exited the pub and made our way to the coffee shop where the meeting was taking place.

Our chat literally lasted eight minutes, much of it being about our travel and our experience with the course. These were topics that Brent could engage in with the level of energy he was able to muster. The meeting ended with a promise to stay in touch and he quickly departed to catch his train. Brent and I stayed in the coffee shop, his back towards the crowds for a few minutes longer. We both needed to take a moment to catch our breath.

The weeks following our return from London were challenging. It seemed as though Brent had been transported back in time, feeling out of place and disconnected. Being away from our home meant he couldn't access his exercise equipment or prepare meals in a full kitchen, adding to his frustration. Even something as basic as showering became a challenge due to the water being shut off at the campground. Our routines were disrupted, and it was taking a toll on both of us.

These changes manifested in various ways, primarily in Brent's struggle to access and engage his coping strategies. It was disheartening to see him face setbacks and realize that he wasn't yet well enough to pursue his interest in consulting. It felt like he was trapped in a cycle of grief, with each attempt at progress leading back to the beginning. I found myself wanting to help him break free from this cycle, but I knew that ultimately, he had to find his way through it.

Recognizing this pattern was a significant moment for me. It was like a lightbulb went off in my mind. The process of grief was one that I knew all too well. It was the first time that I thought I could somewhat relate to what he was going through, and it deepened my understanding of his struggles. It also reminded me that, as much as I wanted to help him, this was his path to navigate. I could be there to hold his hand, listen, and provide comfort, but it was up to him to continue making choices and taking control of his future. Understanding this allowed me to be more patient and compassionate towards him. It was a reminder that healing takes time and that progress is not always linear.

Each step forward, even if followed by a step back, was still a step in the right direction.

25

IN EARLY NOVEMBER 2014, after living in our RV for weeks, we stepped into our new home. The anticipation of this moment had been building, and as the doors swung open that evening, excitement flooded my senses. The three of us gathered around a simple foam mattress pad that we'd pulled from the RV. The living room floor became our dining room table and boxspring, a space where laughter and anticipation mingled in the air. The glow of the fireplace cast dancing shadows on the walls, and its warmth thawed away the lingering chill of the outside world.

With the aroma of freshly delivered pizza wafting through the room, we shared more than just a meal; we shared a moment frozen in time. Perched on the floor like children having a picnic, we savoured every bite, every laugh, every plan for the future that we etched into the evening.

As we lay there, side by side by side, the allure of slumber embraced us in its gentle arms. The night held the promise of a new dawn, when the sun would illuminate our home and our belongings would find their new place. With the warmth of each other's presence and the thrill of what tomorrow held, we drifted into dreams, united in our excitement for the morning to come.

Driven by a natural inclination for organization and structure, I wholeheartedly engaged in the process of unpacking. Time became an abstract concept as I methodically sifted through our possessions, ensuring each found its rightful niche in our new home.

Amidst the bustling activity of setting up our new space, there were boxes sheltering fragments of the past, memories lovingly preserved but carrying their own weight of bittersweet sentiment. Among them, Brent's cherished RCMP memorabilia and artwork, each piece encapsulating a period of his dedicated service. The plaques, trinkets, and artwork told a story of his postings through different detachments and units, a narrative etched in symbols that only he could truly understand.

There were also boxes from the North, tokens of kindness and condolences that had found their way to me after Chris' passing. These items bore the imprints of a life once lived, a past that I held dear in my heart but that I wanted to keep at a distance. Brent and I shared a mutual understanding that some pieces of our past were best kept tucked away. We chose to keep some of these emotional artefacts safely packed and placed them in the storage room. It was a conscious choice, a commitment to ushering in a fresh chapter unencumbered by the heavy burdens of our individual histories.

In planning the design of the interior of our new home, we poured our hearts into selecting decor, artwork, and furnishings that mirrored our joint vision. Each piece was chosen with intention, reflecting not only our personal tastes but also our combined vibe. And while we did allow a handful of sentimental mementos from our "old lives" to grace our living spaces, the overarching theme was one of renewal.

When a piece needed replacing or an update was due, it was an opportunity for us to collaborate, a chance to continue shaping the narrative of our family brand.

Part of building our family brand included empowering Alexis to organize and decorate her own room. It was such an exciting time for all of us. As she grew older, we knew it was time for her to have a bigger bed, so she happily upgraded to the double bed I had bought for Brent on his birthday back when he was living in Hay Lakes. Seeing her enthusiasm and taking charge of organizing and decorating her new room brought a smile to my face. We got cube furniture and bins, and she meticulously placed her books, stuffed animals, and keepsakes exactly where she wanted them. Her closet was organized by colour, with clothes hanging in rainbow order. I couldn't have been prouder of her independence and creativity.

At the age of nearly eight, Alexis was becoming more and more self-reliant, especially during her bedtime routine. She preferred to handle things on her own and would call us only when she was ready to be tucked in. However, my heart sank when I noticed that it was taking longer and longer for that call to come. As a concerned mother, I couldn't help but wonder what was going on behind the closed bathroom door as she spent about twenty minutes in there with the water running intermittently. Something felt off, and I wished I could peek in to reassure myself that she was okay.

After the bathroom routine, Alexis would spend another twenty minutes tidying her room, arranging her stuffed animals just right and giving each of them a goodnight kiss. If one accidentally fell off the bed, she would start the entire process again from the beginning. I worried about her, seeing her meticulous actions and the growing time she spent on each step.

I knew these behaviours could be signs of anxiety, and my heart ached at the thought of my little girl going through such emotions. Brent and I were both dealing with our own challenges, and the added concern for Alexis weighed heavily on my mind. We decided to seek guidance from Dr. Andre, who had a few sessions with Alexis, teaching her techniques to reduce her bedtime anxiety. He taught her how to focus on her senses, allowing her to relax and stay in the present moment. Breathing exercises were introduced to settle her nervous system, and he suggested gradually implementing change by removing one stuffed animal from the bed each week. I felt a mixture of relief and hope knowing that she was receiving support, but I still wished I could take away her worries completely. I desperately wanted to help her find her way to a calmer and more confident state of mind.

One evening shortly after Alexis' ninth birthday she came into my bedroom while I was reading. She was teary-eyed and said, "Mamma, I can't control my equals."

I put my book down and asked her to sit beside me and talk to me about the "equals." She explained that when she goes into her closet and her left shoulder touches the clothes, she needed to turn and make her right shoulder touch as well. What she did with one side of her body needed to be balanced out on the other side. She needed to touch all her stuffed animals with both hands at the same time or it didn't feel right and she wouldn't sleep. I listened to my little girl tell me her biggest secret. As we sat together, her head nestled into my shoulder, my head was spinning. *How can I help her?*

We consulted with Dr. Andre, who referred us to a child psychologist named Dr. Armstrong. Dr. Armstrong's focus was on exploring the impact of music on gifted children dealing with obsessive-compulsive disorder (OCD). Alexis met the criteria for this study, and alongside individual sessions, she became a part of Dr. Armstrong's research group. Over the next three months, Alexis embraced a routine of weekly assignments, an endeavour aimed at conquering what she dubbed the "bug," her personal term for her OCD.

Collaborating with Dr. Armstrong, Alexis constructed a toolkit of diversions to deploy whenever the urge to engage in her compulsions emerged. One particularly effective exercise was deliberately touching an object with one hand and intentionally avoiding contact with the other. Though this experiment triggered waves of unease and tension, Alexis engaged in predetermined distractions to help navigate through these unsettling emotions. She diligently documented her progress within a dedicated journal and celebrated each milestone with a pre-established reward system. The incentives she chose were as tangible as they were motivating: beanie boos, new sets of markers, and new books to nourish her love for reading.

Within the domain of our home, Alexis' bathroom, bedroom, and closet posed the most significant challenges. Collaboratively, Brent and I became integral components of her diversionary tactics. A phrase as simple as "I'm planning to touch the sink and then I'll be back here so we can bake cookies together" became her means of keeping us in the loop. This approach fostered a sense of companionship and support.

Alexis's adeptness at playing the piano and guitar proved to be a valuable asset. The instruments provided an outlet for her fingers and mind, channelling her energies away from the pull of her compulsions. With nimble fingers and a focused mind, she found a soothing distraction from the compelling urges to balance and touch.

This period of exploration and intervention marked a significant growth period in Alexis's struggle with OCD. It highlighted her resilience, her ability to adapt, and the transformative power of combining therapy with her innate talents and familial support. As her parents, Brent and I stood by her side, witnesses to her incredible determination to overcome the "bug" that had been such a challenge in her life.

As Alexis made progress in her therapy sessions and participated in the research study we witnessed a remarkable transformation in her ability to communicate her emotions and needs. The therapy not only helped her tackle her OCD "bug" but also equipped her with a language to articulate her feelings in a way that resonated with us as a family. She began using words to express her emotions, describing how she felt and what she needed with newfound clarity.

This shift in Alexis's communication style had a profound impact on our household dynamics. It created an atmosphere of openness and understanding, where we could openly discuss our emotions and support each other through difficult times. Alexis became the catalyst for change in our family's approach to emotions, teaching us the power of words.

As Alexis introduced us to the feeling wheel tool[4], it was as if she had handed us a compass that pointed the way to a deeper connection with ourselves and each other. Each segment of the wheel represented a distinct emotion, beautifully arrayed like a painter's palette of feelings waiting to be explored. With its vibrant colours and neatly organized categories, the feelings wheel became a bridge that connected us to the intricate landscape of our inner world. Through the simple act of pointing to a segment on the wheel, Alexis communicated volumes. A glance, a nod, and we understood—the unspoken was made tangible, the intangible was given a name.

---

4 A visual representation of the Feelings Wheel can be found in Part 3, Chapter 36 - Use Helpful Language

It was a language of the heart, a lexicon that transcended the limitations of words. As we engaged with the wheel, we felt the bonds between us strengthen, the walls crumble, and the barriers dissolve.

Where once there might have been frustration and silence, there were now words, strung together with a profound honesty. Alexis was no longer just navigating the complexities of her own mind; she was inviting us into her world, giving us a glimpse into her thoughts and feelings. She began to verbalize her emotions, capturing nuances and shades of her experiences that were previously hidden.

This shift, though gradual, had a ripple effect throughout our household. The atmosphere became infused with a sense of vulnerability and empathy. We found ourselves sitting around the kitchen table, engaging in heartfelt conversations about feelings and fears. Alexis's courage in sharing her feelings emboldened Brent and I to be more open about our emotions, to peel back the layers and reveal our vulnerabilities. It was as if the emotions wheel gave us permission to be authentic and genuine, to acknowledge that emotions were not just transient experiences but integral parts of our human experience.

Using the feelings wheel as a family taught us that emotions were not to be feared or avoided, but to be acknowledged and embraced. And in doing so, we discovered a deeper understanding of ourselves, a profound connection with each other, and the art of expressing our hearts through the language of emotions.

We learned that by articulating our emotions, we could not only understand one another better, but also provide the support and comfort that we all needed.

Witnessing Alexis's growth and witnessing how her therapy positively impacted our family's emotional well-being filled me with immense pride and gratitude. It was a testament to the power of seeking help and embracing the tools and resources available to us. Through Alexis's journey, we learned that vulnerability and open communication are essential components of a strong and connected family. We had come a long way since the early days of Brent's PTSD diagnosis, where we grappled with the unknown and felt isolated in our struggles. Now, we had found a shared language of emotions that bound us together, fostering a sense of unity and resilience in the face of adversity.

The impact of Alexis's growth and the emotional growth of our entire family was transformative.

26

•••••

AS I GRAPPLED with the reality that another member of my family was also facing emotional challenges, I found myself questioning why the universe was presenting me with yet another profound lesson just as things were starting to improve with Brent. It felt overwhelming to navigate through these complex emotions while also trying to be a pillar of strength and support for both of them.

Supporting both Alexis and Brent during this time required a delicate balancing act, one that demanded a new level of adaptability from me. Navigating the intricate web of emotions and responsibilities that came with this role was like traversing uncharted territory. I found myself treading the fine line between being present for Alexis's needs, providing a steadfast shoulder for Brent, and still remembering to extend that same support to myself.

My work schedule, which remained part-time, granted me a degree of flexibility that turned out to be a lifeline. It meant that I could be there for Alexis when she needed me. The alignment of her summer break with her treatment timeline was a silver lining amidst the cloud of uncertainty, affording us precious moments together without the constraints of school routines.

Yet, within this dynamic of caregiving and support, there was an ongoing internal struggle that often played out like a relentless tug-of-war. Self-doubt crept in as I wondered if I was striking the right balance, if I was giving enough to each role without compromising my own well-being. It's a familiar sentiment to anyone who's navigated complex situations—that nagging uncertainty that you're not doing enough, or that you're spreading yourself too thin.

At times, I felt like I was juggling a fragile ecosystem of emotions and responsibilities. It required an almost constant recalibration of my priorities and a deep introspection into my own needs. There were moments of frustration and vulnerability, when I questioned whether I was being the mother Alexis needed, the partner Brent deserved, and the person I needed to be for myself.

In the midst of the whirlwind of emotions and challenges that accompanied supporting Alexis and Brent, my work became more than just a job—it became a haven, a place where I could temporarily step away from the weight of my personal circumstances. As a part-time commitment, it offered me a crucial breather, a space where I could momentarily set aside the complexities of our situation and immerse myself in a different world.

When I entered the doors of my workplace, it was as if I was entering a different realm, a place where I could shift my focus and redirect my energy. Engaging with colleagues, immersing myself in projects, and tackling professional challenges provided a much-needed diversion. It allowed me to take a step back, to recharge and gather my thoughts, so that when I returned home, I could do so with a renewed sense of patience and clarity.

Having those hours at work, where my mind could be absorbed in something other than medical appointments and emotional discussions, became a vital lifeline. It granted me the mental space to regroup, to process my own emotions, and to gain a fresh perspective. It was during those moments of detachment that I found myself better equipped to handle the complexities of Alexis's therapy and Brent's emotions.

When I came home from work, I wasn't just a caregiver; I was a mother and a partner, ready to face the challenges that awaited. The patience and understanding I had cultivated during those work hours became invaluable tools in navigating the delicate emotional landscape at home. It allowed me to listen more attentively to Alexis's concerns, to offer Brent the support he needed, and to lend an empathetic ear to both without becoming overwhelmed by the weight of it all.

Work, unexpectedly, became a place where I could recharge my emotional batteries, a space that empowered me to be present for Alexis and Brent in a way that was compassionate and patient. It gave me the strength to separate myself momentarily from emotional struggles and mood uncertainties, allowing me to return with a clearer mind and a more open heart.

Through this delicate balancing act of work and caregiving, I discovered that sometimes stepping away is just as important as being present. It was a reminder that taking care of myself ultimately enabled me to better care for those I loved. And so, as I navigated the intricate dance between my roles at work and at home, I realized that it was this interplay that allowed me to be the pillar of strength, patience, and resilience that both Alexis and Brent needed during this challenging time in our lives.

At this juncture, choosing to seek professional help became an essential part of my journey. With both Brent and Alexis receiving therapy to address their respective challenges, I recognized the importance of having my own support system as well. It was crucial for me to have a safe space where I could freely express my feelings, fears, and anxieties without judgment. Navigating the complexities of our new reality required emotional strength, and having a psychologist by my side helped me regain a sense of balance and resilience while releasing the pressure that had been building up within me.

Among the various coping strategies I explored to navigate through my grief and navigate Brent's diagnosis, the one that resonated most was the pursuit of control. Embracing the role of a proficient project manager, which I often regarded as my superpower, seemed like a lifeline. However, I began to realize that this proficiency might actually be a shield, limiting my ability to embrace the entirety of my emotions. My energy was disproportionately invested in orchestrating the outside world, a deliberate attempt to preserve a semblance of tranquility within.

This approach proved to have both pros and cons. While it momentarily provided a sense of stability, it also restricted the natural ebb and flow of emotions that form an integral part of the human experience. The shield of control was distancing me from the raw authenticity of my feelings, leaving me disconnected from the healing power that comes with acknowledging and processing those emotions.

This realization was transformative. I recognized that this strategy, though seemingly efficient, was not sustainable in the long run. The time had come to embrace new methods of coping. I embarked on a journey of self-discovery, seeking out alternative ways to navigate my life's challenges while supporting Alexis and Brent with theirs.

This transition was akin to embarking on a new adventure, relinquishing the familiar safety of control and venturing into uncharted territories of vulnerability. As I learned to befriend my emotions and accept them as integral parts of my narrative, I began to see the potential for growth and healing that lay in embracing the entire spectrum of human feelings.

In this evolution, I discovered that true strength wasn't just for orchestrating external circumstances, but could also be created by fostering an internal environment that could weather the storms and cherish the calm moments alike. The path ahead was about balance—acknowledging the emotions, creating space for them, and harnessing my organizational skills to support, rather than suppress, my journey towards healing and understanding.

Leaning on evidence-based research and the words of others helps me learn and grow. One of my favourite authors to read and listen to is Brené Brown. Her work was introduced to me when I sought out a psychologist for myself in Ottawa. Dr. June told me to read "Rising Strong," which is a transformative book that explores the process of getting back up after experiencing setbacks, failures, or disappointments. Drawing on extensive research and personal anecdotes, Brown reveals that the key to resilience lies in embracing vulnerability and engaging with our emotions.

The book introduces the concept of the "reckoning, rumble, and revolution," which forms the foundation of rising strong. It encourages readers to reckon with their emotions, face their stories of struggle, and challenge the narratives they tell themselves. By engaging in the rumble, which involves exploring difficult emotions, owning our mistakes, and seeking understanding, we can move towards personal growth and transformative change. It helps readers navigate the complexities of vulnerability, shame, and failure. It is a guidebook for embracing our imperfections, developing empathy, and finding the courage to rise stronger after life's inevitable falls. It helped me to embrace vulnerability, learn from my struggles, and cultivate resilience, to transform my life and relationships. This book changed the way I view the world and the relationship with my family. It allowed me to let go of my need to control the situation and "fix" things. I could now look through the lens of choice and learning. It is hard work to examine where you are and how you feel when you are in the "arena." The quote that formed much of the inspiration of Brené's written words comes from a speech from Theodore Roosevelt that reads:

> *It is not the critic who counts; not the man who points out how the strong man stumbles, or where the doer of deeds could have done them better. The credit belongs to the man who is actually in the arena, whose face is marred by dust and sweat and blood; who strives valiantly; who errs, who comes short again and again, because there is no effort without error and shortcoming; but who does actually strive to do the deeds; who knows great enthusiasms, the great devotions; who spends himself in a worthy cause; who at the best knows in the end the triumph of high achievement, and who at the worst, if he fails, at least fails while daring greatly, so that his place shall never be with those cold and timid souls who neither know victory nor defeat.*[5]

5 Brene Brown, *Rising Strong: How the Ability to Resent Transforms the Way We Live, Love, Parent, and Lead* (New York: Random House, 2017), xx-xxi.

Day by day, the three of us—Brent, Alexis, and myself—stepped into that arena. We showed up, wholeheartedly and resolutely. It wasn't about perfection; it was about commitment. Each day was a chance to learn, to rise above the obstacles, and to push our boundaries. There were days when the battle seemed easier, the progress evident, and the triumphs tangible. And then there were days when the struggle felt more pronounced, and the victories were small, subtle shifts in the right direction.

The arena wasn't just a physical space; it was the metaphorical ground where what mattered was that we were in the ring, giving our very best. Where we embraced the imperfections, let go of control, confronted our fears, and where we strived to be better versions of ourselves. In those moments of perseverance, we were creating the opportunity to learn, to evolve, and to foster the strength that emerges from embracing adversity.

The arena became a sacred space where we were not defined by our struggles, but by our unwavering willingness to confront them. It was a place where setbacks didn't equate to defeat, but were seen as stepping stones towards progress. In this arena, growth wasn't an abstract concept; it was our daily reality. And though the path wasn't alway linear, each day we showed up, fought our battles, and we did it drawing on the support of one another.

Guided by the wisdom of my psychologist, I was introduced to a set of coping strategies that were finely tailored to my unique circumstances. These strategies acted as tools, equipping me to face the daily hurdles with renewed clarity and strength. Gradually, our sessions became a safe haven, a space where I could shed my armour and find comfort in the realization that caring for my own mental well-being was not just acceptable, but essential.

I embraced the art of open conversations that weren't just about addressing problems; they were about creating an environment of empathy and connection. With the lessons from therapy as my guide, I was able to provide the support my family needed in ways that were genuinely beneficial. And as I watched them flourish in the environment of understanding we had collectively nurtured, I found a sense of fulfillment that whispered to me—this is the power of healing, not just for them, but for me as well.

27

•••••

I CHOSE TO be open with my colleagues and the people I worked with about my personal struggles. It was important for me to share this part of my life with them because these individuals were my support system, and I felt comfortable confiding in them and discussing some of the challenges that Brent and I were facing.

On certain days, I found solace in having a listening ear, and my colleagues were always there to lend one. They allowed me to vent and express my feelings, which helped me release the stress and tension I carried. Other times, I actively sought their advice and guidance on how to cope with the difficulties that arose from Brent's symptoms. I considered myself very fortunate to have such understanding and empathetic outlets in my life during those challenging times.

In 2016, a unique opportunity came my way within the RCMP. I was chosen as one of the individuals to be trained as a facilitator for a course known as 'The Road to Mental Readiness' (R2MR). This course had originally been developed by the Canadian Department of National Defense when they realized that their soldiers were returning from Afghanistan with mental health injuries.

The R2MR curriculum was designed in collaboration with medical doctors, psychologists, and front-line soldiers. Its purpose was to outline mental health symptoms along a continuum[6], providing a comprehensive understanding of mental health challenges. As a facilitator, I had the chance to pass on this invaluable knowledge and support to others within the RCMP and beyond.

Being part of this initiative was not only personally fulfilling but also allowed me to contribute positively to the mental well-being of my colleagues and those around me. The training I received gave me a deeper insight into mental health issues, equipping me with the tools and skills to assist others in their mental wellness journey.

Overall, my decision to be open about Brent's diagnosis with my colleagues turned out to be a blessing. It not only strengthened our team but also led to an incredible opportunity to make a difference in the lives of others through my involvement delivering the R2MR course. As we all learned together about the importance of mental health and supporting one another, we created a stronger, more compassionate community within the workplace.

The course focused on observable behaviours that one could notice in daily life, aiming to reduce the stigma surrounding mental health issues within first responder communities. It covered various aspects, including stress, its causes, strategies for managing it, techniques to regulate emotions, goal setting, and how to engage in conversations with loved ones or colleagues about mental health.

For me, teaching this course marked my formal introduction to speaking about mental health publicly. It came naturally to

6 The Mental Health Continuum can be found in Appendix A

me, and I quickly earned credibility with the audience due to my experience as both an RCMP spouse and employee. My personal life provided numerous examples that I could relate to the curriculum's teaching points, which made the delivery more authentic and relatable.

The impact of teaching this course was profound. During almost every session, someone from the class would approach me afterward to share how they had been struggling, and the course had provided them with the reassurance that they were not alone. It inspired them to seek the help they needed, which was incredibly fulfilling for me. It felt like I was making a difference and having a positive impact.

This sense of fulfillment contrasted with my feelings at home, where I often felt helpless in assisting Brent's recovery. However, as he moved from the more challenging ill/injured sections of the continuum to the more positive healthy/reacting section, my hopefulness grew. During the years when Brent was injured and unwell, it had been difficult to feel like I was making a significant contribution. However, this was slowly changing.

His formal separation from the RCMP lifted an immense burden that Brent didn't even realize he had been carrying. Slowly, he was re-entering the "upward turn" stage of the grief cycle and rediscovering his identity outside his strong ties to the RCMP. This process would undoubtedly take time, but he was determined to find his footing once again. Working outdoors in our new yard became his sanctuary.

Though his moods still fluctuated, there was a noticeable improvement. His emotional range now hovered between three to six on his scale, an improvement from the previous range of two to five. That single point made all the difference in his interactions with the world. It meant he could engage more comfortably with neighbours, exchange more than just a head nod, and even initiate conversations with genuine interest. Brent's newfound sense of stability allowed him to be present with Alexis, sharing genuine smiles while playing together.

With the weight of the past slowly lifting, Brent became more open to connecting with others, including our family. He was willing to host them for visits or travel to see them, fostering a stronger sense of connection within our support system. Most importantly, he could engage in more meaningful conversations with me and others. The air seemed a little easier to breathe on most days, and we held onto the hope that the worst was behind us.

Becoming an R2MR facilitator was the catalyst for my formal development in the area of mental health education. I became a contract trainer with the Mental Health Commission of Canada to deliver the civilianized version of R2MR called The Working Mind and The Working Mind for First Responders. I received training in Applied Suicide Intervention Skills Training and Mental Health First Aid. I contributed to the RCMP policy on line of duty death and worked to update the Critically Ill and Fallen and Member's Guide. I am trained as an RCMP Peer-to-Peer advisor where I am kept informed about internal and external resources to offer to coworkers who approach me when they are going through difficult times in the workplace or in their homelife. I was also part of the woman's advisory committee and the employee wellness committee. At every opportunity, I worked to normalize the conversation around mental health.

In January 2019, an exciting opportunity presented itself when I was asked to speak for RCMP Bell Let's Talk Day, an event organized to support mental health within the RCMP. The organizers approached me to deliver a seven-minute speech, sharing my personal story. I wholeheartedly agreed, recognizing the power of storytelling to inspire and provide hope to others facing similar challenges. Standing before my peers, I spoke candidly about my experiences as an RCMP spouse, sharing my journey through traumatic grief and the valuable lessons I had learned in supporting loved ones living with mental health challenges hoping to make a positive impact on their lives.

The speech opened doors for me, leading to an unexpected invitation to become a divisional mental health champion. This role granted me direct access to the senior leadership team, giving me a unique opportunity to advocate for mental health support and policies within the organization. However, when they first approached me in February 2019, I was cautious and skeptical about accepting the role.

Having seen instances in my career where well-meaning initiatives were merely superficial checkboxes, I was adamant about not becoming another token figurehead. I refused to accept the role until I was convinced that their intentions were genuine and that they were willing to take tangible action to support their employees' mental health needs. I believed that if they were truly committed, they would provide the necessary resources and implement concrete steps to make a positive difference in the lives of their workforce.

I wanted to ensure that my involvement as a mental health champion was more than just a symbolic gesture, but a meaningful commitment that would bring real change and support to those who needed it most. It was essential for me to be part of an initiative that genuinely cared for the well-being of all employees and actively worked towards fostering a psychologically safe and supportive workplace environment.

Ultimately, I needed to see evidence of their dedication and sincerity before I embraced the role of a divisional mental health champion. I watched with eagerness over the next few months.

In September 2020, I was approached again, but this time it was amidst the challenging backdrop of the COVID-19 pandemic. Like many others, I had been working from home since the outbreak reached Canada in March 2020. Adapting to this new remote setup, I found that I preferred working from the comfort of my living room, as it allowed me to engage more with Brent and Alexis throughout the day. The coffee breaks we shared provided precious moments of connection. Though I made an effort not to discuss work directly during these breaks, Brent could glean insights into my day from the one-sided conversations he overheard as I wore headphones and spoke from a room with minimal insulation.

Fortunately, both Brent and Alexis were managing their symptoms well during this period. However, the pandemic-induced business shutdowns disrupted their routines. Alexis was engaged in online school and was not able to participate in extracurricular activities. Brent could no longer attend the warrior yoga class, which had been a valuable outlet for first responders and military personnel. Additionally, his sessions with Dr. Andre and Dr. Arora shifted to a virtual format. Despite these changes, Brent and Alexis adapted well to the isolation, finding comfort in our bubble. Brent's symptom management remained steady, with his average number ranging between five and seven.

As a couple, we were feeling closer than we had in years. When the opportunity arose for me to expand my involvement as a mental health champion, we discussed it together. Recognizing the potential impact I could make, I proposed taking on an additional fifteen hours per week dedicated to this essential role. To accommodate this commitment, I devised a flexible schedule that spread the hours across all seven days, allowing me to maintain work-life balance and support Brent's and Alexis' needs simultaneously. He was supportive and agreed wholeheartedly with my decision.

Encouraged by Brent's backing, I responded to the Commanding Officer of National Headquarters with my proposal. To my delight, he approved, recognizing the importance of the mental health champion role and the value I could bring to the organization. This marked the beginning of an exciting time for me, as I stepped into a more significant role in driving positive change.

With a comprehensive project outline, an engaging communication plan, and a well-structured learning strategy, I was prepared to actively contribute to this critical initiative. The support and approval I received fuelled my enthusiasm, and I was eager to embark on this new responsibility, ready to make a meaningful difference in the lives of the RCMP employees and their mental well-being.

As the weeks progressed, I dove headfirst into the role, engaging with colleagues and fostering open conversations about mental health. I implemented the "Guarding Minds at Work" framework to promote psychological health and safety in the workplace. My passion for this cause grew with each successful interaction, knowing that I was contributing to organizational culture change.

I became a certified Leader Character Practitioner, a role that has illuminated the significance of one's character in leadership, extending beyond mere actions to encompass the essence of who you are as a leader.

Within this framework, I've found a compass guiding individuals towards the cultivation of personal well-being and sustained professional growth. Through my certification, I've immersed myself in the foundational principles that underlie effective leadership. This exploration has reaffirmed the pivotal role character assumes in shaping quality judgment, decision-making, and overall personal and professional excellence.

Armed with this knowledge and perspective, I am able to facilitate not only my own personal advancement but also to empower others in their journey towards unlocking their highest potential. This achievement solidifies my dedication to creating an environment where character stands as the bedrock of leadership excellence and holistic well-being. By weaving character into the fabric of leadership, I aspire to not only foster success but also nurture fulfillment and lasting positive influence.

As I continued my journey as a mental health champion, I felt a sense of purpose, knowing that the work I was doing had a positive impact on the lives of others. I felt a desire to contribute to a workplace culture that genuinely cared for the well-being of its employees. This newfound responsibility not only strengthened my connection with Brent but also allowed me to be an agent of change, driving forward a vision where mental health support was a priority and stigma reduction in policing was possible.

28

AS THE PANDEMIC continued to reshape our lives, and I was deeply involved in supporting employee well-being at the organizational level, I began thinking about how we, as a family, were fostering well-being within our own home. Each of us had developed our individual coping mechanisms and stress management techniques that proved effective. We prioritized a healthy lifestyle, ensuring proper nutrition, regular exercise, and showering one another with love and kindness. Despite these efforts, I felt that something was amiss. It dawned on me that our immediate environment might not be conducive to our collective thriving.

Living in the nation's capital city had its challenges, particularly regarding the language requirements for professional growth. Both Brent and I struggled with the necessity of being bilingual to access higher leadership positions in our respective careers. This limitation impacted our upward mobility and created a sense of frustration. Alexis was attending a French-immersion school, as we were determined to break the cycle of language limitations for her. Still, the reality remained that the existing system hindered our full potential.

To add to the complexity, Brent was living several provinces away from his other children and family, which posed emotional challenges and feelings of distance. Although we resided in a beautiful home, it became evident that the larger system surrounding us needed a transformation to truly support our family's well-being and growth.

My heart ached as I came to the realization that Brent was simply surviving, and I yearned for him to truly live and thrive.

In my talks with employees, I often emphasized the importance of taking an active role in recognizing when they needed help and to seek support early and consistently. As I shared this advice, I realized that I, too, needed to heed my own words.

We needed to address the limitations we faced and actively pursue changes that could improve our quality of life. By identifying areas where we needed support and taking steps to create a more nurturing environment, we could move toward a more fulfilling and harmonious life together. I felt empowered to make these changes, knowing that the potential positive outcomes for our family would be nothing short of incredible.

As I reflected on our life in Ottawa, I began to question the reasons for staying. Our decision to remain in the city had been primarily driven by two factors: Alexis's proximity to Chris' family and the convenience of my job. However, the past year, with all its pandemic-induced changes, had shifted my perspective on what was possible. The widespread adoption of video chats had revolutionized communication, making it easier to stay connected with loved ones even from a distance. Alexis was now at an age where she could fly independently to visit family, reducing the necessity to be geographically close.

In addition, I had personally experienced that my work could be effectively performed remotely. The need to physically stay in Ottawa for my job was no longer an issue. As these realizations sunk in, I knew it was time to reconsider our current situation.

During a Thursday night conversation in February 2021, after Brent had experienced a few more challenging days within the lower range, I broached the subject of a potential move. Together, we discussed how relocating could present an opportunity to change our system and improve our overall well-being.

The next morning I spoke with my manager about the possibility of working remotely from Alberta, and to my delight, they approved the arrangement without hesitation. On Saturday, we met with a realtor. By Sunday, photographs of our house were taken, and we were ready to list it on the market. The momentum carried on, and by Wednesday, we had accepted an offer.

In a whirlwind of action, our plans were swiftly set into motion. As we prepared to leave behind the familiarity of our lives in Ottawa, my heart weighed heavy with mixed emotions. The memories and connections we had built there made the idea of starting anew bittersweet. Yet, deep within me, I held onto the belief that change was essential for growth and that the potential gains from this move far outweighed the uncertainties. The prospect of venturing westward filled us with both thrilling excitement and nerve-wracking anticipation, but we were resolute that it was the right choice for our family's well-being and future.

When we shared our decision to leave Ottawa, the responses we received from people were mixed. Some questioned the timing of our move, expressing concerns about making such a significant change during uncertain times. However, I was determined to explain the realization that had prompted our decision. Residing in Ottawa had taken a toll on Brent's well-being. He was merely surviving, not truly living, let alone thriving. Recognizing that we had the power to change our circumstances, we were willing to take that chance for the betterment of our family's quality of life.

As we prepared to leave Ottawa we were filled with a sense of empowerment. The changes we were making in our lives demonstrated our resilience and determination to build a more supportive system for our family. We were ready to embrace the opportunities that lay ahead in our new home, and we were eager to discover how this shift would positively impact our overall well-being.

As we began our search for a new home, there were two essential criteria that we had. The first was finding a space that would accommodate Brent's interest in woodworking. His newfound enjoyment for it had become a grounding and healing experience for him. The prospect of having a workshop where he could organize and access his tools was crucial. Working with natural materials had an incredible therapeutic effect on him, and he poured his heart and soul into each piece he created. Not driven by profit, Brent crafted purely for the joy of it and gifted his creations to friends and family, a reflection of his generous spirit.

The second of our two criteria was finding a location close to nature paths. Nature held a special purpose for us, and we recognized its power to ground and rejuvenate. Being able to immerse ourselves in the beauty of nature offered a sense of peace and harmony that supported our overall well-being.

The proximity to paths in nature was not just about convenience but a conscious choice to integrate nature's therapeutic influence into our daily lives. The lush greenery, the calming sounds of rustling leaves, and the fresh air became a source of rejuvenation for our entire family.

As we scoured the real estate market, we held these two criteria as non-negotiables. We knew that finding a home that fulfilled both of these desires would not only enhance our living space but also contribute positively to our overall well-being. It became clear that the new home we sought was not just about the physical structure but about finding a place that aligned with our values, passions, and the desire for a harmonious and fulfilling life.

With each potential property, we envisioned the joy and peace that Brent's woodworking sanctuary and our proximity to nature would bring to our lives. This vision fueled our excitement and dedication to finding the perfect place where we could thrive as a family.

As the project manager of our relocation, in all healthy meanings of the title, I was on top of every detail. The excitement of this next chapter in our lives energized me in a way I hadn't felt in a long time. With newfound enthusiasm, I became incredibly productive, accomplishing a lot in my waking hours. Despite the enormity of the task ahead, I felt a deep sense of confidence that we could achieve our goals. Our moving date was set for June 28th, with the closing date on the new house scheduled for July 6th. Having a week between these dates worked in our favour, as our household effects needed to travel nearly 3500 kilometres to our new destination.

To make the transition smoother for Brent, Alexis, and Jak, we decided they would leave Ottawa together in our motorhome and drive cross-country. This way, they could escape the chaos of having movers in our home during the final preparations.

This strategy would also provide me the opportunity to finally sift through the boxes that I had left untouched since departing Hay River. In my determined pursuit of fully immersing myself in my emotions, I acknowledged the importance of setting aside both space and time for a personal exploration of these long ignored containers. This act, I believed, marked another significant step in the process of letting go and surrendering.

I had a strong desire to allow the emotions to come as I unpacked the contents of these boxes in solitude, shielded from external influences and distractions. This endeavour extended beyond mere material examination; it was about rekindling memories, reliving moments, and granting myself the privilege of processing the emotions attached to each item. It was a conscious choice to engage with my past, with the confidence that the progress I had made in my healing journey would lend a fresh perspective to this experience.

As I carefully lifted the lids of these boxes, I anticipated a unique connection to the items stored within. The strides I had taken in my healing journey had equipped me to interact with these artefacts in a way that was markedly different from the last time I saw them. Each item held its own significance, eliciting emotions that I was now prepared to confront, explore, and ultimately release.

In the midst of this process, a thought emerged—a contemplation of Alexis's growth. Now that she was 14, I felt a yearning to consider the items that might hold value for her in the future. These objects were potential gateways to stories, to shared experiences and sentiments. *What stories might these objects hold for her? How might she choose to interact with these fragments of the past when the time was right?*

This exploration carried a deeper layer of meaning; it was an acknowledgment of the passage of time and the evolution of relationships. It provided an opportunity to assemble a collection of memories and experiences that could be cherished and shared when she embarked on her own journey of self-discovery.

At this juncture, the interplay between the past, the present, and the future converged. Engaging with these items was not solely an act of personal reflection; it formed a bridge to the legacy of memories I wished to preserve and pass on. The healing I had embraced was now intricately linked with the legacy I intended to leave behind, and this endeavour stood as a commitment to the continuum of growth, connection, and love that tied us together. I was ready to take another step forward.

I joined Brent and Alexis just in time for Canada Day celebrations. I also reunited with my sister Sandy and her family, who lived only a couple of hours away from our new home. It was a heartening moment, a thread of connection against a backdrop of transition. At the same time, Jordan and his fiancée, McKenzie, had moved into their home in Edmonton, a mere twenty-five-minute drive from our new place. This marked a large milestone, a reunion that closed a twelve-year gap of physical separation between father and son and ushered in a newfound closeness that infused our family with an unmistakable warmth.

The days inched forward, each one tinged with mounting excitement and eager anticipation as we counted down to the momentous arrival of our new keys. Staying with Jordan and

McKenzie not only allowed us to revel in the embrace of family but also transformed the waiting period into an occasion of shared joys. Our westward voyage encompassed more than a simple change of address; it was a conscious choice to embrace a fresh chapter, an opportunity to flourish, and a means to draw closer to the Baulkham family's heart.

29

•••••

THE INITIAL MONTHS in Alberta felt like a whirlwind, accompanied by an unexpected heatwave. The day we stepped into our new house, there were nearly record high temperatures, as if the universe was welcoming us with an intense embrace. The warmth of the weather seemed to mirror the warmth of our anticipation and the bustling activity that came with settling in.

While the pandemic restrictions were gradually easing, there still lingered an aura of isolation that made it somewhat challenging to connect with unfamiliar faces. The world was beginning to open up, yet there was a sense of caution that lingered, creating a subtle barrier between us and the broader community. Our interactions were limited to the familiar, to the circle of family and friends whose presence added a sense of comfort to the newness around us.

Inside the flurry of getting accustomed to our new surroundings, we hosted loved ones from Ontario and British Columbia. Their presence injected an extra layer of energy into our busy days, and the house buzzed with a delightful chaos. Even amidst the unpacking and settling, it was heartwarming to have familiar voices and laughter echoing through the halls.

In the midst of the heat, the shifting pandemic landscape, and the company of family, those initial months etched themselves into our memory as a time of adjustment, reconnection, and adaptation. The days were filled with a blend of challenges and joys, forming the foundation upon which we would build our life in Alberta.

Alexis had carried her fervour for playing ringette to Alberta, and as September arrived, she eagerly stepped onto the local rink. Her enthusiasm was infectious, and her commitment symbolized her eagerness to embrace her passions amidst this transition.

Meanwhile, Brent and I were determined to integrate ourselves into our new community. We decided to continue building on our beginner skills and joined the local curling club. This allowed us to exercise and meet people. I transformed one of the downstairs bedrooms into a functional office space, serving as a hub for my work and allowing me to create a productive and comfortable environment.

These deliberate actions signalled our commitment to planting roots in this new community, but there was a crucial matter that needed our attention: finding new healthcare providers for Brent, specifically a psychologist who could offer the guidance and support he required.

While Brent's condition had seemed relatively stable I sensed a certain levelling off on his path towards betterment. I held onto the belief that with fresh healthcare professionals, he could continue advancing on his path toward improved mental well-being. It was a hope that rested on the potential for fresh insights and approaches to invigorate his healing journey.

As Brent extended his reach within his network, diligently seeking referrals for a psychologist through his policing connections, a flurry of emotions stirred within me. A gentle current of anxiety tugged at my heart. The idea of stepping into the realm of the unfamiliar, of entrusting his thoughts and emotions to a new professional, carried a weight of uncertainty that I couldn't help but feel deeply. It meant retracing the contours of painful memories, unveiling those raw and vulnerable corners of his soul that he had so courageously confronted before.

Yet, in the midst of these apprehensions, a quiet recognition emerged—an understanding of the profound significance that this step held for Brent's growth. Dr. Andre and Dr. Arora had been his steadfast guides, but this juncture beckoned for a new perspective, a fresh lens through which to view his progress.

This pursuit wasn't just about replacing one professional with another; it was about embracing change and trusting in the promise it held. I believed in Brent's strength, in his capacity to navigate this uncertain terrain, to unravel the layers of his emotions once again, and to emerge stronger, more resilient, and more connected.

When Brent finally connected with Linda, a swirl of emotions surged within me. A blend of hope and uncertainty left my mind spinning with questions: *Would Linda truly grasp the intricacies of Brent's inner world, as much as his previous therapists had? Would her techniques resonate with his unique needs, crafting an authentic connection that could guide him onward?* These thoughts, like a gentle current of doubt, threaded their way through my mind as he stepped into his first session with her.

My hopes didn't go unanswered. As the weeks passed, I stood as a silent witness to the transformation unfolding within my husband. The process of seeking out new health care professionals yielded positive outcomes that exceeded my expectations. The impact of this change was truly remarkable. The shift to a different care team brought a renewed sense of vitality. It was as if new doors of opportunity had swung open, allowing him to delve deeper into his healing process and make strides he hadn't before.

The imprint of Linda's guidance was unmistakable. The way he spoke about their sessions carried a new sense of clarity and purpose. Her approach had ignited a spark within him, illuminating a path towards understanding and growth.

Every conversation we shared revealed a newfound depth in his insights and a heightened self-awareness. He spoke of the techniques he had diligently practiced. The dedication he exhibited, the conscious effort to integrate these strategies into his daily life, stirred a mix of emotions within me. Pride swelled in my heart, a recognition of his commitment to his own well-being and by proxy, the well-being of our family. Relief followed closely, like a soothing balm, knowing that the darkness that once loomed over him was beginning to yield to the light of progress.

This experience reinforced the idea that change, even if initially daunting, can bring about transformative outcomes. It was a reminder that growth isn't confined to one specific phase; it's a continuous evolution, and new perspectives can infuse our progress with renewed energy. As we navigated this transition together, I saw firsthand the power that comes from resilience and hope.

As we settled into the embrace of our new home and watched Brent's workshop take form, an overwhelming sense of gratitude washed over me. The decision to uproot our lives had demanded a leap of faith, a bold step into the unknown, and its impact had rippled through our existence in ways I could never have foreseen. Brent's smile had never been wider, his laughter reverberated through our spaces more frequently, and my heart couldn't help but swell with warmth and relief. It was as if this new environment had breathed life into him. Seeing Brent flourish in this space and find his stride in his workshop brought an indescribable sense of fulfillment, a realization that we had ventured down the right path. Here he could not only exist but truly thrive.

The puzzle pieces of our lives had clicked into place with an almost poetic precision. Being nearer to our children, rekindling those bonds, and finally uncovering the right path to care for Brent's mental well-being—each piece of this puzzle was a confirmation that we were on the right track, that the challenges we had overcome to get here were worth every effort.

Of course there were still hurdles to navigate, and not every day was a constant stream of ease. But the overall balance of our days tilted markedly towards joy, towards an intangible yet very real sense of fulfillment. Our journey west, one marked by change and courage, had irrevocably transformed the health of our family.

My heart beat with a rhythm of gratitude, love, and the anticipation of what the future held.

30

THE ARRIVAL OF the pandemic in 2020 cast a shadow over the world, ushering in an array of unprecedented challenges. As countries closed their borders and interactions became remote, our carefully laid travel plans were abruptly put on hold. In the midst of this global shift, Alexis and I found ourselves holding onto airline flight credits.

These credits were set to expire within a few months of our westward move. In the midst of adjusting to our new lives, Alexis' school commitments, and the demands of my own work, the task of carving out a window of time to take this trip proved to be a puzzle of its own.

Finding suitable dates that aligned with our responsibilities and allowed us to be away together, was no small feat. The conversations we shared about selecting a destination were rich with contemplation, hope, and an awareness of practical considerations.

After much deliberation, a decision crystallized between us. It was a choice to seize the moment, to embrace the chance for a brief escape. We set our sights a mere hour and a half north—a flight from Edmonton to Yellowknife.

It was Alexis who came up with this idea. A spark of curiosity ignited within her to explore the town where she took her first breaths. The stories she had heard, the names she had encountered only through narratives, beckoned to her like pieces of a puzzle waiting to be assembled. And in her eyes, I glimpsed the eagerness of a young explorer, ready to bridge the gap between the stories and reality. And as her mother, I couldn't help but feel a swelling of emotion—a blend of pride, anticipation, and a touch of vulnerability.

In the aftermath of the trial, my only visit to Yellowknife had been brief and sombre, marked by the shadow of loss as I paid my respects at a friend's memorial. This trip with Alexis held an entirely different significance. The weight of this getaway wasn't lost on me. It was more than a mere break in our routine; it was an opportunity to walk alongside Alexis as she peeled back the layers of the stories that had woven themselves into our lives and trace her roots. This trip held the potential to transform anecdotes into tangible encounters, faces into names, and history into a real presence.

During our time in Yellowknife, we stayed in Michèle's downtown apartment. As the capital of the Northwest Territories, Yellowknife is a city rooted in rock and encircled by lakes, ranging from vast expanses to intimate waters. It boasts all the conveniences of urban living akin to the southern provinces, yet there's an indescribable charm that sets it apart. What struck us most was the strong sense of community, a warmth that radiated as passersby greeted us on the streets.

The landscapes, picturesque and untamed, surrounded us. Our gaze was drawn to the skies, where float planes gracefully danced overhead, eventually touching down on the serene expanse of Great Slave Lake. Along the shoreline, houseboats painted a scene of tranquil living, while the persistent presence of fishing boats reminded us of the community's deep-rooted connection to the water.

For me, this trip was an opportunity to reveal to Alexis the dichotomy that defines Yellowknife. On one hand, there are the more traditional ways of life that still breathe in the Old Town. This stands in contrast to the city centre, where the pulse of modern times beats strong. The prospect of introducing her to the coexistence of these two worlds filled me with an eager anticipation.

At 15 years old, Alexis was venturing into the corridors of time, her curiosity leading her to explore our lives before she came into existence. She was captivated by the imagery of her parents as young newlyweds, living a life that was foreign to her. The notion of her parents' adventures in the North captured her imagination, drawing her closer to a world she hadn't yet experienced.

On the evening we arrived, Michèle had organized a get-together with a few of my closest teacher friends. These friendships had deep roots, tracing back to my beginnings as a substitute teacher. Time seemed to fade away whenever we gathered—as if the years had no hold on our connection. In Michèle's cozy living room, stories flowed freely about the version of me that existed twenty years ago. Laughter echoed around us, leaving its mark for hours. By the time our laughter-filled evening came to an end, my cheeks ached from smiling so much.

Many of these friends hadn't seen Alexis since she was a baby, and watching them interact with her now, as a mature, inquisitive, and vibrant young woman, filled me with a sense of wonder. This meeting highlighted the passage of time—the contrast between their memories of Alexis as an infant and the person she had become was a reminder of life's swift evolution.

As stories and laughter filled the room, Alexis was fully engaged, absorbing the anecdotes that shed light on a version of her mother she had yet to uncover. Through this experience, a profound connection was forged. It was as if these narratives created a bridge between the past and the present, each story adding to the richness of our shared history.

The air was crisp as Alexis and I strolled down the main street the next morning. Each step was a journey back in time, as I told stories of the various stores, eateries, and bars that lined the street. Among these narratives, the "Gold Range" stood out—an iconic establishment that had etched its mark on Yellowknife's landscape, even if not for the best reasons. It was here that Chris had brought me on the day I signed my first teaching contract. A grin spread across his face, and he'd simply said, "When in YK!" I told the story of how we took our seats at the small, round tables cloaked in terry-cloth, a practical touch to minimize the aftermath of spilled drinks. We shared a toast before the place grew too crowded, a preemptive act before the energy of the night engulfed the establishment. The "Gold Range" had a reputation—a place where skirmishes spilled onto the streets, summoning the RCMP on most evenings.

Our tour continued, punctuated by moments like a photo taken in front of a furniture store. A passerby was kind enough to capture the memory. "This is where I felt the first contractions, a day before you were born," I shared with Alexis, the memory painted in vivid detail as we lingered in that spot.

This walk through town became an adventure of anecdotes, each holding a memory, each story a glimpse into the pages of my history. With every step, every memory unveiled, Alexis seemed to become more and more captivated by the tales that animated the corners of the town.

I could see her enthusiasm growing. It was as though I held a key to unlock the past, offering Alexis a glimpse into the moments that had defined me as an individual and us as a family. This was more than a tour of the town; it was an exploration of our personal journey, shared through the lens of the places that had once witnessed my joy, trials, and pivotal moments.

Our steps carried us beyond the courthouse and toward the detachment. The sight of the flagpole was a familiar touchstone, casting elongated shadows over the memorial wall. This unassuming structure bore the weight of significance, adorned with the names of those who had made the ultimate sacrifice in the line of duty while serving in the Northwest Territories. Alexis' gaze fixed upon the wall, her eyes searching until she found Chris' name.

I recalled my previous visit to the wall during my last trip. The elements had cast their mark on the lettering of Chris' plaque, leaving it tarnished and obscured. Ironically, as the newest addition, it bore the signs of age as if it had been there the longest. Moved by this realization, I had reached out to the Commanding Officer. The response was heartening—a commitment to replace the tarnished plaque, ensuring that Chris' name and legacy would be preserved with the respect it deserved.

Standing before the wall with Alexis, a sense of gratitude washed over me as the new plaque gleamed in the light, a tribute to Chris' service displayed for his daughter to see. Alexis' fingers gently grazed the cool metal, tracing the contours of her father's name. I chose to remain silent, allowing her to fully immerse herself in this moment. It was her journey to navigate, her emotions to unravel, and I was there to support her in whatever way she needed.

I held back, letting her dictate the rhythm of our conversation. I answered her questions thoughtfully, allowing her to absorb and reflect, knowing that as time passed and experiences accumulated, she would seek out the deeper layers of insight when she felt ready. Until then, I was content to stand by her side.

Michèle met us later in the afternoon and chauffeured us across town to the arena. It was here that a hockey jersey, bearing Chris' name and the number 22, hung on display. Alongside it were two jerseys paying homage to firefighters who had sacrificed their lives in service to their community. A tradition unfolded annually—a police versus firefighter hockey game that served as a tribute to these three men.

Descending to the ice level with Alexis, I looked up to find a blue and yellow jersey suspended in the rafters, proudly bearing the name "Worden." Yellowknife had not forgotten; the memory of Chris and his fellow comrades was etched into the very fabric of this community.

As Alexis and I stood there, united by shared remembrance, a wave of humility washed over us. The fact that those who had known Chris continued to honour his memory, keeping it alive for those who had not had the privilege of knowing him, was profoundly touching. It highlighted the depth of connection that transcended time and circumstances. It was a reminder of why Yellowknife had always felt like home—a place where relationships, stories, and shared experiences combined to create a sense of belonging that never wavered.

A whirlwind of emotions surged within me, a blend of feelings that I couldn't quite put into words. This trip held a significance that ran deep. For Alexis, this experience marked the first time she could remember stepping beyond the boundaries of the Worden home to explore a place that was part of her origin story—a place where the man who created her had lived and breathed. The weight of this moment wasn't lost on me; it was a special opportunity to share something profound with my daughter.

As I observed Alexis in this context, I was struck by the dynamic nature of memory. It was more than a static collection of stories—it was a living, breathing force that shaped her identity and perspective. His legacy was actively influencing her choices, her curiosity, and her desire to understand the roots from which she came.

I felt a deep reassurance that Chris' presence, even though physically absent, was an enduring force that continued to guide and inspire Alexis on her own unique path.

That evening, after pouring out these stories and experiences to Alexis, as we readied ourselves for bed, Michèle entered our room with an urgent whisper—the aurora borealis was visible in the night sky. Alexis' one fervent desire before our trip was to witness the enchanting dance of the northern lights. The invitation from Michèle ignited a rush of excitement in us.

Stepping outside, we were greeted by a celestial spectacle that exceeded our expectations. Green and yellow hues swirled across the canvas of the sky, like a dance performed exclusively for us. In that moment, pure elation was felt. I stood under the vast expanse of the heavens, in the birthplace of my daughter, while the shimmering aurora borealis painted the night sky.

It was a culmination of emotions and experiences; the storytelling, the reminiscing, the sharing of memories—all of it led to this exquisite moment. As I gazed at the lights, a profound sense of joy washed over me. This was a moment when time seemed to pause, where the universe itself seemed to acknowledge the significance of our journey and the bond between mother and daughter.

That moment is forever imprinted on my heart.

31

IN SPITE OF Alexis being a child who naturally clung to familiarity and hesitated at change, her response to welcoming Brent into her life was truly extraordinary. Right from the instant they crossed paths, she radiated an innate capacity for acceptance, embracing him with an open heart and open arms. It was as if she sensed a kindred spirit in him, a connection that defied her usual reservations.

The ease with which Alexis embraced Brent's presence has been a source of immense gratitude for me. She had the remarkable fortune of having Brent become a constant in her life, and as the years have passed, she can't recollect a time when he was not a part of her memories. This seamless integration of Brent into her world is a gift that I hold close to my heart.

Throughout her life, Alexis has been blessed with the love and support of a strong male figure. Brent's presence offered her stability and reassurance, forming a bond that thrived on trust and care. Even during the most testing times, when Brent's health was at its most fragile, Alexis was at an age blissfully innocent to the intricacies of life's challenges. I remember explaining, "Dad is feeling sick today, he has a headache," and she accepted it at face value, devoid of delving into the gravity that lay beneath those words. This innocence, this unburdened understanding, is another blessing I am deeply thankful for.

The sense of pride and gratitude I feel when I reflect upon the family Brent and I have nurtured is immeasurable. The distinctive qualities that each individual brings to this collective whole are not just noteworthy, they are truly exceptional. The way our unique strengths and personalities meld seamlessly together to craft our family is amazing.

The path of building a blended family came with its share of potential challenges and growth opportunities. It was a road we travelled with anticipation, knowing that there would be moments of adjustment and adaptation. Fortunately we found that the frequency and impact of these challenges were surprisingly minimal, allowing us to focus on the bonds we were forging.

Keegan and Jordan, their hearts wide open and their minds receptive, extended a sincere and genuine welcome to us. Their warm embrace, their acceptance, and their affectionate approach spoke volumes about their innate kindness and maturity. Their ability to navigate the nuances of change and to seamlessly integrate new dynamics into their lives stands as a remarkable testament to their character.

Amidst the geographical expanses that sometimes separated us, our visits held a magic of their own. It was a magic infused with the essence of love, the sound of laughter, and the shared moments that felt like gifts in the vaults of memory. Through those fleeting periods of togetherness, the relationships between siblings, between father and children, and between stepmother and children found fertile ground to flourish.

Stepping into the role of a stepmother to teenagers who were already navigating the terrain of having two living parents introduced a distinct and enriching dimension to our family.

Within this role, I discovered my place as not just a guardian figure, but as a companion and confidante. It was as if I found a path that allowed me to merge the roles of friend and ally, creating a space where support, guidance, and an extra layer of affection could develop naturally. The fifteen year age gap between Brent and I proved to be a segue between worlds with the boys. It wasn't just a matter of years; it was a bridge of understanding, a gateway to building connections that transcended mere titles. This proximity in age facilitated a natural resonance, allowing us to share thoughts, laughter, and experiences in a way that felt like we were speaking the same language. Conversations flowed effortlessly, and common interests served as stepping stones to deeper connections that were underpinned by mutual respect.

Being a stepmother wasn't about replacing, but about complementing. I wasn't here to replace their parents; I was here to complement their lives, to add a dimension of care and companionship that was unique to our relationship. We navigated this journey together, bound by a common thread of growth, mutual support, and a shared understanding that family isn't solely defined by blood, but by the bonds that are nurtured over time.

My role as a stepmother wasn't predefined, but rather it unfolded organically as our connections deepened and evolved. I stood beside them as a friend, a mentor, and an advocate, offering a perspective that was different yet aligned with their own journeys. It demonstrated the fluidity of love and the limitless possibilities that arise when hearts open to the beauty of connection.

Both Keegan and Jordan have earned master's degrees in psychology and counselling. Their formal education about how the mind reacts to trauma has unlocked a deeper comprehension of their father's experiences. This newfound insight serves as a key to unravelling the behaviours and actions exhibited by Brent during their upbringing. While Brent's official diagnosis occurred in 2010, the undiagnosed symptoms of PTSD had silently plagued him for years. These were crucial years, shaping the foundations of Keegan and Jordan's growth.

It's not mere coincidence that both sons ventured into careers centred around mental health and well-being. As the boys pursued their master's programs, Brent found the strength to unveil more about the scars of his past. The knowledge and training Keegan and Jordan received through their education allow them to receive this information with a fresh perspective, fostering a richer understanding. Additionally, Brent has grown to embrace greater responsibility for his actions as a younger father. These candid conversations, fueled by newfound understanding, have propelled their healing journey forward.

Keegan and Jordan stand as incredible individuals whose evolution has been a source of pure joy to witness. From the days of their teenage years, when their passions revolved around the thrill of hockey and basketball, to this moment where they've grown into thoughtful and accomplished young men pursuing impactful careers in counselling and education, their journey has been filled with growth and inspiration.

The transformation from adolescence into adulthood is a remarkable process that the boys have embraced with grace and determination. Witnessing their futures unfold, from the pursuit of personal passions to the cultivation of their professional paths, has been a privilege that has filled my heart with pride.

In the realm of love, their stories have continued with beauty and grace. Keegan's heart has found its place in the presence of Jessica, a spirit who complements his life with shared dreams and unwavering support. Jordan, too, has discovered a deep connection with McKenzie, a bond that radiates warmth and understanding. Our family circle has now expanded to encompass these two incredible women, effectively turning us into a united and affectionate family of seven. The introduction of Jess and Kenz has breathed a fresh vitality into our family dynamics. Our gatherings are punctuated by shared stories, inside jokes, and the joyful sound of collective laughter. Our bonds have expanded, creating an environment where every individual feels cherished, understood, and valued. In Jessica and McKenzie, we've found not just new family members, but individuals whose presence has enriched our lives. With their inclusion, our story has taken on new dimensions, creating a legacy of unity, love, and a sense of belonging that warms our hearts and brings light to our lives.

For Alexis, the addition of the girls as loving and caring sisters has been an invaluable source of support and comfort, especially during the challenging times of adolescence. Their strong bonds have cultivated a nurturing and empathetic environment, providing Alexis with strength and encouragement.

Observing the closeness between all the kids is a treasured gift, a symbol of the unbreakable ties of family. As they move through the complexities of life, they've found comfort and understanding in one another. Their shared experiences create a deep well of empathy, fostering a sense of companionship, motivation, and unwavering affection.

As a parent, stepmom, and mother-in-law, being a guiding presence for all the children has been immensely rewarding.

Nurturing their growth and offering them guidance to navigate life's intricate pathways is a responsibility that fills me with purpose. Within these moments of teaching, comforting, and sharing, I find profound fulfillment. It's a privilege to be asked to offer them the tools necessary to navigate life's challenges, providing steadfast support and knowledge gained from experience.

Vulnerability demands tremendous courage. Over recent years, each member of our family has exhibited this bravery. Brent, by bravely sharing his traumatic experiences and extending heartfelt apologies for the pain he inadvertently caused in their youth. Keegan and Jessica, who tenaciously pursued their aspirations despite challenges. Jordan and McKenzie, who humbly sought guidance while navigating the complexities of both their professional and personal lives. Alexis, who embraced change by immersing herself in a new school environment during our relocation. And myself, taking the steps to pen this book, sharing our collective stories and my personal experiences. These moments of courage have shaped our story of resilience, growth, and unity that binds our family together.

As a united family, we understand that life's journey may include moments of stumbling and setbacks for each one of us. In these times, our commitment remains—we stand as steadfast advocates, firmly by the side of our loved one in the midst of their challenges. Like watching a teammate who is in the arena, we offer our collective strength and encouragement. We become their loudest cheerleaders, providing unwavering support from the sidelines, and readily stepping in when the need arises. This is the embodiment of love and devotion in its most profound and active form.

In our marriage, Brent and I have reached a level of connection and understanding that surpasses anything we've experienced before. Our love has grown deeper, and our bond has strengthened as we faced the challenges of life as a united front. We discovered the importance of communication, compassion, and empathy within our family dynamic. We found that in our most vulnerable moments, we could lean on each other for support and find comfort in knowing that we were not alone in our struggles. Together, we built a foundation of trust and resilience, one that has become the bedrock of our family's way of being. We have come to understand that surviving together is not just about getting through the tough times; it's about growing together, learning from each other, choosing our narrative, and finding joy, no matter how small.

The lessons we've learned on this path from survival to thriving have shaped us into a stronger, more connected couple and family.

32

REFLECTING ON BOTH my past and the path ahead, I'm reminded of a quote by musician and author Jann Arden: "Good things come out of bad things." It's a sentiment that resonates deeply with me as I contemplate the chapters of my life. The sum of these moments and narratives has sculpted the person I stand as today. In the absence of the tumultuous grief that followed Chris' tragic passing, I might not have cultivated the wellspring of empathy and compassion that fuels my unwavering support for Brent. Absent the years I devoted to aiding loved ones grappling with trauma and mental health battles, I wouldn't have stepped into the role of educator and advocate, championing the cause of stigma reduction and mental well-being.

Empowering others through the dissemination of knowledge, the cultivation of empathy, and the dismantling of stigma has been a calling for me. Witnessing the transformative power it holds, both for individuals and the larger community, has deepened my conviction in its importance. By contributing to the evolution of a more all-encompassing society, by bolstering individuals with knowledge and fostering the dismantling of biases, I've embarked on a mission that has not only changed me but has the capacity to bring about lasting change, one conversation at a time. The resonance of this journey continues to stir my soul and propel me forward with determination to create enduring impact.

The way we perceive and engage with the world is a conscious decision we make. Our mindset serves as one of our most formidable tools, wielding a remarkable influence over our lives. In "The Choice: Embrace the Possible,"[7] Edith Eger eloquently delves into the concept of victimhood:

> *...(S)uffering is universal. But victimhood is optional. There is a difference between victimization and victimhood. We are all likely to be victimized in some way in the course of our lives. At some point we will suffer some kind of affliction or calamity or abuse, caused by circumstances or people or institutions over which we have little or no control. This is life. And this is victimization. It comes from outside. It's the neighborhood bully, the boss who rages, the spouse who hits, the lover who cheats, the discriminatory law, the accident that lands you in the hospital.*
>
> *In contrast, victimhood comes from the inside. No one can make you a victim but you. We become victims not because of what happens to us but when we choose to hold on to our victimization. We develop a victim's mind -- a way of thinking and being that is rigid, blaming, pessimistic, stuck in the past, unforgiving, punitive, and without healthy limits or boundaries. We become our own jailors when we choose the confines of the victim's mind.*

7 E.E. Eger, E. S. Weigand, and P.G. Zimbardo, P. G., *The Choice: Embrace the Possible* (New York: Scribner, 2017), 7-8.

Eger emphasizes a pivotal truth—that we possess the agency to shape our own destiny through our thoughts and actions. Her words echo the power we hold within us to redefine our narrative and craft our own path by the choices we make and the perspectives we embrace.

In August 2022, I took a significant step towards fulfilling my aspirations by enrolling in a program that meets the educational requirements for obtaining my International Coaching Federation credentials. Within this program, one of the core principles resonated deeply with me: the belief that every individual is inherently whole, capable, resourceful, and creative. We all carry a wealth of wisdom inside us, guiding us towards our destined path if we choose to listen.

This belief has become a cornerstone of my perspective, and I have consciously embraced it in all aspects of my life. In retrospect, I realized that I had already been embodying this belief for years. I deliberately made choices that nurtured a positive mindset and helped me move forward despite the challenges life threw my way.

Instead of getting mired in a state of helplessness or asking *why is this happening to me?* I shifted my focus to a more empowering question: *what do I do now?* This simple but profound reframing altered my perspective and motivated me to take positive action towards growth and healing. By adopting this perspective, I propelled myself forward, stepping into a space of resilience and determination.

The choice to believe in the inherent wisdom within ourselves is transformative. It shifts our mindset from victimhood to empowerment, encouraging us to see challenges as opportunities for growth. Through this belief, I discovered my capacity to overcome obstacles and embrace life with a proactive attitude.

As a coach, when I engage with others on their own journeys I am reminded daily of the power of this belief. I witness the positive impact it has on others, encouraging them to tap into their inner resources and embrace their inherent capabilities. It is a belief that fuels hope, nurtures resilience, and fosters the courage to take bold steps towards a fulfilling and joyful life. This journey is one of continuous learning and growth. I remain committed to exploring this belief and sharing its transformative potential with others. It has become the guiding light that illuminates my path, pushing me towards a life of purpose, authenticity, compassion, and joy.

Life's journey is not always a straight and smooth path. There will be moments when unforeseen events take us off course. However, these detours are not setbacks; they are opportunities for learning and growth. Each challenge we face adds to our strength and aligns us even more with our purpose and shapes us into who we are meant to become.

As Edith Eger beautifully states: "Our painful experiences aren't a liability—they're a gift. They give us perspective and meaning, an opportunity to find our unique purpose and our strength." These gifts in disguise provide us with valuable perspective and meaning, offering us an opportunity to discover ourselves and uncover hidden reservoirs of strength within us. It may be difficult to see or feel this truth in every moment, but holding on to this belief can help carry us through the challenging times.

Embracing the idea that challenges are transformative gifts enables us to navigate through the ups and downs of life with resilience and hope. Each twist and turn in our journey shapes us, moulding us into individuals capable of facing anything that comes our way. We become stronger, wiser, and more aligned with the path that leads us towards our true purpose.

Giving myself permission to explore my life vision and aspirations was a process that took time and self-reflection. For years, my focus had been on supporting others, leaving little room for me to dream big and pursue my own ambitions. Yet, deep down, I knew that I wanted to share my story and empower others on a larger scale.

The turning point came unexpectedly, with a breast cancer diagnosis in October 2022. The months of recovery from multiple surgeries provided a unique opportunity for introspection. It was during this time that I could delve into the question that had been brewing within me: *How can I utilize my life to create a positive impact on others, discover profound fulfillment, and immerse myself in the activities I am passionate about?*

Through countless iterations and much soul-searching, I finally found my answer: to write this book and pursue a path as a coach. This realization ignited a stir within me like never before. I understood that by sharing my experiences and insights, I could have an impact on others, empowering them to navigate their own challenges with resilience and hope.

Becoming a professional certified coach would enable me to offer space and support to individuals seeking transformation and growth. It felt like the perfect blend of my desire to help others, my passion for teaching, and having one-on-one conversations.

Embracing this newfound direction brought a sense of clarity and purpose to my life. It allowed me to envision a future where I could make a positive difference in the lives of others while also finding fulfillment and joy in my everyday.

Writing a book has been an incredibly fulfilling experience for me. It provided a meaningful platform to share not only my knowledge and insights but also the unique events of my life experiences. Through this creative process, I discovered the power of storytelling, recognizing how our words can profoundly impact others, guiding them on their own paths of growth and understanding. It is a way of fostering a sense of connection and shared experiences. This process has taught me the importance of vulnerability and the courage it takes to share our stories openly, knowing that it can touch the lives of others in unexpected ways. This experience has enriched my life in ways I could never have imagined, and it has fueled my desire to continue using words as a vehicle for positive change and empowerment in the lives of others.

I invite you to embark on a transformative journey inspired by the profound words of well-known psychologist, speaker, and author Dr. Jody Carrington in her book "Feeling Seen,"[8] where she outlines the importance of being able to reconnect, repair and re-engage after we've been wronged, alienated or hurt. She explains that feeling seen is about connection. It's about recognizing our shared humanity and embracing our common experiences. When we make an effort to see others, we open the door to empathy, understanding, and true human connection.

In a world often overshadowed by disconnection, let us come together and intentionally see one another. Let us pause, listen attentively, and extend our hearts to truly witness the joys, struggles, and triumphs of those around us.

Resilience is at the heart of this journey. It is the choice to engage with adversity, to find strength in the face of challenges, and to empower ourselves and others. By choosing resilience, we can create a space where every individual's story

8 Jody Carrington, *Feeling Seen: Reconnecting in a Disconnected World* (Toronto: HarperCollins Canada, 2023).

is acknowledged and where their resilience becomes a source of inspiration.

This call to action asks us to set aside preconceptions and judgments, replacing them with curiosity and genuine interest. It encourages us to harness the power of choice—to choose empathy and understanding. Together, we can create brave spaces where authenticity is celebrated, and where the power of vulnerability paves the way for profound human connection.

By embracing this call to action, we have the power to make a lasting impact on the lives of those around us. Let us cultivate a world where feeling seen is the norm—a world where our shared humanity is celebrated, resilience is honoured, and where the power of empathy transforms lives.

As you dive into the final part of this book, you will discover valuable lessons from my journey towards greater resilience, acceptance, understanding, and true human connection. I invite you to embrace these lessons and use them as tools to support your own path of growth and transformation.

Amidst the stories and lessons explored in this book, one resounding theme emerges—the importance of choice in finding joy in our lives. Life may present us with challenges and unforeseen circumstances, but within these moments lies the power to choose our responses and reactions. It is through conscious choices that we can rewrite our narratives, transcend adversity, and craft a life that aligns with our deepest desires and aspirations.

Harnessing choice also means acknowledging that happiness and joy are within our reach, waiting to be discovered and cherished. Joy is not an elusive concept; it is an intentional decision to seek out moments of happiness and gratitude. Finding joy in the simplest of things—laughter, nature's beauty, the warmth of a loved one's embrace, in the beauty of a sunrise, or in the warmth of a heartfelt conversation - serves as a reminder that happiness can be found even in the midst of adversity and in the face of pain. By choosing joy, we cultivate an attitude of gratitude and appreciation for the beauty that surrounds us, however small or ordinary it may seem. It is a journey of discovering the extraordinary in the everyday and finding contentment in the present moment.

When we choose to infuse our lives with joy, we create a positive ripple effect that extends not only to ourselves but to those around us. As we journey together towards greater resilience, acceptance, understanding, and true human connection, let us remember that choice and joy are potent tools. We have the power to shape our narratives, embracing vulnerability, empathy, and compassion. By making mindful choices and finding joy in the journey, we transcend limitations and unlock the door to a life of fulfillment and purpose. By embracing joy, we discover a wellspring of resilience that helps us navigate through difficult times.

So, as you embark on your own journey of growth and transformation, harness the power of choice and the beauty of joy. Let them guide you towards a life filled with purpose, empathy, and heartfelt connections. Together, we can create a world where every individual is valued and celebrated, a world where the pursuit of joy becomes a transformative force for all. Choose joy, embrace it, and allow it to lead you towards many more happy tomorrows.

Part 3: The Lessons Learned

MY EXPERIENCES OVERCOMING traumatic grief and supporting my loved ones as they grappled with mental health challenges have etched within me valuable lessons that shed light on the path to resilience and growth. As a professional certified coach, I've been fortunate to witness the transformative power of these lessons for myself and those I've worked with. As I reflect upon my journey, I've distilled these lessons into contemplative reflections, each acting as a guidepost on the road to understanding and healing.

Every lesson holds its distinct significance, and to truly embrace their transformative power, I've crafted thought-provoking coaching questions that act as guiding lights, leading us through the maze of emotions and insights. These questions are not mere words, but invitations to explore our emotions, thoughts, and actions. Engaging with these questions unlock a multitude of benefits, all interconnected to lead us toward a deeper connection with ourselves and the world around us.

Through self-awareness, we unravel the complexities of our emotions, motives, and triggers. I've seen how asking questions about our reactions and thoughts allows us to uncover layers of understanding that were previously concealed. Personal empowerment emerges from this self-awareness; we recognize the agency we possess to shape our responses and decisions. With reflection, we evolve into active participants in our own lives, driven by a renewed sense of purpose and direction.

A positive mindset is nurtured through these reflections. The questions guide us to focus on the bright spots, encouraging us to seek lessons amid challenges. I've observed how this mindset acts as a shield against negativity, fostering resilience in the face of adversity. As the burdens of the past are gently lifted, a sense of joy emerges that is rooted in our ability to find meaning in even the darkest corners.

As we embark on this journey of reflection, the benefits ripple outward, impacting our relationship with ourselves, others, and our overall well-being. This isn't a mere exercise but a voyage of self-discovery and growth. The reflections become the framework upon which we construct our narratives of strength, acceptance, and transformation. It is how we employ our power of choice. The outcome that emerges from this process is one of enhanced well-being, draped in the stories of our experiences, connected with the lessons we've embraced.

In confronting the challenges that life presents, engaging with these reflective questions becomes an act of self-care and compassion. It's a way to honour our stories, to acknowledge the struggles, and to celebrate the victories. I've witnessed first hand that after delving into the depths of our experiences, we emerge stronger, wiser, and more attuned to our life—a journey that leads to a deeper self-awareness, personal empowerment, a positive mindset, joy, and an overall enriched sense of well-being. It all starts with you: your strength, your courage, and your choice to step into self-discovery and open yourself up to the wisdom within.

Visit www.jodiebaulkham.com to download a free version that contains these lessons learned and has room for you to journal and capture your reflections.

33

The Importance of Self-Discovery and Strength of Character

•••••

I learned the importance of self-discovery and how strength of character is the foundation for emotional and professional wellbeing.

"Strength of character" refers to when an individual possesses each of the eleven dimensions of character in balance with each other (shown below). A person with strength of character is internally and externally self-aware. They have implemented positive habits in their life that allow them to approach situations with a regulated body and mind. They focus on who they are becoming while they are busy doing.

Through introspection and my life experiences, I've come to realize that having strength of character serves as the bedrock for both emotional and professional well-being. The process of self-discovery involves delving into one's values, beliefs, strengths, and weaknesses. By recognizing and embracing these facets of oneself, individuals can build a solid foundation for personal growth and overall fulfillment.

Strength of character acts as a guiding compass, steering individuals towards making informed decisions and maintaining harmonious relationships. When we are aware of our values and beliefs, we can align our choices with what truly resonates with us. This alignment not only boosts our self-confidence but also fosters authenticity in our interactions with others. As we embrace our strengths and acknowledge our weaknesses, we develop resilience, humility, and our overall character. This self-awareness allows us to tackle challenges with a positive mindset and seek opportunities for growth.

Emotional well-being thrives on the principles of self-discovery and a strength of character. Understanding our emotional triggers, responses, and needs empowers us to manage stress and cultivate emotional resilience. When we are in touch with our emotions, we can communicate effectively, empathize with others, and establish meaningful connections. Strength of character enables us to approach relationships with empathy, patience, and understanding, nurturing a supportive network that contributes to our emotional well-being. From this place of emotional alignment, we are better able to show up as our best self in both our personal and professional life.

The connection between self-discovery, a balanced strength of character, and professional success is undeniable. In the realm of work and leadership, self-awareness helps us identify our passions and talents, guiding us towards careers that align with our values. Strength of character drives quality decision-making and judgment to lead effective teams that are motivated and inspired; essential qualities for building a successful and respected professional reputation. By continually exploring our strengths and limitations, we can set realistic goals, adapt to changing circumstances, and persistently improve our skills, ultimately advancing our careers.

The journey of self-discovery culminating in strength of character is a transformative process with far-reaching implications. This foundation not only shapes our emotional well-being but also propels our professional growth. By understanding our inner selves and nurturing strength of character, we equip ourselves with the tools needed to navigate life's challenges, build meaningful relationships, and achieve both personal and professional fulfillment.

Leader Character Framework[9]

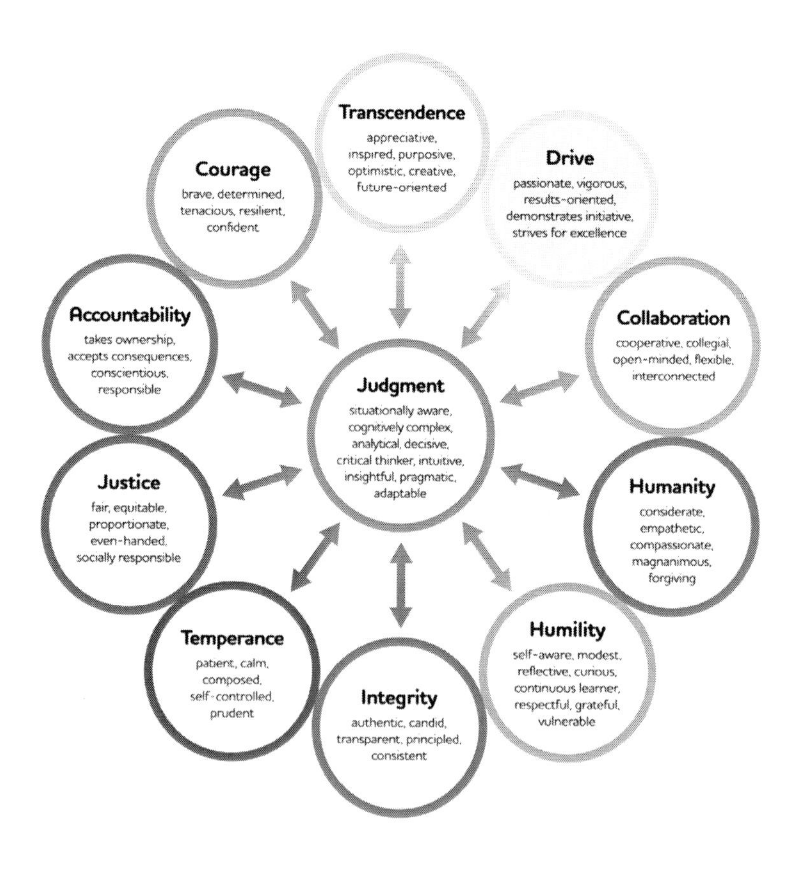

9 "Leader Character Framework," accessed 18 September, 2023, https://virtuositycharacter.ca

Consider these questions:

1. Consider the feedback you've received from friends, family, or colleagues recently. What are the recurring themes or patterns in the feedback you've been given? How does this feedback align with your self-perception or self-assessment, and how might it motivate change, exploration, or celebration? If you haven't received feedback, what can you do to seek out this information?
2. Take a moment to look at the Leader Character Framework. Which areas do you feel are strengths and which areas may require loving/compassionate attention? Which daily habits, patterns, or behaviours can you adapt to bring yourself closer to balance?
3. How do your actions, patterns, and behaviours align with your core values and beliefs? Reflect on instances when you made decisions that were aligned with your principles, and those that weren't. What did you learn from these experiences? How would you adapt your responses to better align your actions with your values?
4. Sit with your thoughts during moments of self-doubt or insecurity. Are there common unhelpful self-talk patterns that arise? How might you challenge and reframe these thoughts to align with a more helpful self-perception?
5. What are the areas in your life where you tend to seek external validation? Reflect on why you may feel the need for validation and how this might impact your self-worth, self-esteem, and confidence. Consider how cultivating self-awareness, self-compassion, and

self-assurance can contribute to a more balanced and resilient character.

6. Examine your daily routines and habits. Which patterns energize and positively impact your day, and which ones tend to drain your energy supply? How might prioritizing value-based activities improve quality of life and life satisfaction?

34

Stop Taking Things Personally

•••••

I learned to stop taking things personally when others appear angry or withdrawn. I realized that their behaviour was not my fault or a reflection of our relationship. This changed the way I engage with them.

Learning to stop taking things personally when others appear angry or withdrawn is a valuable skill that can greatly enhance one's emotional well-being and relationships. Often, people's negative emotions or behaviours are not directed specifically at us, but are a result of their own internal struggles, stressors, or past experiences. Recognizing this allows us to detach ourselves from their negative energy and avoid unnecessary self-blame or guilt. By understanding that their behaviour is not our fault, we can approach the situation with empathy and compassion, which can potentially defuse the tension and open up opportunities for meaningful communication and resolution. This approach also provides space for the other person to process what they are going through. Rather than reacting and expecting them to meet our needs, we can contribute to their wellbeing by allowing them to move through their emotions to meet their own needs first.

Taking things personally can create a cycle of negativity and escalate conflicts unnecessarily. When we internalize someone else's anger or withdrawal, we may react defensively or with equal negativity, further worsening the situation. By reframing our perspective and realizing that their behaviour is not a reflection of our relationship, we gain the power to respond in a more constructive manner. Instead of getting caught up in a cycle of blame and defensiveness, we can take a step back, assess the situation objectively, and respond with patience and understanding. This shift in mindset allows us to break the pattern of personalizing the actions of others and enables us to maintain healthier and more productive relationships.

Not taking things personally fosters a sense of emotional resilience and self-confidence. When we constantly internalize others' behaviour, we may start questioning our worth or the quality of our relationships. This can lead to feelings of self-doubt and have a negative impact on our self-esteem. By recognizing that their anger or withdrawal is not a reflection of our value, we free ourselves from unnecessary self-criticism and can focus on nurturing our own emotional well-being. This newfound emotional resilience allows us to navigate difficult situations with a clearer mind and a stronger sense of self, enabling us to make better decisions and maintain healthy boundaries in our relationships.

By letting go of the need to personalize others' actions, we can cultivate more harmonious and fulfilling relationships.

Consider these questions:

1. In what situations do I tend to take things personally? What about these situations activate a reaction within me?
2. How does taking things personally affect my emotional well-being and relationships? What unhelpful patterns or cycles does it create and/or maintain?
3. What are some potential reasons why others may display anger or withdrawal? How can I broaden my perspective to consider *their* internal struggles, stressors, or past experiences?
4. What strategies or techniques can I employ to detach myself from others' negative energy? How can I avoid unnecessary self-blame, guilt, or shame?
5. How does reframing my perspective empower me to respond more constructively in challenging situations?
6. How can I practice letting go of personalizing the actions of others? How can this cultivate more harmonious and fulfilling relationships?

35

Ask Questions That Support Communication

•••••

I learned how to ask questions that support communication and dialogue rather than provoke confrontation.

Learning how to ask questions that support communication and dialogue rather than provoke confrontation is a transformative skill that can greatly improve relationships and foster understanding. When faced with a disagreement or a potentially confrontational situation, asking open-ended and non-judgmental questions from a place of caring and genuine curiosity can create a safe and inviting space for open discussion. By adopting this approach, we encourage the other person to share their thoughts and perspectives, fostering a climate of understanding and empathy.

By asking open-ended questions and giving space for them to answer, we invite the other person to express their feelings and thoughts more fully and thoughtfully. Instead of framing questions in a way that suggests a particular answer or implies judgment or that can be answered with a simple "yes" or "no," open-ended questions allow individuals to explore their own perspectives, thoughts, and emotions, and share their experiences. This approach helps uncover underlying motivations, fears, or concerns that may not be initially apparent and promotes active listening and demonstrates a genuine interest in understanding the other person's point of view, creating an environment where both parties feel heard and respected.

Examples of open ended questions include:

- Can you tell me more about that?
- How do you feel about this situation?
- What are your thoughts on [topic]?
- What has been your experience with [subject]?
- How would you describe your perspective on [issue]?
- In what ways do you think we could approach this differently?
- What do you think might be the underlying causes of [problem]?
- Could you share an example that illustrates your point?
- What are some potential solutions that come to mind?
- How has [event] affected your feelings or thoughts?
- What would you like to achieve in [area of interest]?
- Can you describe your goals and aspirations regarding [topic]?
- What are your hopes for the future in terms of [subject]?

Non-judgmental questioning promotes a sense of safety and trust within conversations. It also helps to minimize defensiveness and encourage a more collaborative approach to problem-solving. When questions are asked with a judgmental or confrontational tone, they can easily put the other person on the defensive, hindering productive communication. On the other hand, by using non-judgmental language and genuinely seeking to understand, we create an atmosphere of trust and openness. This encourages the other person to engage in the conversation without feeling attacked or criticized, paving the way for more effective problem-solving and resolution. By encouraging others to share their perspectives openly, we create an environment that values diverse viewpoints and promotes active listening, which in turn builds stronger connections and fosters empathy.

Asking questions that support communication and dialogue allows for a deeper exploration of underlying emotions and concerns. Often, confrontations arise from underlying issues or unmet needs that have not been adequately addressed. By using questions that promote reflection and introspection, we encourage the other person to delve deeper into their own emotions and motivations. This can lead to a greater understanding of the root causes of the conflict and open up avenues for finding mutually beneficial solutions.

Adopting this skill enhances interpersonal relationships and enables us to navigate difficult conversations with greater tact and effectiveness that lead to healthier and more meaningful relationships.

Consider these questions:

1. How do my questions tend to provoke confrontation or invite communication and dialogue? What impact does this have on my relationships?
2. Can I recall specific instances where asking open-ended and non-judgmental questions led to a more productive and understanding conversation? How did this approach contribute to creating a safe and inviting space for dialogue?
3. What are some common barriers or challenges I face when attempting to ask open-ended questions? How can I overcome these challenges to foster better communication?
4. Reflecting on past experiences, how have confrontational or judgmental questioning hindered productive communication and problem-solving? How did defensiveness impact the outcome of those interactions?
5. What role does empathy play in asking questions that support communication and dialogue? How can I cultivate empathy in my questioning approach?
6. How can I integrate communication and dialogue-promoting skills into my daily interactions and relationships? What steps must I take to consistently apply these transformative skills?
7. What are three questions I can ask to promote communication with someone I care about?

36

Use Helpful Language

•••••

I learned a helpful approach to language and vocabulary related to stress, anxiety and emotion. I was able to use it to support Brent and Alexis, as well as helping to manage my own stress and anxiety.

This is a valuable skill that promotes effective communication and emotional well-being. When there is a heightened level of emotion, the likelihood of using confrontational language is increased. When we are able to pause, regulate, and then shift to language that focuses more on gaining insights, we are better able to work towards solutions.

Examples of confrontational and insightful language include:

Confrontational Language	Insightful Language
"We need to tackle this problem head-on and defeat it."	"Let's consider how we can address your feelings and find a solution that brings comfort."

"I won't back down until you see things my way."	"Let's collaborate to find a solution that eases the tension and improves the situation for both of us."
"This is your fault; you need to fix it."	"What can we do to ensure both of us feel heard and respected?"
"I'm going to fight for what I want."	"I want to work together to meet both our needs. Let's approach this with the goal of maintaining a positive and supporting environment for both of us."

Acquiring insightful language equips individuals with the tools to better understand and express their own emotions, as well as provide targeted support to their loved ones.

Expanding one's vocabulary allows us to be more precise when describing our personal experiences and feelings. When we can accurately label and express our own emotions, we gain a deeper understanding of our stress and anxiety triggers. This heightened self-awareness enables us to take proactive steps in managing our own well-being. Additionally, possessing a richer vocabulary empowers individuals to communicate more effectively with their loved ones, enhancing the overall level of understanding and empathy in the relationship.

Engaging in helpful language also introduces individuals to various coping strategies and techniques for managing stress and anxiety. Exploring mindfulness, relaxation techniques, or cognitive reframing can provide us with a broader range of tools to effectively manage our emotional well-being. By implementing these strategies in our lives, we can model healthy coping mechanisms for our loved ones, leading by example and promoting overall well-being within the relationship.

By understanding and using the same language as each other, individuals within a relationship can better empathize with their loved one's experiences and challenges. This facilitates a deeper level of understanding, enabling individuals to provide more meaningful support. Being able to communicate using this shared vocabulary helps individuals navigate conversations around stress and anxiety more effectively, fostering an environment of trust, compassion, and support.

The feelings wheel is a visual tool that categorizes and illustrates a wide range of emotions and feelings. It consists of a circular diagram divided into different sections, each representing a category of emotions. The wheel starts with broad categories in the centre sections, such as happiness, sadness, anger, fear, surprise, and disgust. As you move toward the outer perimeter of the wheel, more nuanced and specific emotions are displayed. These choices allow individuals to pinpoint their feelings with greater accuracy. An example of a feelings wheel created by Dr. Gloria Willcox is shown below.

The purpose of this tool is to help individuals increase their emotional vocabulary and develop a deeper understanding of their own emotional experiences. This can be valuable for self-reflection, communication, and emotional regulation.

The Feelings Wheel[10]

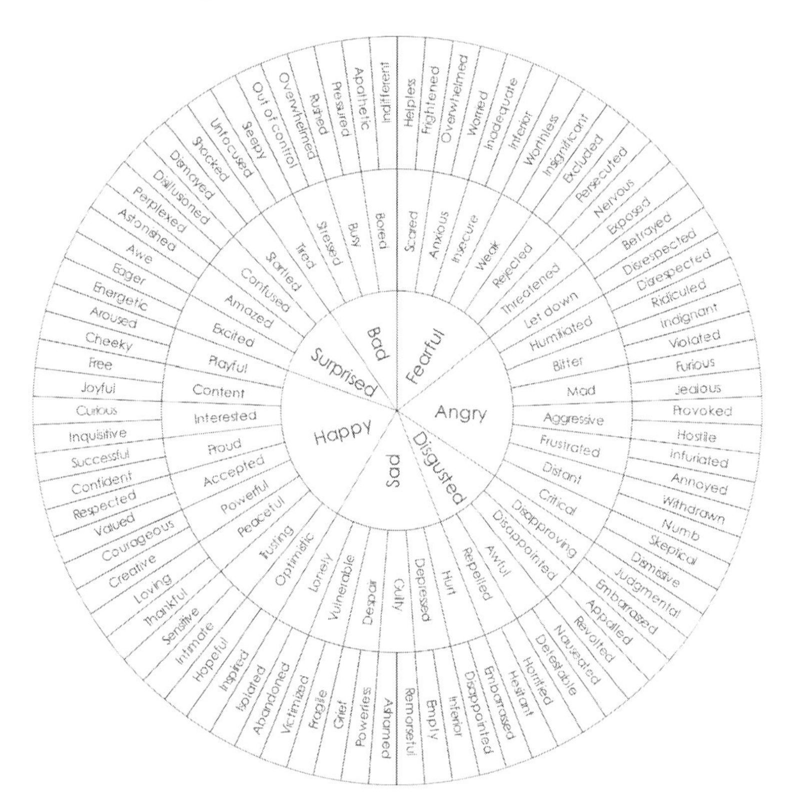

Having this shared language strengthens the ability to support and empathize with a loved one, fostering a deeper connection and promoting a supportive environment. By developing and using helpful language, we enhance our capacity to support and nurture the well-being of both ourselves and our loved ones.

10 "Feelings Wheel," RewardCharts4Kids, accessed 18 September, 2023, https://www.rewardcharts4kids.com/feelings-wheel/.

Consider these questions:

1. How would acquiring new communication skills around stress and anxiety benefit my own emotional well-being? How would it influence my ability to support my loved ones?
2. Reflect upon a scenario that a lack of shared language around stress and anxiety led to misunderstandings or hindered emotional support in my relationships. How can I work towards fostering a shared understanding and language in those situations?
3. What are some specific stress and anxiety moments in my life that I struggle to articulate? How could expanding my vocabulary help me better understand and express these emotions?
4. Have I noticed any patterns in my loved one's stress and anxiety levels that could be better addressed through a shared vocabulary and understanding? How can this improve our communication and support with each other?
5. How can the use of a feelings wheel or other visual tools contribute to my emotional vocabulary and self-awareness? In what ways can this help me in self-reflection, communication, and emotional regulation?
6. How can I integrate the use of a shared vocabulary into my daily interactions with my loved ones? What resources or strategies can I apply to expand my emotional vocabulary and strengthen the connections with those I care about?
7. Which words on the emotions wheel best describe how I am feeling in this moment?

37

Speak Authentically

•••••

I learned to speak authentically, communicating honestly to say what I mean and ask for what I need.

Learning to speak authentically is an empowering and transformative skill that can greatly enhance communication, assertiveness, personal relationships and overall well-being. Often, people hesitate to express their true thoughts and needs due to fear of judgement, rejection, conflict, or the desire to please others. However, by developing the ability to communicate authentically and assertively, individuals can foster stronger connections, establish boundaries, and ensure their own needs are met while creating healthier relationships and navigate life with greater confidence.

When you speak authentically to say what you mean, you communicate your thoughts and feelings honestly and directly. This allows others to understand your intentions and desires clearly. This clarity eliminates ambiguity and reduces the potential for misunderstandings. It promotes open and authentic communication. By expressing yourself genuinely, you enable others to understand your perspectives and make informed decisions. This promotes healthier and more productive interactions, as everyone involved has a clear understanding of where you stand, reducing confusion and potential miscommunication. This fosters mutual understanding, trust, and respect within relationships.

Learning to speak authentically and say what you mean and ask for what you need is essential for personal growth and fulfilment. By clearly articulating your needs, you empower yourself to take ownership of your well-being and create opportunities for others to support you. Whether it is asking for emotional support, help with a task, stating a preference, or setting boundaries, communicating your needs allows you to create a supportive network and cultivate relationships that are based on mutual respect and understanding. When you assertively ask for what you need, you also demonstrate self-worth and the confidence to advocate for yourself.

Expressing your true thoughts and needs fosters authenticity and deepens connections with others. By sharing your genuine thoughts and feelings, you invite others to do the same, creating a space for open and honest communication. This vulnerability can lead to more meaningful and fulfilling relationships, as it allows for a deeper level of understanding and emotional intimacy. When you communicate authentically, you encourage others to reciprocate, fostering trust and building stronger connections based on mutual respect and support.

By mastering this skill, you can cultivate healthier and more fulfilling relationships, while also nurturing your own growth and self-advocacy.

Consider these questions:

1. How comfortable am I with expressing my true thoughts and needs? What patterns or tendencies in my communication style hinder my authentic and/or assertive self-expression? What skills can I use to become more aware of these patterns and make intentional efforts to improve my communication?
2. In which instances have I felt unheard or unsupported because I didn't effectively communicate my needs or desires? How can I learn from those experiences and approach similar situations differently in the future?
3. What common fears or concerns prevent me from saying what I mean or asking for what I need? How can I address or overcome these fears?
4. How does expressing myself honestly and assertively contribute to building stronger connections and establishing boundaries within relationships? Can I think of examples where setting clear boundaries would have been beneficial for my well-being?
5. How can I balance expressing my needs with actively listening and considering the perspectives of others? What can I do to ensure my communication is respectful and open-ended while still advocating for myself?
6. How can I actively practice saying what I mean and asking for what I need in my daily interactions? Are there specific scenarios or relationships where I can focus on applying this skill?

38

Confide in Someone You Trust

•••••

I learned the benefit of having a trusted person who I could talk to without judgment about my feelings.

Learning the benefit of having a trusted person whom you can talk to about your feelings without judgement is a valuable asset for emotional well-being and personal growth. When faced with confusion or frustrations, it is natural to experience a range of emotions that can weigh us down if left unexpressed. Having a trusted friend, coach, therapist, spiritual leader, support group, or social worker to confide in provides a safe space to unload those negative emotions, allowing for a release and a sense of relief.

Sharing your feelings with a trusted confidant offers a cathartic experience. Verbalizing and externalizing your emotions can be a powerful way to process and make sense of them. By expressing your confusion or frustrations to someone you trust, you gain the opportunity to organize your thoughts and gain perspective on the situation. This process helps in relieving the burden and prevents the negativity from lingering and affecting other aspects of your life. It can also help you uncover new perspectives, challenge any limiting beliefs, and gain a deeper understanding of yourself.

Speaking openly to a non-judgmental person allows you to be vulnerable and authentic. In a safe and accepting environment, you can share your deepest concerns and fears without fear of being criticized or invalidated. Having someone who listens without judgment helps you feel heard and validated, which promotes emotional well-being and strengthens your connection with that friend. It also cultivates a sense of trust and intimacy within the relationship, allowing for more meaningful and supportive interactions.

Confiding in someone you trust helps to foster personal growth and self-awareness. This person can offer guidance, provide empathy, or simply be a sounding board for you to reflect on your feelings. This supportive dynamic encourages self-reflection, allowing you to gain clarity and develop new insights about yourself and the challenges you face. As a result, you become better equipped to navigate future experiences and manage your emotions effectively.

By having such a person, you can alleviate emotional burdens, foster personal growth, and enhance your overall well-being.

Consider these questions:

1. What is the benefit of having a trusted person to confide in about my feelings? Can I recall specific instances where sharing my feelings provided relief?
2. What qualities do I look for in a trusted confidante? What can I do to identify individuals in my life who are non-judgmental and supportive?
3. How have open and non-judgmental conversations contributed to my being authentic and vulnerable? How has being able to express my concerns and fears impacted my overall well-being?
4. Can I think of specific instances where confiding in another has helped me foster personal growth and self-awareness? How did their support and insights contribute to my development?
5. Have there been times when I hesitated to confide in someone due to fear of judgment or criticism? What do I need in a relationship to overcome this fear and cultivate trust in them?
6. How can I actively nurture and maintain the bond with my trusted person? What steps can I take to strengthen our connection and create an ongoing space for open and authentic conversations?

39

Appreciate All Your Days

•••••

I learned that there will be good days and better days and to appreciate each.

Learning to appreciate both good days and better days is a valuable lesson that fosters gratitude, resilience, and a positive mindset. Recognizing that not every day will be perfect and that there is value in every moment allows us to embrace a more positive and balanced perspective. Life is filled with ups and downs, and recognizing and cherishing the moments of joy and positivity, regardless of their intensity, can lead to a more fulfilling and contented existence.

Appreciating good days cultivates gratitude and mindfulness. When we acknowledge and savour the small victories, simple pleasures, and moments of happiness, we train ourselves to be present and fully experience the positive aspects of our lives. By practising a habit of gratitude for the good days, we develop a more optimistic outlook, which in turn can contribute to enhanced mental and emotional well-being. This mindset shift helps us to find happiness in the present moment, rather than constantly chasing after an elusive state of perfection.

Better days are those in which we may face challenges but still manage to find moments of joy, personal achievement, or meaningful connections. Recognizing and valuing better days fosters a sense of progress and growth. These days remind us of our resilience and ability to overcome obstacles. By appreciating the progress made on these better days, we gain a sense of accomplishment and motivation to continue moving forward, even during more difficult times.

Appreciating both good days and better days helps us develop resilience and adaptability. It allows us to find silver linings and positive aspects even when faced with adversity. By recognizing the good within the spectrum of experiences, we can reframe challenging situations and find strength in the midst of difficulty. This mindset shift helps us maintain a balanced perspective and navigate through life's ups and downs with greater ease and emotional stability.

Learning to appreciate each type of day promotes a healthier and more sustainable approach to happiness. It reminds us that happiness is not solely dependent on extraordinary or exceptional moments but can be found in the everyday joys and the progress we make. By embracing this mindset, we cultivate a deeper sense of contentment and fulfilment in our lives, rather than constantly chasing after fleeting moments of intense happiness. We develop a greater capacity to adapt, find meaning, and appreciate the journey rather than fixating on a destination.

By appreciating each type of day, we cultivate a sustainable and fulfilling approach to happiness and a more enriched experience of life.

Consider these questions:

1. What practices do I engage in to show appreciation for the good days in my life? What are some specific habits that help me cultivate gratitude and mindfulness during those moments?
2. Are there days that have been challenging, yet bring about moments of joy and personal growth? How did I recognize and value those moments, and how did they contribute to my resilience and progress?
3. Do I tend to focus more on extraordinary moments or exceptional experiences when it comes to seeking happiness? How can I shift my perspective to appreciate the everyday joys and small victories that make up good days?
4. Can I recall how self-awareness, appreciation of progress, and determination allowed me to overcome challenges? What motivated me to keep moving forward and overcome difficulties?
5. How can I incorporate a daily practice of appreciation and gratitude that fosters a healthier and more sustainable approach to wellbeing? What specific actions or reflections can help me cultivate a deeper sense of contentment and fulfilment in my life?
6. What steps can I take to embrace the journey and appreciate each moment? What challenges can arise that cause me to fixate on a specific destination? How can I develop a greater capacity to adapt, find meaning, and savour the progress and growth I experience on both good days and better days?

40

Talk Regularly about Mental Health

•••••

I learned to make the topic of mental well-being a daily conversation in our home, at work and in social settings.

Making the topic of mental well-being a daily conversation in all interactions, but especially in our home is a transformative practice that promotes open communication, support, and overall emotional health. By prioritizing and normalizing discussions about mental well-being, we create a safe and nurturing environment for ourselves and our loved ones.

Regular conversations about mental well-being help to break down the stigma surrounding mental health. By openly discussing emotions, stress, and self-care, we challenge the notion that mental health is a taboo topic. A culture of acceptance and understanding is created. This helps to foster an atmosphere where everyone feels comfortable expressing their feelings and seeking support when needed. It also encourages a more empathetic and understanding approach towards mental health, fostering a sense of compassion and acceptance.

Making mental well-being a daily conversation creates opportunities for early detection and intervention. Regular discussions allow us to identify any changes or challenges that may arise in our emotional well-being or that of our loved ones. By being attuned to the well-being of each family member, we can recognize signs of distress, anxiety, or other mental health issues. This early awareness enables us to provide timely support, seek professional help if necessary, and prevent potential crises from escalating. By checking in with each other and actively listening to each other's experiences, we create space for empathy and connection. Family members can offer guidance, encouragement, and a listening ear, providing valuable emotional support. This practice fosters a sense of togetherness and strengthens the familial bond, promoting a shared understanding of each other's emotional needs.

Regular conversations about mental well-being cultivate emotional intelligence and resilience. By discussing emotions and coping strategies, we equip ourselves and our loved ones with the tools to navigate life's challenges more effectively. These conversations foster self-awareness, emotional regulation, and the development of healthy coping mechanisms. They also encourage problem-solving and a growth mindset, enabling family members to approach difficulties with resilience and a proactive attitude.

When we openly share our feelings, concerns, and triumphs, we create a space of vulnerability and authenticity. This fosters deep connections and strengthens the support system within the family. By actively listening and supporting one another's mental well-being, we demonstrate care, empathy, and validation, strengthening the bonds that hold our relationships together.

By prioritizing mental well-being in daily conversations, we create a foundation for a healthier and happier environment and contribute to stigma reduction.

Consider these questions:

1. How can I initiate and maintain regular conversations about mental well-being within my family/workplaces/social circles?
2. What are some strategies I can implement to create a safe and nurturing environment where everyone feels comfortable discussing their emotions and asking for support?
3. How can I challenge the stigma surrounding mental health within my family/workplaces/social circles and foster a culture of acceptance and understanding?
4. What can I do to actively listen and be attuned to the emotional well-being of each family member? How can I recognize signs of distress or mental health challenges?
5. What are some coping strategies and healthy mechanisms I can establish within my family to navigate life's challenges more effectively?
6. How can I ensure that my conversations about mental well-being promote compassion, validation, and authentic connections within our family?

41

Hope Can Save A Life

•••••

I learned that being vulnerable and sharing my story offers hope to those who may be struggling with similar challenges. Hope can be a lifeline to foster a pathway towards healing and recovery.

This is a profound realization that highlights the power of positivity, compassion, and support. In times of darkness and despair, a glimmer of hope can make an immense difference, offering solace, motivation, and the belief that better days lie ahead.

Hope provides a sense of purpose and meaning, even in the face of adversity. When someone feels lost or overwhelmed by life's challenges, offering a message of hope can ignite a spark within them, reigniting their determination to persevere. Hope reminds individuals that their current circumstances do not define their future, and that with resilience and support, they can overcome obstacles and find a path towards fulfilment and well-being.

Bringing hope can inspire resilience and foster a positive mindset. By offering encouragement, empathy, and reassurance, we help individuals reframe their perspectives and see beyond their immediate struggles. Hope shifts the focus from despair to possibility, reminding individuals of their inherent strengths and potential for growth. It helps them envision a better future. This renewed sense of optimism empowers individuals to take proactive steps towards positive change, propelling them towards a brighter future.

Hope has the power to uplift spirits, build connections, and strengthen communities. Bringing hope can create a ripple effect, impacting not only the individual but also those around them. By sharing messages of hope, we create an environment of support and understanding, where individuals feel valued and encouraged. This sense of unity and shared purpose generates a collective resilience that can transform lives and communities.

In times of crisis or when someone is battling mental health challenges, hope can be a lifeline. It reminds individuals that they are not alone, that there are people who care and believe in their potential. Hope instills a sense of belonging and gives individuals the courage to reach out for help, fostering a pathway towards healing and recovery.

Leaning into the space of supporting those affected by trauma or living with mental health issues has been a transformative journey for me, deeply contributing to my sense of purpose. As I began gaining and sharing knowledge, raising awareness, and promoting understanding about mental health, I witnessed how this encouraged others to speak up, seek help, and challenge the societal structures that perpetuate stigma.

When I educate others about mental illness, I feel a tremendous sense of fulfillment and purpose because I know I am making a positive difference. By dispelling misconceptions and breaking down stigma, I am actively working towards creating a more inclusive and supportive society. Witnessing the transformation in their confidence and their ability to advocate for themselves and others gives me a deep sense of purpose. I am fueled by the belief that I am playing a part, no matter how small, in reshaping the narrative around mental health and fostering a more compassionate and understanding world for those affected by trauma and mental illness.

Educating others about mental illness has forced me to confront my own biases and misconceptions. As I dug deeper into the subject, I realized that I, too, held certain stigmatizing beliefs that needed to be addressed. Through self-reflection and an openness to learning, I have been able to challenge and reshape my perspectives, leading to personal growth and a deeper understanding of the complexities of mental health. This ongoing journey of self-discovery has infused my sense of purpose with a profound sense of authenticity and integrity. Knowing that my efforts have helped someone navigate the challenges of mental health and find solace and support brings immense meaning to my life.

By sharing messages of hope, we hold the potential to make a meaningful difference in the lives of others, reminding them of their worth and the endless possibilities that lie ahead.

Consider these questions:

1. How can I cultivate a mindset of hope and positivity in my own life, so that I can effectively bring hope to others?
2. What are some practical ways I can offer messages of hope and support to individuals who are going through challenging times?
3. How can I create a supportive and compassionate environment where individuals feel safe to express their struggles?
4. What steps can I take to challenge the stigma surrounding mental health and promote understanding within my communities?
5. How can I show compassion to those who are facing trauma or mental health issues, while respecting their individual journey?
6. What resources or organizations are available that can connect individuals with the supports needed on their path of healing and/or recovery?

42

Grief Is Complex

•••••

I learned that grief is not a linear process but a complex and individual journey. It is unpredictable, comes in waves, and disrupts rational thought.

Grief, as I've come to understand it, is a force of nature that defies predictability and disrupts the logical flow of thoughts and emotions. It manifests as an ocean, where waves of sorrow, anger, confusion, and even moments of unexpected clarity crash against the shores of our consciousness. What strikes me most about grief is its inherent unpredictability; it arrives unannounced and lingers without a set timetable. In the throes of grief, one can never anticipate when the next wave of emotion will wash over them, nor can they fully prepare for its intensity. This unpredictability is what makes grief such a formidable force, capable of catching even the most composed individuals off guard.

Grief possesses the uncanny ability to disrupt rational thought and cloud the clarity of the mind. In its wake, we often find ourselves grappling with thoughts and feelings that seem irrational or contradictory. It can lead to self-doubt, guilt, and a sense of disorientation. I've experienced moments when grief has transformed my once logical and ordered mind into a maze of conflicting emotions and thoughts. It's as if grief has its own language, one that I don't understand and which doesn't adhere to the conventions of reason. In these moments, it's crucial to remind oneself that these disruptions are a natural part of the grieving process, and they don't diminish the validity of our emotions or experiences.

One of the most profound lessons I've learned on my journey through grief is that it is inherently personal and unique to each individual. No two people grieve in precisely the same way, and there is no universal roadmap for navigating the complexities of loss. While some may find solace in seeking company and sharing their feelings, others may prefer solitude and introspection. The duration and intensity of grief can also vary greatly, with some finding healing over time, while others carry the weight of grief with them for years. This diversity of experiences underscores the individuality of grief and the need for compassion and understanding when someone is experiencing grief. It is a reminder that there is no right or wrong way to grieve, only the way that feels authentic to the one experiencing it.

Experiencing grief has taught me the profound depths of human emotions and the resilience of the human spirit. I have learned that it is okay to feel a range of emotions, from sadness and anger to guilt and confusion. Each emotion is valid and serves a purpose in the healing process. Grief has taught me the importance of allowing myself to fully experience and process these emotions without judgment or expectation, giving myself permission to grieve in my own unique way.

Through grief, I have learned the significance of self-care and self-compassion. I realized that healing requires patience and gentleness with oneself. It is essential to prioritize self-care activities that nourish and replenish the mind, body, and soul. Whether it's seeking support from loved ones, engaging in therapy or counseling, practicing mindfulness and meditation, or engaging in activities that bring joy and comfort, I have learned that self-care is an integral part of my healing process. Grief has taught me to listen to my own needs and honour my healing journey.

Grief reinforced the importance of connection and support. It has shown me the power of leaning on others for comfort, understanding, and empathy. I have learned that it is okay to ask for help and to lean on my support system. Sharing my feelings and memories with others who have experienced loss has provided a sense of validation and solace. I have learned that connecting with others who have walked a similar path can provide a sense of understanding and community. Grief has taught me that healing is not a solitary journey but one that is best navigated with the support and love of others.

This is my experience of grief told through metaphor:

When mired in the early stages it was like I was barely treading water in an ocean of grief. My feet couldn't touch the ocean floor and my arms and legs were exhausted from supporting my struggle. Often my head would dip below the water line, where it felt like I was drowning. A break in the heavy waves would allow a brief moment for me to catch a small breath of air before the next wave overtook me. The lifeguard could throw the life ring within an arm's length of me, but I did not have the strength to reach for it. I remember when the undertow carried me out so far in the water that I could barely see the shore or the life ring bobbing beside me. I'd hear voices far off in the distance. When the winds shifted just slightly, the voice would get louder. It was a bright, light voice that said "Mamma" and gave me the strength to grab onto the life ring. Holding tightly, I allowed myself to be pulled back to shore. The waves were still relentless, but the pull of the life ring was ever-present. Soon I was able to feel the ocean bottom. A mixture of soft sand and hard shells on the soles of my feet. After having been in the waters so long, my flesh was tender. I knew I could easily get injured.

I was careful with each step and used the support of the life ring to help stabilize me. The weight and the power of the waves began to dissipate. As I made each step forward through the water and more of my body began to feel the sun on my skin, I felt a feeling of safety returning. I was more confident, more stable with each step I took. When the water was just above knee level, I let go of the life ring. I was close enough to the shore to see the people who had been working together to pull me in. I saw my mom, dad, and sisters. My northern friends from Yellowknife and Hay River were near the front of the line. Behind them was an army of people I didn't know. They had come to lend support to those who were supporting me. My Ottawa girlfriends were standing in a line together, gripping the rope tightly. They had been pulling on the rope even when I'd let it go. I continued to wade through the waters towards the shore. I could see Alexis happily playing at the edge of the water. She was trying not to get her feet wet. She was content to build sandcastles and find shells along the shoreline. At this point, I had the strength and curiosity to look behind me towards the horizon. I could see others in the ocean of grief, all at different depths and distances from the shore. Some were holding life rings, others had not been able to reach theirs just yet.

I could take a few moments to raise my face up towards the sun and feel the warmth on my face. I inhaled deeply, filling my lungs with air. It was as if I hadn't been able to do that forever. I held my breath for a few moments. When I exhaled, I let go of the feeling that I needed to rescue the others. They were each on their own journey. I was hoping that they saw me grab the life ring and watched as I made my way back to shore. With the help of others, they could escape the wrath of the waves and reach calmer waters. My feet and legs were still wet, but the weight of the water was gone.

As I stood in the shin-deep water looking out at the others floating in the ocean of grief, I felt a warm hand take mine. Brent had waded into the shallow waters to meet me. His presence was enough to make me turn around and face the shore. Hand in hand we watched Alexis playing on the beach, her feet still dry. We walked together toward her.

There would be times when I returned to grief beach. Sometimes when the winds were high the waves splashed water on my feet. Other times I felt the need to wade ankle deep. Other times I'd sit down on the sand and watch the waves roll in. When I visit this beach on the edge of the ocean of grief, this is how I watch the water, from a place of dry ground with greater clarity and awe. The wind is not as strong as years ago, and the waters are moving more gently. The ocean will always be in motion, but sitting quietly on the sand, I don't feel it. I can watch it from a distance and find peace.

Questions to consider:

1. How has the experience of grief and loss affected my emotional well-being?
2. In what ways have I granted myself permission to grieve authentically and fully experience and process my emotions during grief, without judgment or expectation? How has this impacted my ability to heal and find meaning in my loss?
3. What strategies or coping mechanisms have I developed to navigate the unpredictable nature of grief? Have I found any effective ways to prepare myself for its waves of emotion?
4. What aspects of the grieving process have been particularly challenging? Why have these challenges been particularly difficult?
5. How have my relationships with others changed as a result of my grief?
6. Have there been any moments of growth or personal insights that have emerged from my experience of grief? How have I integrated these insights into my daily life?
7. How have I applied the importance of self-care and self-compassion in my own healing process? Can I identify specific self-care activities or practices that have been particularly effective for me?
8. How can I honour and remember my loved one while still allowing myself to heal and move forward?

43

The Value of Seeking Professional Help

This is how to foster an environment that promotes recovery and overall well-being.

Seeking professional help for oneself when experiencing personal challenges or supporting loved ones with mental health challenges is a crucial step towards maintaining one's own well-being and providing effective support. Often, when we care deeply about someone who is struggling with their mental health, we may neglect our own needs and emotions, leading to burnout, increased stress, and a decline in our own mental well-being. Engaging in therapy or counselling sessions allows us to gain valuable insight into our own emotions, develop coping strategies, and receive the necessary support to navigate the challenges associated with supporting our loved ones.

Professional help provides a safe and non-judgmental space for individuals to express their thoughts and emotions. When supporting loved ones with mental health challenges, it's natural to experience a range of emotions, including sadness, frustration, or even guilt. However, it can be challenging to process and manage these emotions on our own. Seeking professional help allows us to explore and understand our feelings in a supportive environment, helping us gain clarity and perspective. Therapists and counsellors can provide valuable guidance, helping us develop healthy coping mechanisms and strategies to navigate the emotional complexities that arise when supporting someone with mental health issues.

In addition to emotional support, professional help equips individuals with practical tools and knowledge. Mental health professionals possess specialized expertise and can offer insights into the nature of mental health challenges, various treatment options, and effective communication techniques. This knowledge empowers individuals to provide more informed and effective support to their loved ones. By learning about different coping strategies, understanding the dynamics of mental health disorders, and acquiring communication skills, individuals can play a more active and supportive role, fostering an environment that promotes recovery and overall well-being.

Another significant benefit of seeking professional help is the validation it provides. Supporting loved ones with mental health challenges can sometimes be isolating, as others may not fully understand or acknowledge the complexities involved. Engaging in therapy or counselling allows individuals to share their experiences in a non-judgmental space and receive validation for their feelings and efforts. This validation can be immensely empowering and reassuring, reminding individuals that they are not alone in their struggles and that their experiences are valid and worthy of attention.

A complimentary option to support yourself is engaging with a professional certified coach. Psychological therapy and certified coaching are two distinct approaches that aim to support individuals in navigating life's challenges. While they share some similarities in promoting well-being and personal growth, there are key differences in their focus, objectives, and methodologies.

Therapists are trained to diagnose and treat mental health disorders, psychological distress, and emotional difficulties. They work with individuals to explore and address deep-rooted issues, unresolved traumas, and patterns of thinking or behaviour that contribute to emotional and psychological challenges. Therapy involves a therapeutic relationship where clients can delve into their past experiences, gain insight, and develop coping strategies. Therapists employ various therapeutic modalities such as cognitive-behavioural therapy (CBT), psychodynamic therapy, or mindfulness-based approaches to facilitate healing, personal growth, and improved mental health.

Certified coaching, on the other hand, is dedicated to bridging the distance between your current state and your desired future, all while acknowledging that your next steps emerge from your inner wisdom. This form of coaching encompasses a diverse range of strategies aimed at propelling you towards your envisioned outcomes. These strategies encompass nurturing personal strengths, cultivating adaptability, and fostering personal growth, all of which are guided by the belief that your innate wisdom holds the keys to your journey.

Certified coaches partner with individuals navigating setbacks, confronting challenges, searching for deeper understanding of themselves, or seeking to refine their abilities to thrive in their life. During this process, a coach serves as a guide, helping you tap into your potential to successfully navigate adversity. Within the realm of certified coaching, the spotlight during coaching sessions frequently falls on the cultivation of practical skills, transformative shifts in perspective, and empowerment to translate your inner wisdom into decisive actions. Through this collaborative journey, a coach serves as a facilitator, guiding you to recognize and embrace the wisdom that resides within you. This wisdom, combined with expert coaching guidance, becomes the compass that navigates you toward your aspirations and a future that resonates deeply with your inner values and insights.

Seeking professional help for oneself when supporting loved ones with mental health challenges is essential for maintaining personal well-being and providing effective support. By engaging in therapy, counselling, and/or coaching, individuals can gain valuable insights, emotional support, and practical tools to navigate the complexities associated with supporting someone with mental health issues. This proactive step not only enhances their own mental well-being but also equips them with the knowledge and skills to create a supportive environment for their loved ones. Ultimately, seeking professional help is an act of self-care that allows individuals to provide the best possible support while preserving their own mental health and resilience.

Consider these questions:

1. Have I been prioritizing or neglecting my well-being? How have I supported my wellness journey and what habits get in the way?
2. What are the potential consequences of neglecting my own needs and emotions? How will this affect the support I provide for myself and others?
3. How can seeking professional help for myself enhance my ability to support others?
4. What are some specific emotional reactions I have faced while supporting someone with mental health challenges? How have these emotions impacted my own mental well-being?
5. How can my self-care and personal growth positively influence my ability to provide effective support to my loved ones?
6. What are some alternative modalities of care, such as certified coaching, that I can consider to better support myself in providing care to others?

Visit www.jodiebaulkham.com to download a free version that contains these lessons learned and has room for you to journal and capture your reflections.

Conclusion

•••••

AS I REFLECT upon the journey recounted in these pages, I am filled with an overwhelming sense of gratitude. The path I have travelled has been anything but smooth, strewn with immense challenges, heart-wrenching grief, and relentless battles. Yet, through it all, I have discovered an incredible resilience within myself, a strength that I never knew existed. This memoir has been a testament to the strength of the human spirit and a reminder that joy can be found in even the most difficult of circumstances.

Surviving grief is a deeply personal and intricate process, one that cannot be neatly packaged or universally understood. It is a journey that forces us to confront our vulnerabilities, our fears, and the profound ache of loss. Losing a loved one leaves an indelible mark on our souls, forever altering the fabric of our existence. There is an additional layer when the justice system is part of the process. But amidst the darkness, there is also a glimmer of hope. It is through our grief that we can rediscover the true essence of life and learn to cherish each moment.

Supporting a loved one with PTSD is an ongoing commitment, requiring unwavering patience, empathy, and understanding. It demands that we become warriors of compassion, willing to stand by their side through the darkest nights and fiercest battles. The journey of healing is non-linear, filled with setbacks and small victories, but it is a journey worth embarking upon. By educating ourselves about PTSD and cultivating a safe and nurturing environment, we can provide the love and support necessary for our loved ones to reclaim their lives and find solace within themselves.

Raising a child with OCD adds an additional layer of complexity to our lives. It requires us to be both advocates and confidants, guiding them through their anxious thoughts and behaviours. The journey can be overwhelming, at times, but witnessing the sheer resilience and strength of our child demonstrates the power of love and determination. Through patience, therapy, and a supportive network, we can help our children navigate their fears, encouraging them to embrace their uniqueness and find their own paths to fulfilment.

Amidst the turbulence of grief, PTSD, and OCD, I have discovered an enduring truth: joy can coexist with pain. Life is composed of moments of immense beauty and profound sadness. It is in embracing the full spectrum of human emotions that we truly appreciate the vibrant essence of joy. It is in finding the courage to live authentically, despite the storms that rage within and around us, that we unearth the strength to savour every ounce of happiness that comes our way.

Throughout my life, I have learned that resilience is not born out of an absence of struggle but rather through an unwavering commitment to endure and grow. It is in acknowledging the scars that mark our souls and accepting them as part of our story that we can truly find peace. By sharing my experiences and exposing my vulnerabilities, I hope to inspire others on their own journeys, reminding them that they are not alone and that hope is a flame that can never be extinguished.

In the end, this memoir is not solely about surviving grief or supporting a loved one with PTSD or raising a child with OCD. It is about the resilience of the human spirit and the power of love. It is a celebration of the countless moments, both big and small, that make life worth living. It is a reminder that even in the face of unimaginable challenges, there is always room for joy, growth, and healing.

The significance of choice cannot be overlooked throughout this narrative. In the face of adversity, we are confronted with choices— to succumb or to fight, to despair or to hope, to retreat or to persevere. It is in these choices that we exercise our agency, shaping the course of our tomorrows and finding the strength to embrace the joy of living.

May these words serve as a beacon of hope for those grappling with grief, PTSD, OCD, or any other trial that weighs upon their hearts. I implore you to harness the power of choice within your own journey. Even in the face of unimaginable grief and daunting challenges, remember that you hold the key to shaping your narrative. Through the tears, the laughter, and the love that threads its way through our lives, choose to lean into the pain, to seek support, and to find solace in the joy that still exists. It is through the realm of choice that we tap into our inherent resilience, foster personal growth, and embrace the joy that emerges in our lives.

This is my story. May it be a reminder that even in the darkest of nights, the sun will inevitably rise, and your tomorrow holds the promise of joy.

With unwavering belief in the transformative power of choice, connection, and an enduring commitment to embrace life's joys,

Epilogue

CHOOSING TO HARNESS the power of choice is a lifelong commitment.

As this book entered production, our family has been confronted with another legal hurdle as the man convicted of Chris' murder has applied for the opportunity to seek early parole before his twenty-five years are served. He is doing so under section 745.6 of the Criminal Code, sometimes known as "The Faint Hope Clause."

Prime Minister Harper was able to enact some of his tough on crime initiatives during his tenure as the leader of our country. On December 2, 2011, the section of the Criminal Code of Canada being used by Chris' murderer to seek parole was repealed. Unfortunately for our family, this change cannot be applied to crimes committed prior to this date.

This process has once again put my resilience to the test. I have come to acknowledge that this will always be an undercurrent in my life, until Chris' murderer dies.

My approach to moving through the adversity that flows my way, including my breast cancer and double mastectomy and now this legal process, is rooted in my lessons learned through navigating tragedy. It's not about denying the pain or difficulty. It's about making the conscious choice to remain positive and look to make an impact, practicing gratitude, finding joy in the small and larger moments in my life, and choosing to show up tomorrow. The power of choice and the pursuit of joy have become my guiding stars on this journey of resilience and I will continue to draw on those principles for the rest of my life.

April 2009, Seattle Washington

November 2011, Banff Alberta

November 2011, Banff Alberta

November 2011, Banff Alberta

November 2011, Banff Alberta

Summer 2014, Sanca, British Columbia

Summer 2015, Ingersoll Ontario

December 2014, Ottawa Ontario

September 2015, Henderson New York

February 2015, Puerto Aventuras México

September 2014, London England

September 2018, Ottawa Ontario

December 2021, Edmonton Alberta

April 2022, Yellowknife Northwest Territories

November 2022, Disneyland California

Appendix A

Mental Health Continuum[11]

HEALTHY (Green)	REACTING (Yellow)	INJURED (Orange)	ILL (Red)
Normal mood fluctuations Calm/confident	Irritable/impatient Nervous Sadness/ overwhelmed	Anger Anxiety Pervasive sadness/hopeless	Easily enraged/ aggression Excessive anxiety/ panic attacks Depressed mood/ numb
Good sense of humour Taking things in stride In control mentally Can concentrate/ focus	Displaced sarcasm Distracted/loses focus Intrusive thoughts	Negative attitude Recurrent intrusive thoughts Constantly distracted Can't focus on tasks	Non compliant Cannot concentrate Loss of memory/ cognitive ability Suicidal thoughts/ intent

11 "Mental Health Continuum Self Check," accessed September 21, 2023, https://the-workingmind.ca/continuum-self-check

Normal sleep patterns Few sleep difficulties Physically well Feeling energetic Maintaining a stable weight	Trouble sleeping Lack of energy Changes in eating patterns Some weight gain or loss	Restless disturbed sleep Some tiredness/ fatigue Fluctuations in weight	Can't fall asleep or stay asleep Sleeping too much or too little Physical illnesses Constant fatigue/ exhaustion Extreme weight loss or gain
Physically and socially active Performing well	Decreased activity/socializing Procrastination	Avoidance Tardiness Decreased performance	Withdrawal Absenteeism Can't perform duties/tasks
Limited alcohol consumption, no binge drinking Limited/ no addictive behaviours* No trouble/ impact (social, economic, legal, financial) due to substance use	Regular to frequent alcohol consumption, limited binge drinking Some regular to addictive behaviours Limited to some trouble/impact (social, economic, legal, financial) due to substance use	Frequent alcohol consumption, binge drinking Struggles to control addictive behaviours Increasing trouble/impact (social, economic, legal, financial) due to substance use	Regular to frequent binge drinking Addiction Significant trouble/impact (social, economic, legal, financial) due to substance use

Acknowledgments

•••••

John, MaryAnn, Cathy, Micheal, and Peter - I am deeply grateful to each of you. Thank you for shaping Chris into the man he was, for sharing him with me, and for keeping his memory alive.

Mom and Dad - Thank you for raising us in a loving home and showing me how a partnership can grow and evolve over years of marriage. The way you gave me space when I needed it, yet always opened your arms when I returned, means more than words can express. Mom, thank you for snapping photos at seemingly inappropriate times and meticulously scrapbooking e-v-e-r-y-t-h-i-n-g!

Deb - You are my person.

Kendra - Your unwavering belief in my story's power, both on paper and on stage, ignited a spark of possibility within me. Your own equilibrium and perspective are truly inspiring. Thank you for being so well adjusted!

The Ringette mom gang - Kristen, Alicia, and Danielle; thank you for your friendship and support. I hope our girls remain as close as we when they are our age!

Friends and mentors - Michèle, Karla, LeeAnne, Lindsay and Lorelei; your support and guidance have contributed to my ability to remain positive and make aligned choices. Your wisdom and guidance continue to help me choose my tomorrows.

The Baulkhams - Thank you for welcoming Alexis and I into your family. The love you've shown us has truly enriched our lives.

My big kids - Keegan, Jessica, Jordan, and McKenzie; your role as cheerleaders has been immeasurable. Boys, your professional insights have been invaluable. Your education was money well spent! You fill my heart with love and I am so grateful for each of you.

Alexis - Your very being radiates joy into my life. Your laughter, your humour, and the light you bring are irreplaceable. Munchkin, I love you to the moon and back.

Brent - Thank you for trusting me to tell our story. Your support and encouragement means the world to me. I love you and look forward to many more happy tomorrows together.

Author Bio

•••••

Jodie is a licensed teacher, professional coach and certified Leader Character practitioner who focuses on cultivating character, igniting passion, and fortifying resilience for herself and others. She is a leadership and mental health curriculum design specialist, trainer and advocate. Jodie's expertise has touched thousands of people in the first responder community and beyond.

Alongside sharing her story to provide a sense of connection and hope, Jodie's mission is to inspire and coach heart-centred, motivated, and open-minded individuals, guiding them towards the realization of their best lives. With unwavering support, she offers world-class professional coaching services, creatively designed courses, and transformative programs dedicated to enhancing overall well-being. By providing tools for self-discovery, resilience-building, and leadership excellence, she aims to create a profound impact on the lives of those she serves, fostering a global community where authenticity, empathy, and growth intertwine to create lasting joy and positive change.

As an author and speaker, Jodie harnesses the written and spoken word to ignite the flames of perpetual learning and transformation. By nurturing vulnerability, encouraging self-reflection, accessing inner wisdom, strengthening resilience, and advocating for the sharing of personal journeys, she strives to continuously encourage individuals on their pathways of growth.

Jodie lives in Alberta with her husband, daughter, and mini goldendoodle. When she is not teaching, training, writing, or coaching, Jodie enjoys curling, watching her daughter play ringette, camping, and eating meals with family and friends that were prepared by someone other than her.

You can connect with Jodie by visiting her website:
www.jodiebaulkham.com

Photo: Sheila Bell Brands

Can You Help?

Thank You For Reading My Book!

I really appreciate all of your feedback and
I love hearing what you have to say.

Please take two minutes now to leave a helpful review
letting me know what you thought of the book.

Thanks so much!

- Jodie Baulkham

Choose Your Next Best Steps

•••••

Claim your free gifts by visiting my website www.jodiebaulkham.com.

Book a discovery call to learn about participating in a coaching engagement to support your personal evolution.

Book me to speak at an upcoming event.

Connect with me through:

@jodiebaulkham

Choose YOUR tomorrow

Manufactured by Amazon.ca
Acheson, AB

13024237R00226